VISIONARIES

Fantastic Four Visionaries: John Byrne Vol. 4

STORY & ART:
john byrne with
kerry gammil, penciler, *Fantastic Four #266*
ron wilson, penciler, *Thing #10*
hilary barta, inker, *Thing #10*

LETTERS:
jim novak with **michael higgins, diana albers & rick parker**

COLORS:
glynis wein with **julianna ferriter** & **andy yanchus**

COLOR RECONSTRUCTION:
jerron quality color

COVER COLORS:
chris sotomayor

EDITORS:
carl potts, bob budiansky & denny o'neil

COLLECTIONS EDITOR:
jeff youngquist

ASSISTANT EDITOR:
jennifer grünwald

SALES MANAGER:
david gabriel

PRODUCTION:
jerry kalinowski

BOOK DESIGNER:
carrie beadle

CREATIVE DIRECTOR:
tom marvelli

EDITOR IN CHIEF:
joe quesada

PUBLISHER:
dan buckley

fantastic four # 258

SEPTEMBER 1983

STAN LEE PRESENTS PERHAPS THE STRANGEST ISSUE EVER OF THE FANTASTIC FOUR!

INTERLUDE

THE TIME IS SEVERAL MONTHS AGO. IN **NEW YORK** THE MEMBERS OF THE **FANTASTIC FOUR** ARE RE-COUPERATING FROM AN ALL-OUT BATTLE WITH THE SHAPE-SHIFTING **SKRULLS** AND AN ALIEN SUPER-SOLDIER KNOWN AS **GLADIATOR**.

BUT THIS IS NOT NEW YORK, AND THIS SOMBER, BROODING FIGURE IS NOT ONE OF THE FF. HE IS, IN FACT, THEIR GREATEST ENEMY, A MAN OF VAST KNOWLEDGE AND AWESOME POWER.

HE IS **DOCTOR DOOM!**

MY BELOVED LATVERIA SUFFERED MUCH UNDER THE RULE OF THE USURPER SORBA. HE BROUGHT CRUEL LAWS AND GREAT PAIN TO THESE, MY LOYAL SUBJECTS.
IT WAS AS IF A HUGE AND TERRIBLE PLAGUE HAD FALLEN UPON THIS LITTLE COUNTRY, TOPPLING IT FROM ITS PLACE AS ONE OF THE MOST POWERFUL NATIONS ON EARTH...
TO A PITIFUL JOKE OF A COUNTRY, TOTTERING ON THE BRINK OF ANNIHILATION.
JOHN BYRNE STORY AND ART
JIM NOVAK LETTERING
GLYNIS WEIN COLORING
CARL POTTS--EDITOR
JIM SHOOTER EDITOR-IN-CHIEF

BUT NOW THE RULE OF DOOM IS RESTORED. THE PEOPLE PROSPER ONCE AGAIN. THE FIELDS ARE LUSH WITH GRAIN, THE SHOPS BULGE WITH LUXURIES.
ONCE MORE THERE IS NO CRIME, NO HUNGER, NO UNEMPLOYMENT IN ALL THE LAND. THE PROCESS OF REBUILDING DOOMSTADT GOES QUICKLY. THE PEOPLE ARE HAPPY AND CONTENT.
AS I HAVE COMMANDED THEY BE...
3

BUT, EVEN THE MUSINGS OF ONE OF THE WORLD'S LAST REIGNING ABSOLUTE MONARCHS DO NOT GO UNINTERRUPTED.
FORGIVE MY INTRUSION, MASTER. A GYPSY GIRL HAS ARRIVED AT THE MAIN GATE. SHE BEGS AN AUDIENCE WITH YOU.
DO NOT DISTRESS YOURSELF, LOYAL BORIS. IT IS TIME I TURNED MY MIND TO OTHER THINGS. HAVE THE GIRL BROUGHT IN.

AND, TIMID IN THE PRESENCE OF HER KING, THE WOMAN TELLS HER STORY...
...THUS IT HAS COME TO PASS THAT DOCTOR STRANGE IS WITHOUT A DISCIPLE. AS A MASTER OF BOTH SCIENCE AND SORCERY, HERR DOKTOR, I THOUGHT YOU WOULD WANT TO KNOW.
YOU HAVE SERVED YOUR LIEGE WELL, MY CHILD. I SHALL NOT FORGET THIS.

LEAVE ME NOW. I HAVE MUCH TO PONDER.
SO, THE MAN REPUTED TO BE EARTH'S SORCERER SUPREME IS BEREFT OF DISCIPLE, EH? IT WOULD BE UNSEEMLY FOR VICTOR VON DOOM TO ACKNOWLEDGE ANY MAN HIS MASTER...

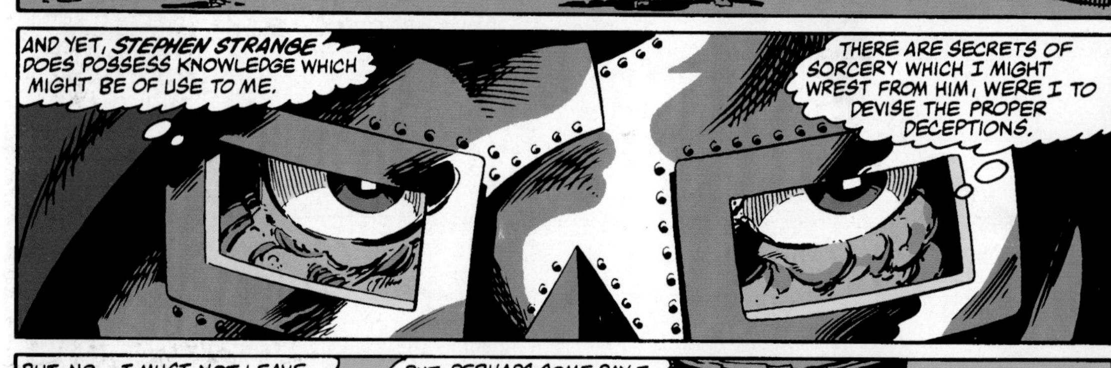
AND YET, STEPHEN STRANGE DOES POSSESS KNOWLEDGE WHICH MIGHT BE OF USE TO ME.
THERE ARE SECRETS OF SORCERY WHICH I MIGHT WREST FROM HIM, WERE I TO DEVISE THE PROPER DECEPTIONS.

BUT, NO... I MUST NOT LEAVE MY PEOPLE NOW. THEY NEED THE FIRM HAND OF DOCTOR DOOM IN THIS HOUR, TO GUIDE THEM BACK TO PEACE AND PROSPERITY.
BUT, PERHAPS SOME DAY I SHALL MEET THIS DOCTOR STRANGE, AND THEN HE SHALL LEARN WHICH OF US IS TRULY THE MASTER.
AYE, SOME DAY...
BUT FOR NOW THERE ARE OTHER MATTERS TO CONCERN ME.
4

FIRST AND FOREMOST...

I MUST LOOK IN ON YOUNG KRISTOFF...
AND SO IN 1876 THE HEREDITARY MONARCHY OF LATVERIA PASSED FROM... OH...
GOOD MORNING, HERR DOKTOR.
MASTER?

MASTER!
MUCH OF THE WORLD LIVES IN FEAR OF THE MAN CALLED DOOM, BUT THE JOY THAT BLOOMS NOW IN THE CHILD'S HEART IS TOTALLY GENUINE...

AS IS THE WARMTH WHICH IS RETURNED.
THIS IS A SIDE OF DOCTOR DOOM THE WORLD RARELY SEES. THIS IS NOT THE CRUEL TYRANT, THE WIELDER OF DEATH AND DESTRUCTION.
EVIL DOOM MAY BE, BUT ALSO A MAN OF HONOR, A MAN WHO PAYS HIS DEBTS.
KRISTOFF'S MOTHER DIED WHILST UNDER DOOM'S PROTECTION. IN THAT MOMENT, THOUGH HE DID NOT KNOW IT, THE CHILD BECAME A WARD OF THE STATE. SINCE THEN HE HAS WANTED FOR NOTHING...
LEAST OF ALL PARENTAL LOVE...

AND GOOD MORNING TO YOU, FRAULEIN MUELLER. HOW ARE THE LESSONS PROCEEDING?
OH, VERY WELL, HERR DOKTOR. KRISTOFF IS A WONDERFULLY BRIGHT CHILD. IT HAS RARELY BEEN MY PLEASURE TO TUTOR SO QUICK AND ATTENTIVE A STUDENT.
EXCEL-LENT.

THEN YOU WILL NOT MIND IF I BORROW HIM FOR AN HOUR OR SO. THERE ARE CERTAIN MATTERS OF STATE I MUST ATTEND TO, AND I HAVE REASONS TO WISH THAT KRISTOFF BE AWARE OF SUCH THINGS...
5

FIRST, KRISTOFF, SINCE MY RETURN TO POWER I HAVE NOT HAD AN OPPORTUNITY TO REVIEW THE ROBOTS I EMPLOY FOR SOME OF MY MORE MENIAL OPERATIONS.
THIS SEEMS AS GOOD A TIME AS ANY TO DO JUST THAT.
YES, MAS-TER.
SILENTLY, THE STEEL-CLAD MONARCH PACES BEFORE HIS DUPLICATES, UNTIL...
ROBOT A 76, YOU HAVE A SCRATCH ON THE SHOULDER OF YOUR ARMOR. YOU ARE NOT A COMBAT UNIT. HOW DID YOU COME TO BE DAMAGED?
THE HUMAN ARCADE STRUCK A MATCH THERE DURING OUR RECENT CON-FRONTATION WITH THE MUTANT X-MEN, SIRE. *
I SEE. AND IN WHAT MANNER DID YOU TERMINATE ARCADE FOR THIS AFFRONT TO THE PERSONNAGE OF DOOM?
I DID NOT TERMINATE HIM, MASTER. I JUDGED IT CONCEIVABLE YOU MIGHT HAVE NEED OF HIM LATER.
*SEE ISH #145-147 OF THAT MAG.
NEED?
DOOM NEEDS NO ONE.
6

REMEMBER THAT, KRISTOFF, IT IS AN IMPORTANT LESSON. A RULER MAY SURROUND HIM-SELF WITH MANY UNDERLINGS, FOR HE CANNOT BE IN ALL PLACES AT ALL TIMES. BUT HE MUST NEVER FORGET THAT HE, AND HE ALONE IS MASTER.
Y-YES, MASTER.

PAY CLOSE ATTENTION TO ALL I HAVE TO TELL YOU, KRISTOFF. FROM NOW ON YOUR LIFE WILL BE A SINGLE, LONG EDUCATION--AND AN INVALUABLE ONE.
ONE THAT WILL TAKE YOU FAR. VERY FAR.

FOR CONSIDERABLY MORE THAN "AN HOUR OR SO" THE BOY STANDS BY DOOM, AS THE MASTER OF LAT-VERIA PRACTICES HIS UNIQUE BRAND OF JUSTICE.
ONE BY ONE THE DAY'S LIST OF SUPPLICANTS COME BEFORE HIM, AS LIKE SOME LATTER DAY SOL-OMON, DOOM HANDS DOWN HIS RULINGS.
IN EACH INSTANCE HE RULES QUICKLY. FOR THE MOST PART HE IS FAIR...

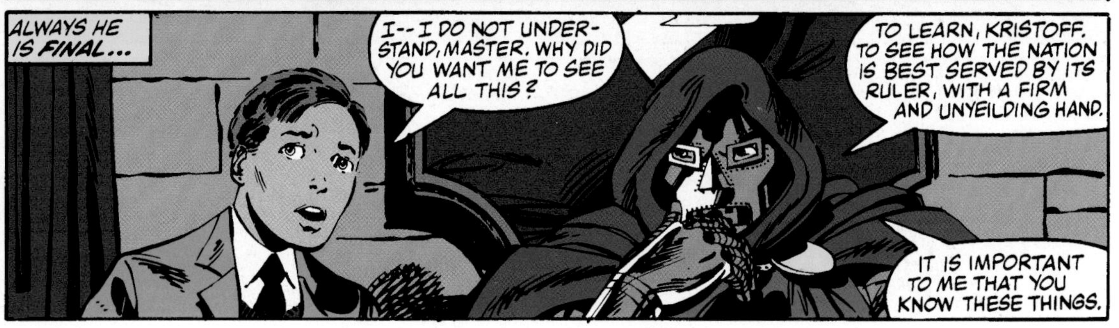
ALWAYS HE IS FINAL...
I-- I DO NOT UNDER-STAND, MASTER. WHY DID YOU WANT ME TO SEE ALL THIS?
TO LEARN, KRISTOFF. TO SEE HOW THE NATION IS BEST SERVED BY ITS RULER, WITH A FIRM AND UNYEILDING HAND.
IT IS IMPORTANT TO ME THAT YOU KNOW THESE THINGS.

OF THIS MATTER NO MORE IS SAID FOR THE PRESENT, AND SO THE BOY IS LEFT TO PONDER THE CRYPTIC WORDS OF THE KING OF LATVERIA...
THE DAYS ROLL SLOWLY BY...
SOME WEEKS LATER, AS THE FIRST LIGHT OF DAWN TINTS THE MIGHTY TOWERS OF CASTLE DOOM...
...THE PEOPLE OF DOOMSTADT BEGIN TO STIR.

BUT IN THE CASTLE ITSELF, DOCTOR DOOM HAS NOT WAITED FOR THE SUN TO BEGIN HIS DAY.
YOUR ARMOR IS READY FOR YOU, MASTER.

ROBOTIC HANDS MOVE WITH QUICK PRECISION, AS THE MANY PARTS OF DOOM'S COMPLEX GARB SLIP AND CLICK INTO PLACE.
ONLY THESE FOREVER LOYAL SERVANTS ARE PERMITTED IN THE PRESENCE OF THE UNARMORED DOOM, AND THOUGH THEIR DULL PHOTO-ELECTRIC EYES PASS OFTEN ACROSS HIS RUINED FACE...
...THEY REACT NOT AT ALL TO THE HORROR THEY FIND THERE.

WITHIN THE HOUR...
BREAKFAST IS TO YOUR LIKING, MASTER?
EXCELLENT, AS ALWAYS, PIERRE. YOU NEVER CEASE TO EXCEL YOURSELF.
BZZKT!

WHO DARES DISTURB DOOM AT TABLE?
IT IS I, HAUPTMANN, MASTER. YOU ORDERED ME TO CALL YOU...
THE MOMENT THE PROJECT WAS COMPLETE...
8

WITHIN SECONDS, IN AN ELEVATOR PLUNGING INTO THE CASTLE'S DEPTHS...
AT LAST! AT LONG LAST!
THIS PROJECT HAS BEEN UNDER WAY SO MANY MONTHS I HAD ALMOST DESPAIRED OF EVER SEEING IT REACH FRUITION.

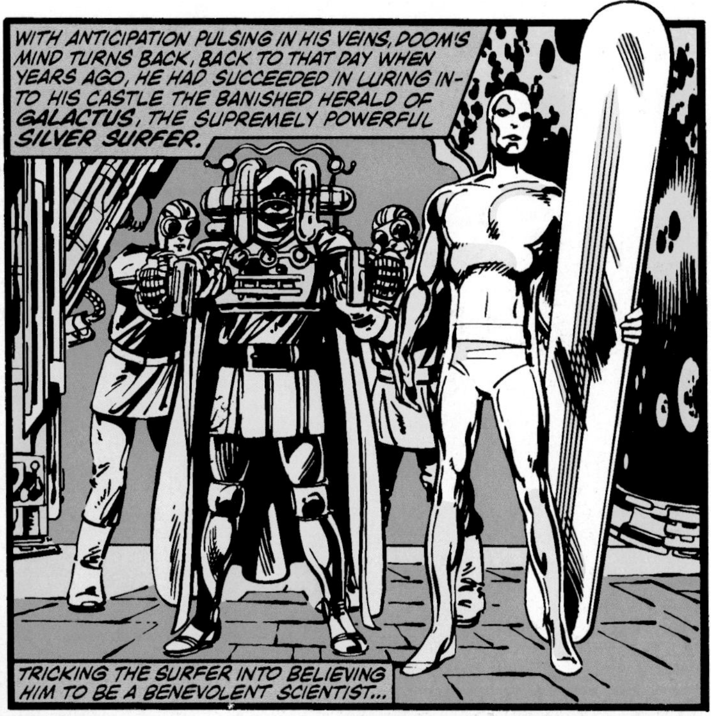
WITH ANTICIPATION PULSING IN HIS VEINS, DOOM'S MIND TURNS BACK, BACK TO THAT DAY WHEN YEARS AGO, HE HAD SUCCEEDED IN LURING INTO HIS CASTLE THE BANISHED HERALD OF GALACTUS, THE SUPREMELY POWERFUL SILVER SURFER.
TRICKING THE SURFER INTO BELIEVING HIM TO BE A BENEVOLENT SCIENTIST...

...DOOM WAS ABLE TO USE HIS VAST TECHNOLOGICAL SKILLS TO CATCH THE SKY-RIDER UNAWARES,
AND THE DICTATOR DRAINED FROM HIS ARGENT FORM THE STAR-SPANNING POWER.

THUS ELEVATED ALMOST TO GODHOOD DOOM WENT MAD, AND SET FORTH UPON A CAMPAIGN OF CONQUEST AND DESTRUCTION.
NO ONE, IT SEEMED, COULD STAND AGAINST HIM.

BUT REED RICHARDS, LEADER OF THE FANTASTIC FOUR, WAS ABLE TO TRICK DOOM.
CLUTCHING A MECHANISM HE BELIEVED HAD BEEN DESIGNED TO STRIP HIM OF THE POWER COSMIC, DOOM FLEW TO THE VERY THRESHOLD OF SPACE...
THERE TO SMASH AGAINST THE BARRIER GALACTUS HAD SET TO HOLD HIS REBELLIOUS SILVER HERALD FOREVER PRISONER ON EARTH.*
*FOR A MORE COMPLETE VERSION SEE FF #'S 57 THRU 60.
9

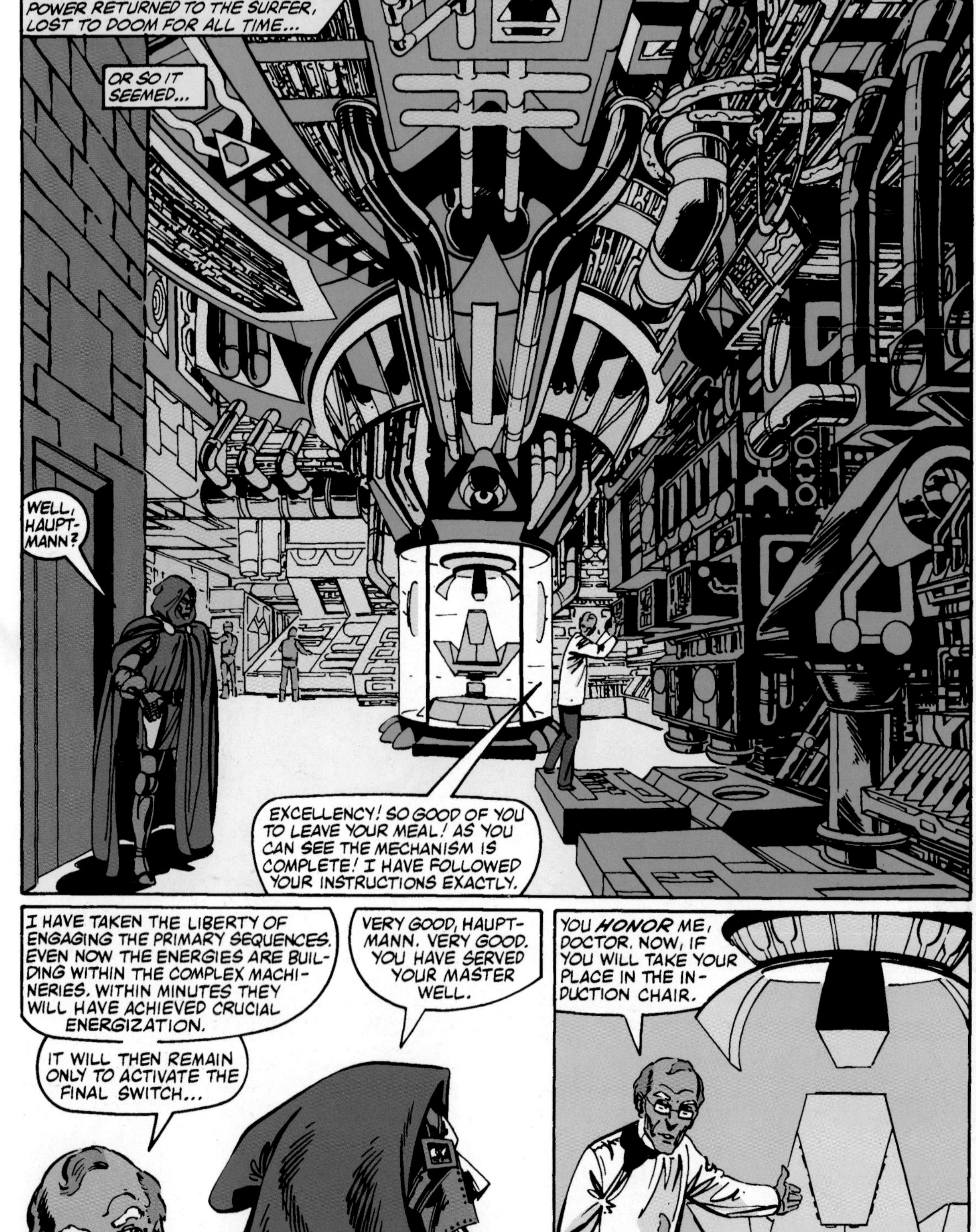
THOUGH DOOM SURVIVED, THE COSMIC POWER RETURNED TO THE SURFER, LOST TO DOOM FOR ALL TIME...
OR SO IT SEEMED...
WELL, HAUPTMANN?
EXCELLENCY! SO GOOD OF YOU TO LEAVE YOUR MEAL! AS YOU CAN SEE THE MECHANISM IS COMPLETE! I HAVE FOLLOWED YOUR INSTRUCTIONS EXACTLY.
I HAVE TAKEN THE LIBERTY OF ENGAGING THE PRIMARY SEQUENCES. EVEN NOW THE ENERGIES ARE BUILDING WITHIN THE COMPLEX MACHINERIES. WITHIN MINUTES THEY WILL HAVE ACHIEVED CRUCIAL ENERGIZATION.
IT WILL THEN REMAIN ONLY TO ACTIVATE THE FINAL SWITCH...
VERY GOOD, HAUPTMANN. VERY GOOD. YOU HAVE SERVED YOUR MASTER WELL.
DOOM IS PLEASED.
YOU HONOR ME, DOCTOR. NOW, IF YOU WILL TAKE YOUR PLACE IN THE INDUCTION CHAIR.
VERY SOON THE POWER OF THE SILVER SURFER WILL BE YOURS AGAIN.
10

NO, NO, DEAR, LOYAL HAUPTMANN. FOR YOUR LONG LABORS ON MY BEHALF IT IS ONLY FITTING THAT THE HONOR OF BEING SO EMPOWERED BELONG TO **YOU!**
NO, MASTER! NO! NO DON'T!

DO NOT FEAR, HAUPTMANN. THINK ONLY OF THE GLORIES THAT WILL BE YOURS AS POSSESSOR OF THE POWER COSMIC.
NO! DOOM DON'T DO...

NOW, A SINGLE SWITCH NEED MERELY BE THROWN...
AND THE **COSMOS** SHALL BE YOURS...

IT BEGINS...
FROM SOMEWHERE DEEP INSIDE THE ARCANE ENGINES A SOUND BEGINS. A SOUND LIKE NONE EVER HEARD ON EARTH.

RAW POWER CORUSCATES THROUGH HAUPTMANN'S FRAIL BODY. HIS LIMBS EXPAND, HIS MIND FILLS WITH CONCEPTS BEYOND HUMAN UNDERSTANDING.
AND HE SCREAMS.

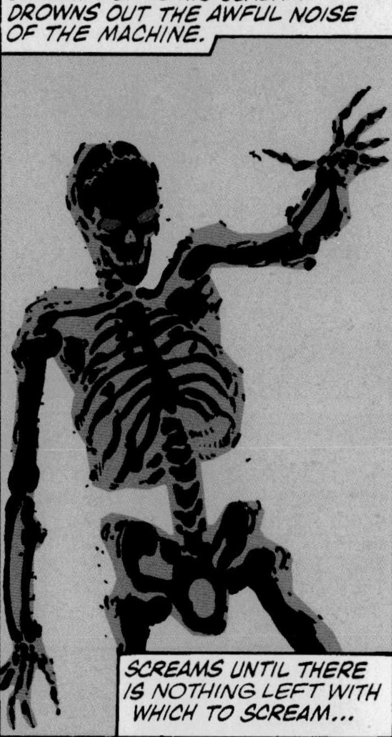
SCREAMS WITH EVERY LAST ATOM OF BREATH IN HIS TORTURED LUNGS. SCREAMS UNTIL HIS SCREAM DROWNS OUT THE AWFUL NOISE OF THE MACHINE.
SCREAMS UNTIL THERE IS NOTHING LEFT WITH WHICH TO SCREAM...

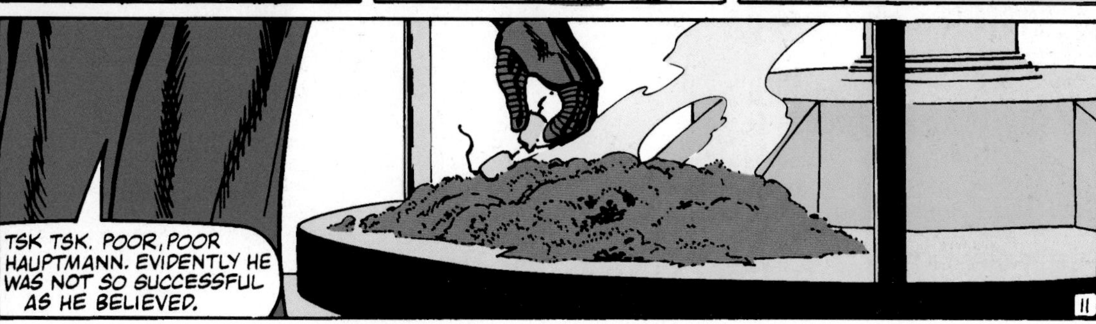
TSK TSK. POOR, POOR HAUPTMANN. EVIDENTLY HE WAS NOT SO SUCCESSFUL AS HE BELIEVED.
11

MASTER, YOUR ACTIONS DISTURB MY PROTECTIVE CIRCUITS. IF HAUPTMANN HAD RECEIVED THE POWER COSMIC HE MIGHT HAVE USED IT AGAINST YOU--HE MIGHT HAVE DESTROYED YOU.
THERE WAS NO DANGER OF THAT EVENTUALITY, A-17.
I HAD SUSPECTED THE ARTIFICIALLY RE-CREATED POWER MIGHT BE TOO UNSTABLE FOR A HUMAN BODY TO CONTAIN. HAUPTMANN'S EAGERNESS CONFIRMED THIS.
HE HAD LONG ME FOR KILLING HIS HAD DEAR HAUPTMANN TRULY SUCCEEDED HE WOULD HAVE ALREADY USED THE MACHINE ON HIMSELF.

BUT, ONE SIDE NOW.
THERE IS MUCH TO DO.

MANY LONG HOURS LATER...
MASTER, ARE YOU BUSY? I HAVE COME TO SAY GOOD-NIGHT.
HMM?
AH--KRISTOFF. COME IN, LAD. COME IN.
WHAT ARE YOU DOING, MASTER?

SEARCHING, KRISTOFF. SEARCHING THROUGH MY ARCHIVES FOR SOMEONE POWERFUL ENOUGH THAT I MAY PLACE WITHIN THEM THE AWESOME POWER OF THE SILVER SURFER, YET CRAVEN ENOUGH THAT I MAY USE HIM TO FURTHER MY GREATEST PLAN.
WHAT OF THE EVIL MUTANT KNOWN AS MAGNETO, MASTER? I HAVE READ THAT HIS POWER RIVALS EVEN YOURS...

...RIVALS...
12

NO ONE RIVALS DOOM!
NO ONE!

DOOM IS SUPREME! THERE IS NO POWER ON EARTH, NO INTELLECT IN ALL CREATION TO EQUAL MINE!
MASTER... YOU'RE HURTING ME!

BE GONE FROM MY SIGHT! YOU HAVE ANGERED ME BEYOND MEASURE. GO TO YOUR QUARTERS AND REMAIN UNTIL I SUMMON YOU AGAIN!
Y-YES, MASTER!

STUPID, INSOLENT CHILD! TO EVEN SUGGEST THAT A FREAK SUCH AS MAGNETO COULD BE A RIVAL TO DOOM--MAGNETO, WHO HAS LATELY PERMITTED FOOLISH HUMAN WEAKNESS TO DILUTE HIS OWN SCHEMES OF CONQUEST.
NO. THE ERSTWHILE MASTER OF THE BROTHERHOOD OF EVIL MUTANTS IS OF NO USE TO DOOM...
BUT THERE MUST BE SOMEONE--AND THIS WRETCHED COMPUTER WILL GIVE ME A NAME OR I WILL SMASH ITS USELESS CIRCUITS TO...
13

WAIT... A NAME APPEARS. A NAME I SHOULD HAVE THOUGHT OF FOR MYSELF!
IF TRULY HE STILL LIVES, HE WILL BE PERFECT FOR MY PLAN, MY GOAL...
THE ULTIMATE DESTRUCTION OF THE FANTASTIC FOUR!

LET FORTY-EIGHT HOURS ROLL QUICKLY BY, AS WE TURN FROM THE VALLEY KINGDOM NESTLED IN THE BAVARIAN ALPS...
...TO THE MAN-MADE MOUNTAINS AND CANYONS OF EARTH'S GREATEST CITY, NEW YORK, NEW YORK.

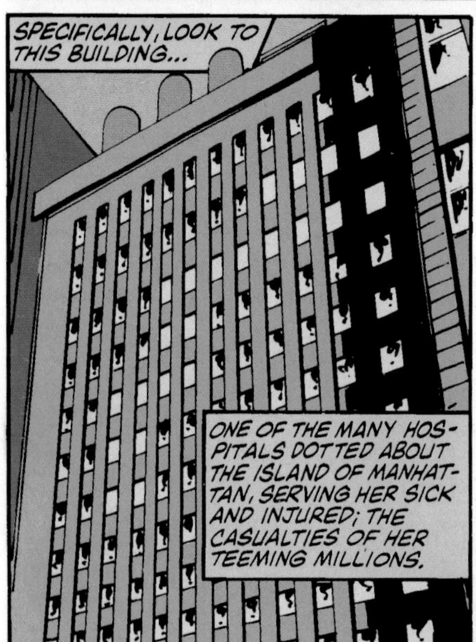
SPECIFICALLY, LOOK TO THIS BUILDING...
ONE OF THE MANY HOSPITALS DOTTED ABOUT THE ISLAND OF MANHATTAN, SERVING HER SICK AND INJURED; THE CASUALTIES OF HER TEEMING MILLIONS.

IN A DARKENED CORRIDOR...
THEY MOVE ALMOST SILENTLY, THE THICK FOAM ON THEIR SOLES CUSHIONING THEIR METAL FEET FROM THE COLD FLOOR...
A GLANCE WOULD BE MORE THAN ENOUGH TO TELL THEY DO NOT BELONG HERE.

...CERTAINLY HOPE BEN WILL RECOVER, IRON MAN. HE'S BEEN THROUGH AN AWFUL LOT, LATELY.
I WOULDN'T WORRY TOO MUCH, CAP. THE THING'S ONE OF THE TOUGHEST MEN ALIVE. HE'LL PULL THROUGH FINE.*
*FOR THE FULL STORY BEHIND THIS DISCUSSION SEE MARVEL 2-IN-1 #96.

CAPTAIN AMERICA AND IRON MAN. THEY SPOKE OF A MEMBER OF THE FANTASTIC FOUR. IF HE IS HERE WE COULD...
NO, UNIT SEVEN. THE MASTER IS AWARE OF THE THING'S LOCATION AND CONDITION.
OUR INSTRUCTIONS ARE TO LEAVE HIM UNMOLESTED. COME, WE HAVE ANOTHER MISSION HERE.
14

MOMENTS LATER...
MORNIN', BOB. HOW'S OUR JOHN DOE TODAY?
UNCHANGED, JIM. I SWEAR, THAT GUY ALMOST MAKES ME BELIEVE IN MIRACLES. THEY FIND HIM STARK NAKED IN A GARBAGE PILE, EVERY MAJOR BONE IN HIS BODY BROKEN...

STILL GOT HIM ON THE GLUCOSE MARTINIS?
YEP. THAT SUGAR AND ALCOHOL SOLUTION SEEMS TO BE HOLDING HIS CONDITION, BUT IT'S HARD TO TELL IF HE'S HEALING OR NOT. NONE OF HIS CHEMISTRIES COME OUT ANYTHING LIKE THE WAY THEY SHOULD BE. IF ONLY HE COULD SPEAK ENGLISH--OR ANY LANGUAGE WE KNOW.
IT SOUNDS CRAZY, BUT I'M HALFWAY CONVINCED HE'S NOT EVEN HUMAN...

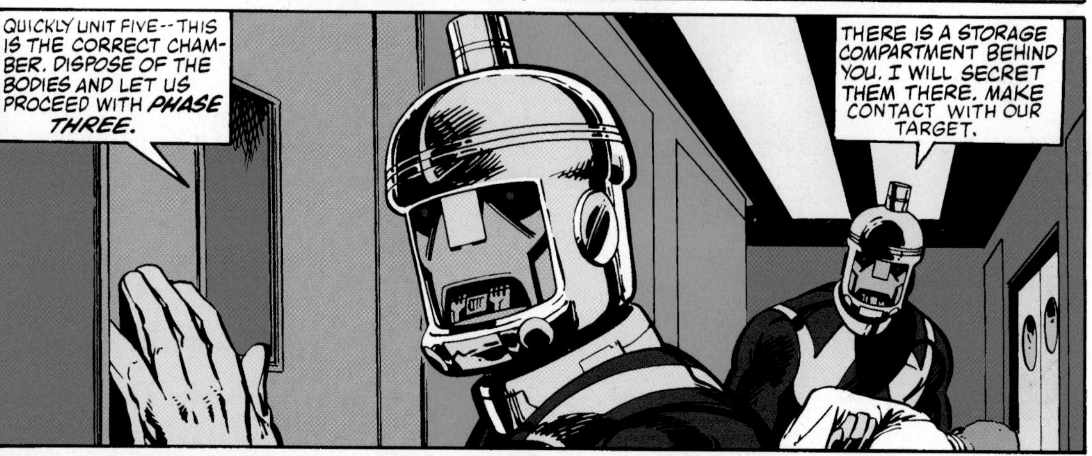
QUICKLY UNIT FIVE--THIS IS THE CORRECT CHAMBER. DISPOSE OF THE BODIES AND LET US PROCEED WITH PHASE THREE.
THERE IS A STORAGE COMPARTMENT BEHIND YOU. I WILL SECRET THEM THERE. MAKE CONTACT WITH OUR TARGET.

THE ROOM IS AS PLEASANT AS A SICKROOM CAN BE, BUT THE ROBOT'S SENSORS TELL HIM ALL IS NOT RIGHT HERE...

...AND THE FIGURE ON THE BED GLARES AT THE INTRUDER WITH TERRIBLE HATRED...
15

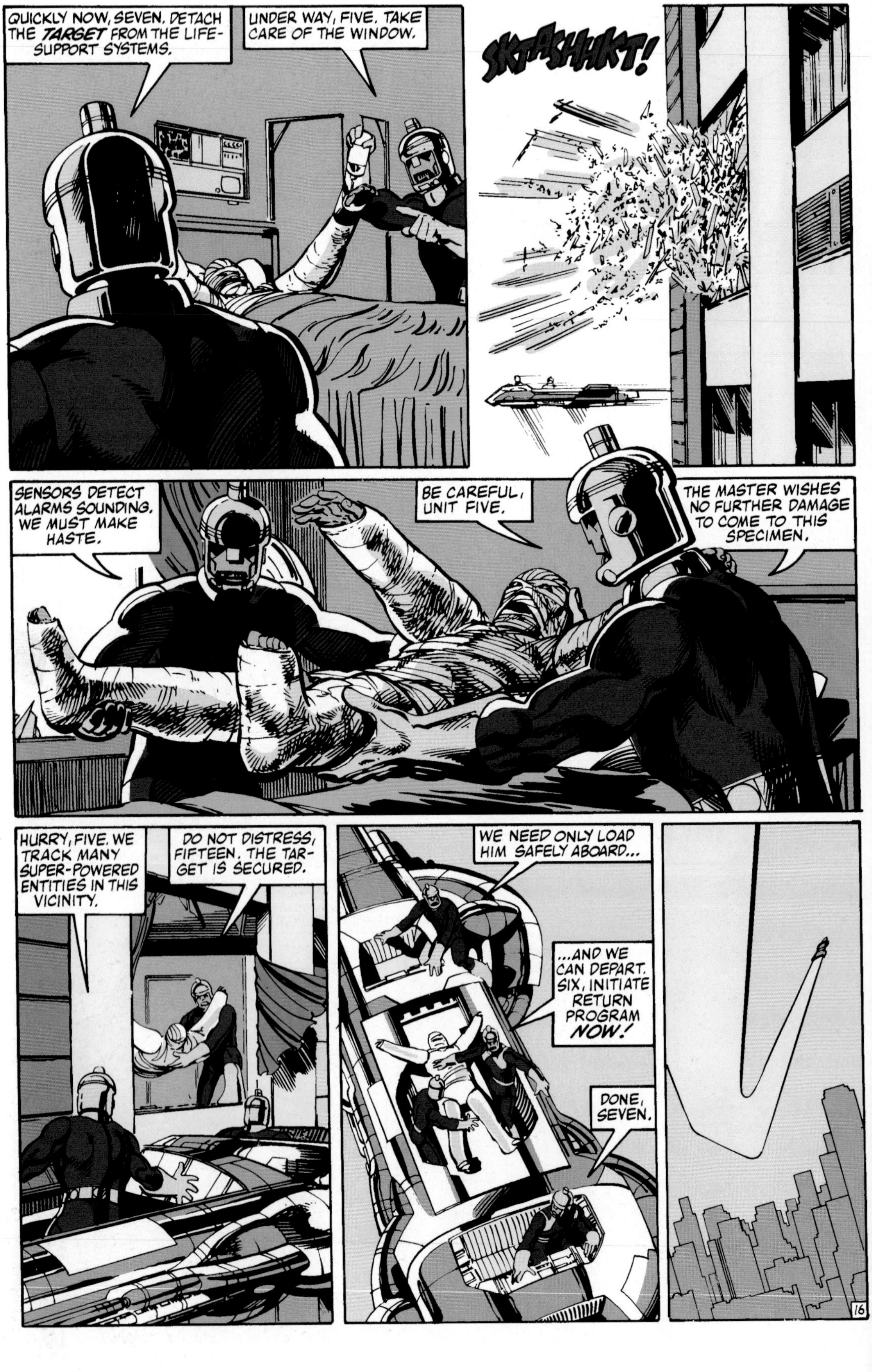

QUICKLY NOW, SEVEN. DETACH THE *TARGET* FROM THE LIFE-SUPPORT SYSTEMS.

UNDER WAY, FIVE. TAKE CARE OF THE WINDOW.

SKTASHHKT!

SENSORS DETECT ALARMS SOUNDING. WE MUST MAKE HASTE.

BE CAREFUL, UNIT FIVE.

THE MASTER WISHES NO FURTHER DAMAGE TO COME TO THIS SPECIMEN.

HURRY, FIVE. WE TRACK MANY SUPER-POWERED ENTITIES IN THIS VICINITY.
DO NOT DISTRESS, FIFTEEN. THE TARGET IS SECURED.

WE NEED ONLY LOAD HIM SAFELY ABOARD...
...AND WE CAN DEPART. SIX, INITIATE RETURN PROGRAM *NOW!*
DONE, SEVEN.

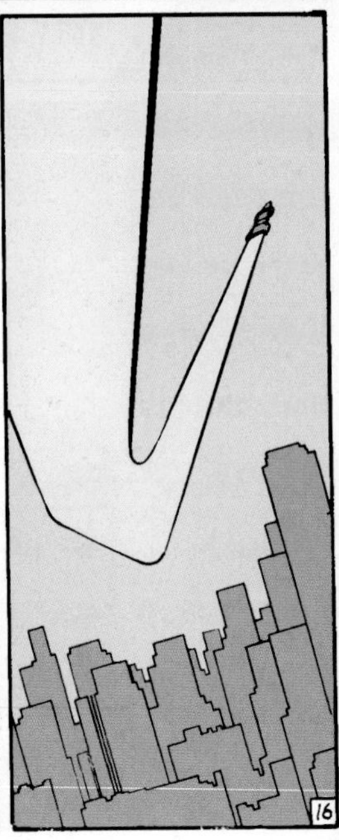

WITHIN FOUR HOURS THE SLEEK CRAFT IS FLASHING ACROSS THE TREETOPS OF LATVERIA, BOUND FOR HOME...

AND, EXACTLY SIX WEEKS LATER...
WELL, PHYSICIAN? HOW FARES YOUR PATIENT?
AH, MASTER, I WAS JUST ABOUT TO CALL YOU. I BELIEVE HE IS READY.

YOU ARE CERTAIN? I AM PREPARED TO WAIT A FEW MORE DAYS IF NECESSARY.
NO NEED, MASTER. HIS BODY HAS COMPLETELY HEALED. THE TREATMENT YOU PRESCRIBED WORKED PERFECTLY. MY ONLY CONCERN WAS THAT HIS ALIEN METABOLISM MIGHT REJECT THE TRANSLATOR IMPLANT, BUT THAT HAS NOT OCCURRED.
EXCELLENT! IT WOULD SEEM THEN TIME THAT I INTRODUCED MYSELF TO OUR... GUEST.

...ER...FORGIVE ME, MASTER, BUT YOUR GARB IS NOT STERILE...
NO MATTER, PHYSICIAN.
AFTER TODAY HE WILL NOT NEED TO BE PROTECTED BY HIS ENVIRONMENTAL CUBE.
AFTER TODAY HE WILL BE MINE TO COMMAND!

WHO DARES! WHO DARES DISTURB TYROS THE TERRIBLE?!
17

PAUSE A MOMENT NOW. STUDY CAREFULLY THE TABLEAU UNFOLDING HERE BEFORE YOU: ONE OF THE MOST POWERFUL HUMANS OF ALL EARTH'S TORTURED HISTORY FACES AN ALIEN BEING ONCE ONE OF THE MOST POWERFUL IN THE COSMOS. HOW CAN WHAT HAPPENS NEXT BODE WELL FOR ANYONE, LEAST OF ALL THE ***FANTASTIC FOUR?***

SO IT IS ***TYROS***, IS IT? THEN I DEDUCED CORRECTLY THAT YOUR RECENT MEMORIES WERE STRIPPED AWAY, ALONG WITH YOUR COSMIC POWERS.

YOU PRATTLE WITHOUT MEANING, ARMORED ONE. WHO ARE YOU? WHAT IS THIS PLACE?

ANSWER QUICKLY, OR BY MARMAN'S SEVEN RINGS I WILL CRUSH YOUR ARMOR FLAT--WITH YOU INSIDE IT!

YOUR RAGE IS MAGNIFICENT, TYROS. AND JUSTLY SO. BUT DIRECT IT NOT AGAINST THE PERSON OF DOOM, FOR YOUR LIFE NOW RESTS IN THE HOLLOW OF MY HAND.
I AM MASTER HERE, TYROS, AND BEFORE YOU PROTEST THAT IRREVOCABLE FACT, YOU WOULD DO WELL TO LISTEN. LISTEN...
AND LEARN.
"DO NOT QUESTION HOW I GAINED SUCH KNOWLEDGE, TYROS, BUT BE ASSURED I KNOW YOU, KNOW WHO AND WHAT YOU ARE.
"ONCE YOU RULED THE CITY OF LANLAK, IN THE NORTHERN HEMISPHERE OF A WORLD CALLED BIRJ, FIFTH MOON OF THE GAS GIANT MARMAN, EIGHTY THOUSAND LIGHT YEARS FROM EARTH.
18

"YOU WERE CONTENT WITH YOUR PETTY TYRANNY, BUT YOU FELL UNDER THE GAZE OF GALACTUS.
"GALACTUS! HE WHO IS POWER PERSONIFIED, THE ONE BEING IN ALL THE UNIVERSE BEFORE WHOM EVEN DOOM MUST TREMBLE. GALACTUS, DEVOURER OF WORLDS, WHO FEEDS ON THE LIFE-ENERGIES OF ENTIRE PLANETS!
"HE HAD NEED OF A NEW HERALD, A NEW SLAVE TO SEARCH THE COSMOS FOR SUITABLE FOOD-WORLDS.
"AND, TYROS OF LANLAK, HE HAD CHOSEN YOU!

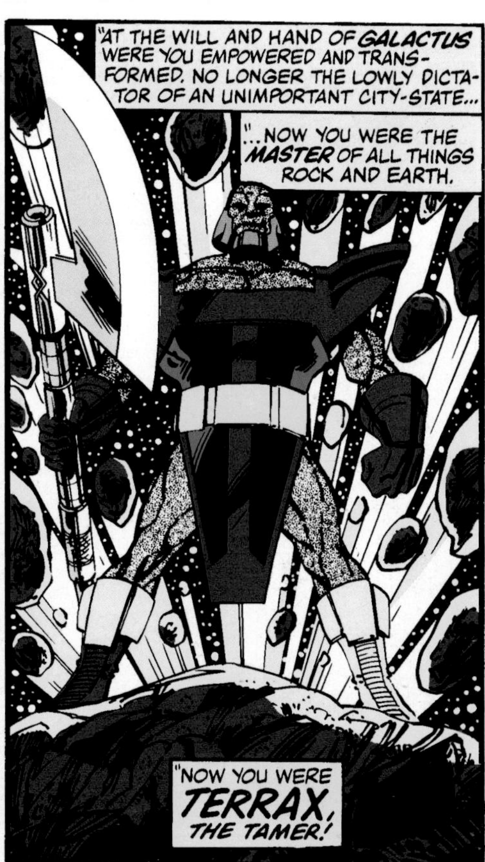
"AT THE WILL AND HAND OF GALACTUS WERE YOU EMPOWERED AND TRANSFORMED. NO LONGER THE LOWLY DICTATOR OF AN UNIMPORTANT CITY-STATE...
"...NOW YOU WERE THE MASTER OF ALL THINGS ROCK AND EARTH.
"NOW YOU WERE TERRAX, THE TAMER!

"BUT, LIKE SO MANY BEFORE YOU, YOU TURNED UPON YOUR MASTER, THINKING YOUR OWN PUNY POWER TO BE A MATCH FOR HIS COSMIC ALL!
"ON EARTH HE STRIPPED YOU OF YOUR ENERGIES.

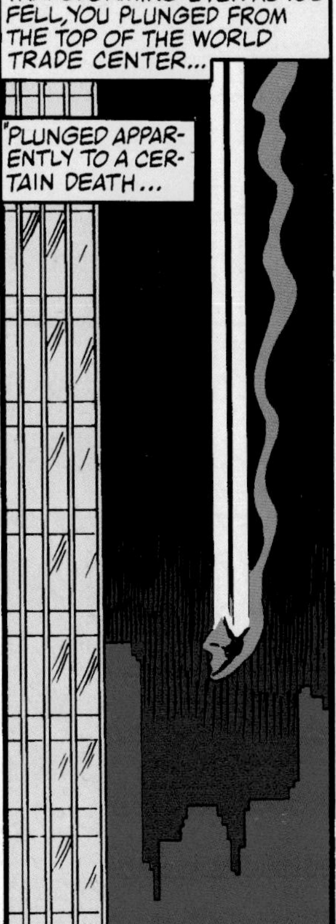
"TRANSFORMING EVEN AS YOU FELL, YOU PLUNGED FROM THE TOP OF THE WORLD TRADE CENTER...
"PLUNGED APPARENTLY TO A CERTAIN DEATH...

BUT, THOUGH YOU FELL, NOT ALL THE FALL WAS IN YOUR MORTAL FORM. YOU WERE SMASHED ALMOST TO JELLY, BUT YOU SURVIVED. AND IT IS YOUR VERY SURVIVAL THAT TELLS ME YOU ARE SUITABLE FOR A PROJECT I HAVE IN MIND.
YOUR STORY HAS A STRANGE RING OF TRUTH, ONE-CALLED-DOOM. SAY ON.
THE TIME FOR WORDS IS PAST, TYROS. TIME IS NOW RIPE FOR ACTION!
19

THUS...
I...DO NOT UNDERSTAND THESE MACHINES, NOR THIS STRANGE GARB.
WITHIN THESE MECHANISMS I HAVE CREATED, ARTIFICIALLY, A TINY SPARK, TYROS, A SPARK THAT IS AS NOTHING BEFORE THE FIRE OF GALACTUS.
YET THAT SPARK IS SUFFICIENT TO GENERATE WITHIN YOUR BODY A FORCE TO EQUAL THAT OF THE FIRST HERALD OF GALACTUS, THE SILVER SURFER.
BUT THAT POWER IS UNSTABLE, AND YOU WILL NEED THAT SPECIAL GARMENT TO CHANNEL AND CONTROL THE ENERGIES PROPERLY.
BUT ENOUGH TALK, TYROS. YOU ARE ABOUT TO BE RE-BORN...
FOR THE SECOND TIME!
AGAIN THE SWITCH IS THROWN...
AGAIN THE MYSTERIOUS ENERGIES BURST FROM THE SURROUNDING MACHINES...
AGAIN A MORTAL FORM IS SUBJECTED TO THE BOMBARDMENT BY POWERS ALMOST BEYOND COMPREHENSION...
AND THOUGH IT IS EXTRAORDINARILY PAINFUL...
THIS TIME, AT LEAST, IT IS NOT FATAL...
YAAAAARGH!
TYROS! ROBOTS, SEIZE HIM!
20

HOLD HIM FAST, MY UNLIVING SLAVES. THE *POWER* SURGES WITHIN HIM.
IT MAY HAVE DRIVEN HIM INTO *MADNESS*...
NO... DOOM...
TYROS IS NOT MAD...

A FEW MINUTES LATER...
WELL, TYROS, IS YOUR QUESTION ANSWERED?
COMPLETELY, DOOM. IT IS AS IF THE SLED IS AN EXTENSION OF MY OWN BODY.
THEN GO, TYROS.
GO AND SEEK YOU OUR ENEMIES.
I AM GONE, DOOM. AND THE LIVES OF THE ACCURSED QUARTET CAN NOW BE MEASURED IN HOURS!
MASTER, I MUST QUESTION THE WISDOM OF THIS COURSE OF ACTION. WITH THE ALIEN TYROS THUS EMPOWERED...
HE PRESENTS NO MORE THREAT TO ME THAN DID HAUPTMANN, ROBOT. I HAVE NOT, YOU SEE, TOLD TYROS QUITE THE ENTIRE TRUTH.
THE TECHNO-SUIT HE WEARS DOES MORE THAN CONTROL THE ENERGIES NOW RAMPANT WITHIN HIM. IT SERVES ALSO AS A LIFE-SUPPORT SYSTEM, DELAYING THE DESTRUCTION MET BY HAUPTMANN.
TYROS HAS NO MORE THAN FIVE HOURS OF LIFE, BEFORE THE SUIT BURNS OUT AND THE POWER COSMIC CONSUMES HIM.
BUT THAT WILL BE ENOUGH TIME FOR HIM TO SUBJUGATE REED RICHARDS AND HIS THREE PARTNERS. THEN I SHALL DELIVER THE COUP DE GRACE...
THE DESTRUCTION OF THE FANTASTIC FOUR!

fantastic four # 259

OCTOBER 1983

STAN LEE PRESENTS A BOLD NEW BEGINNING FOR THE FANTASTIC FOUR!
CHOICES
BELLE PORT, CONNECTICUT. THE SIGN ON THE FRONT LAWN READS SIMPLY "FOR SALE." BUT TO THIS WOMAN IT MAY WELL SAY SOMETHING ELSE...
...HOME.
HELLO? IS ANYONE HERE?
MRS. BENJAMIN? IS THAT YOU?
JOHN BYRNE STORY & ART / GLYNIS WEIN COLORIST / JIM NOVAK LETTERER / BOB BUDIANSKY EDITOR / JIM SHOOTER EDITOR IN CHIEF

OOOPS! I ALMOST ANSWERED "NO". I CHOSE "BENJAMIN" AS AN EASY NAME FOR US ALL TO REMEMBER, BUT IT LOOKS AS IF THIS SECRET IDENTITY BUSINESS MAY BE TRICKIER THAN I THOUGHT.
GUESS I'M TOO USED TO BEING CALLED SUSAN STORM RICHARDS.
YES, I'M SUSAN BENJAMIN. ARE YOU THE LADY I SPOKE TO ON THE TELEPHONE?
MARTHA WINSLOW, YES. I'M IN CHARGE OF SHOWING THIS HOUSE TO PROSPECTIVE BUYERS. I SUPPOSE THAT'S A STEP UP FROM MY NORMAL ROLE OF NEXT-DOOR NEIGHBOR.
OH, THEN I TAKE IT YOU'RE A FRIEND OF THE OWNERS?
YES INDEED! FAITH AND I GO BACK JUST FOREVER AND EVER!

LET ME JUST CLOSE THIS... UMF... DOOR. SOMETIMES IT'S A LITTLE STIFF.
AND THERE GOES ANY THEORY SHE MIGHT BE A PROFESSIONAL BROKER.
THIS SEEMS A VERY PLEASANT HOUSE.

I LOVE THE SIZE OF THE ROOMS--AT LEAST WHAT I'VE SEEN. BUT IS THE WHOLE HOUSE PANELED LIKE THIS?
JUST THE LIVING ROOM AND UPSTAIRS HALL. OH, AND ONE WALL IN THE DINING ROOM.
DON'T YOU LIKE IT?
WELL, IT'S A BIT ...MONOTONOUS. I LIKE VARIETY.

BUT I SUPPOSE IF WE DO END UP BUYING WE CAN ALWAYS REDECORATE.
NICE DINING ROOM.
ISN'T IT, THOUGH? THE KITCHEN IS THROUGH HERE. UMM, I DON'T THINK I ASKED WHAT YOU AND YOUR HUSBAND DO?
REED IS... IN RESEARCH.

I'M NOT DOING MUCH OF ANYTHING JUST NOW. I'M HOPING TO TAKE IT EASY FOR A WHILE.
YOU SEE, MY HUSBAND AND I ARE EXPECTING OUR SECOND CHILD...
OH, HOW WONDERFUL. GEORGE AND I HAVE NO CHILDREN.

YOU'LL WANT TO SEE THE UPSTAIRS NOW, I...
OH...
BY THE WAY, I'M AFRAID THIS ANTIQUE DOESN'T COME WITH THE HOUSE.

IT DOESN'T? OH, WHAT A... PITY.
YES. BUT I'M AFRAID FAITH WAS QUITE FIRM ON THAT.

OH WELL, I SUPPOSE WE'LL JUST HAVE TO MUDDLE THROUGH WITHOUT...
BING BONG
NOW WHO COULD THAT BE?

WHY, HELLO KATIE. HOW ARE YOU TODAY?
FINE THANKS, MRS. WINSLOW. I WAS BABYSITTING DANNY AND WE SAW A LADY COME TO LOOK AT THE HOUSE.
AND YOU THOUGHT YOU SAW BUSINESS?

WELL, I THINK YOU MAY BE IN LUCK. MRS. BENJAMIN, THIS IS KATE DWYER, OUR LOCAL BABYSITTING MAGNATE.
HI, MRS. BENJAMIN. DO YOU HAVE ANY KIDS WHO NEED SITTING?
I HADN'T EVEN THOUGHT OF THAT. IN NEW YORK WE'VE ALWAYS DEPENDED UPON ALICIA OR ONE OF REED'S ROBOT NANNIES...
WHY, YES, KATE. I SUPPOSE WE WILL NEED A SITTER ONCE IN A WHILE.

AN HOUR OR SO LATER...
WELL, THAT'S IT! ALL THE COMPLEX LITTLE REAL ESTATE WHEELS HAVE BEEN SET TO TURNING. IN A FEW DAYS THE FAMILY "BENJAMIN" WILL BE HOMEOWNERS.
WHAT AN EXPERIENCE THIS HAS BEEN! IT'S A LONG TIME SINCE I'VE LIVED IN DARKEST SUBURBIA. NOT SINCE BEFORE REED AND I GOT MARRIED.
FOR SALE
I KNOW THIS ADVENTURE INTO SECRET IDENTITIES IS ABSOLUTELY NECESSARY TO GIVE OUR SON FRANKLIN SOMETHING LIKE A NORMAL LIFE, BUT I HOPE REED AND I WON'T GET CABIN FEVER SO FAR FROM THE BIG CITY.
AH, THERE'S MY FANTASTI-CAR SEGMENT, RIGHT WHERE I LEFT IT.
HER COSMIC-RAY-SPAWNED POWER REACHES OUT, AND LIGHT WAVES BEND AROUND SUSAN RICHARDS AND HER VEHICLE...
IT WAS BEST THAT I DO THE HOUSE-HUNTING, RATHER THAN REED.
THERE ARE THINGS THE INVISIBLE GIRL CAN DO THAT EVEN MISTER FANTASTIC CAN'T.
SO LONG, BELLE PORT. I WONDER WHAT YOU'D ALL THINK IF YOU KNEW THE FANTASTIC FOUR ARE COMING TO TOWN!
I'M OUT OF RANGE OF PRYING EYES NOW. SO, I CAN BECOME VISIBLE AGAIN...
...AND TAKE OFF THIS VERY UNGLAMOROUS WIG!

MEANWHILE, EVEN AS THE FANTASTIC FOUR'S BEAUTIFUL DISTAFF MEMBER GUIDES HER CURIOUS CRAFT WESTWARD TOWARD HOME...
...A SLEEK DC-9 WINGS IN OVER NEW YORK'S BUSTLING LA GUARDIA AIRPORT...

...THERE TO DISGORGE A VERY NERVOUS GROUP OF PASSENGERS...
I...I'VE NEVER HAD SUCH A TERRIFYING FLIGHT!
ME NEITHER! I KEPT EXPECTING US T' GET BLOWN OUTTA TH' SKY!
THIS IS ABSOLUTELY OUTRAGEOUS! YOU HAVE NO RIGHT TO SUBJECT YOUR PASSENGERS TO SUCH DANGERS!
ATLANTA
WHAT GIVES? I THOUGHT THEY HAD GOOD WEATHER...
CHECK THE PASSENGER LIST.

"BEN GRIMM IS ON THAT FLIGHT!"
JUST GREAT! AS IF IT WEREN'T ROUGH ENOUGH FOR ME THE PAST COUPLA DAYS...*
...I GOTTA WIND UP WITH A PLANE FULLA FOLKS WHO TREAT ME LIKE I WUZ TYPHOID MARY!

*SEE FANTASTIC FOUR #'S 256-257 AND THE THING #'S 3-4 -- BOB.

DOES IT HAFTA BE THAT WAY EVERY TIME ONE OF TH' FF USES PUBLIC TRANSPORT?
DOES EVERYBODY THINK ONE OF OUR ENEMIES IS GONNA ATTACK US ANY SECOND?
MEL'S TAXI
AW... NUTS! I JUST NEED TA GET HOME AND INTA A NICE HOT BATH.

TH' BAXTER BUILDING, PAL, AN' STEP ON IT!
H-HOLY CATS! YOU'RE THE THING!
GO T' TH' HEAD OF TH' CLASS, BRIGHT BOY. NOW GET ROLLIN', WILL YA?

THUS THE CAB MERGES INTO THE STEEL AND RUBBER SNAKE SLITHERING SLOWLY TOWARDS THE MIDTOWN TUNNEL...
...AS THE THOUGHTS OF THE MIGHTY-MUSCLED THING TURN TO DARKNESS...

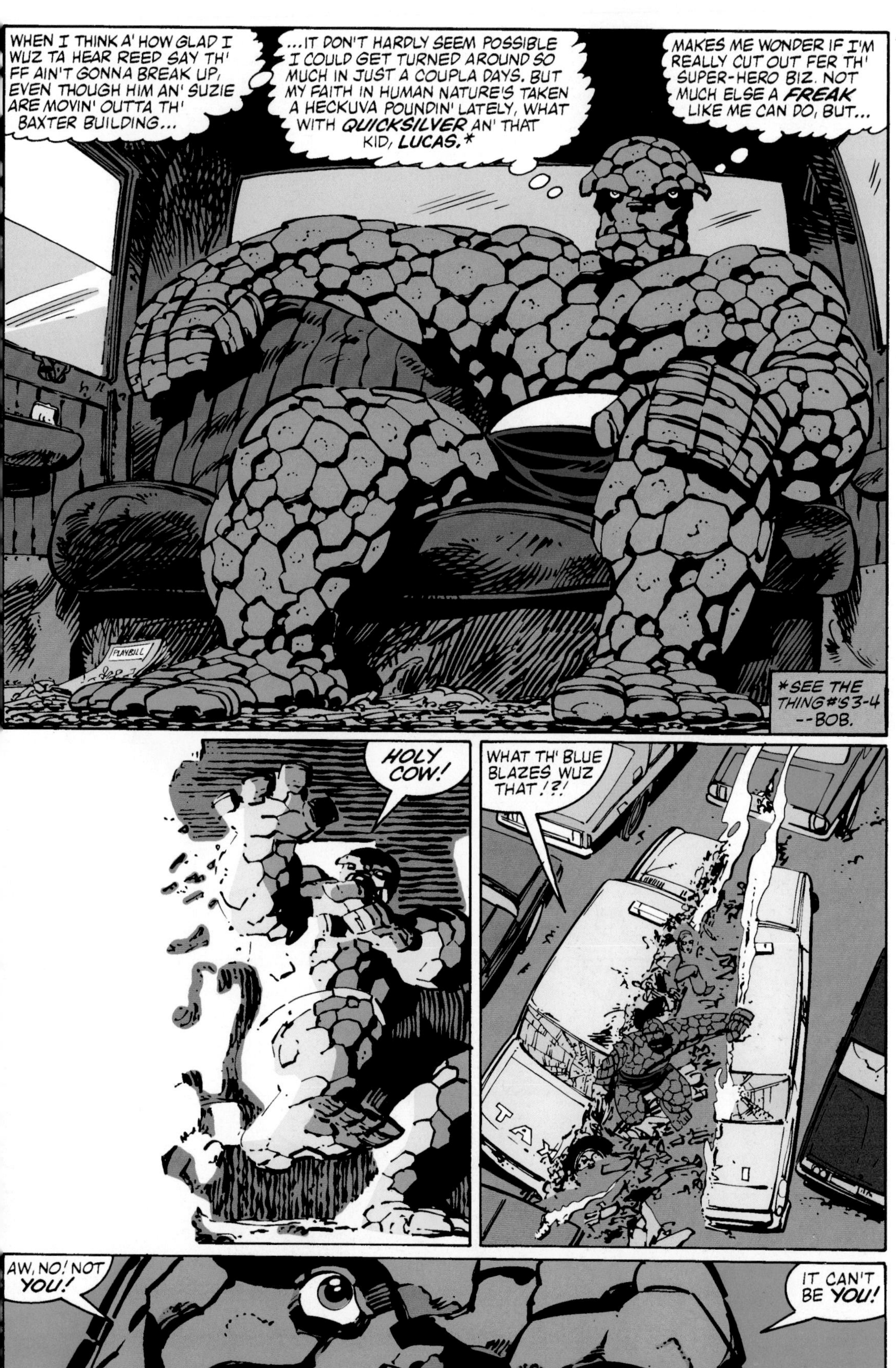
WHEN I THINK A' HOW GLAD I WUZ TA HEAR REED SAY TH' FF AIN'T GONNA BREAK UP, EVEN THOUGH HIM AN' SUZIE ARE MOVIN' OUTTA TH' BAXTER BUILDING...
...IT DON'T HARDLY SEEM POSSIBLE I COULD GET TURNED AROUND SO MUCH IN JUST A COUPLA DAYS. BUT MY FAITH IN HUMAN NATURE'S TAKEN A HECKUVA POUNDIN' LATELY, WHAT WITH QUICKSILVER AN' THAT KID, LUCAS.*
MAKES ME WONDER IF I'M REALLY CUT OUT FER TH' SUPER-HERO BIZ. NOT MUCH ELSE A FREAK LIKE ME CAN DO, BUT...
PLAYBILL
*SEE THE THING #'S 3-4 --BOB.
HOLY COW!
WHAT TH' BLUE BLAZES WUZ THAT!?!
AW, NO! NOT YOU!
IT CAN'T BE YOU!

BUT IT IS, FOOL! IT IS!! THOUGH YOU MAY HAVE THOUGHT ME DEAD BY THE HAND OF WORLD-DEVOURING GALACTUS, I AM RISEN, MORE POWERFUL THAN EVER I WAS BEFORE!
NOW AND FOREVER MORE AM I TYROS THE TERRIBLE!
SO IT'S BACK TA TYROS, HUH? WELL, I WUZ NEVER MUCH IMPRESSED WHEN YA WERE WORKIN' FOR GALACTUS AN' CALLIN' YERSELF TERRAX, EITHER!
TH' WAY I SEE IT, PAL, A BOZO BY ANY NAME STILL AIN'T GONNA SMELL LIKE A ROSE...

...OR, TA PUT THAT ANOTHER WAY...
IT'S CLOBBERIN' TIME!
SKA-RAM!
FOOL! STUPID PUNY FOOL! YOU DARE PIT YOUR PUNY STRENGTH AGAINST THE CON-SUMMATE POWER OF TYROS?
MINE IS THE POWER COSMIC! THE ULTIMATE POWER OF GALACTUS HIMSELF!

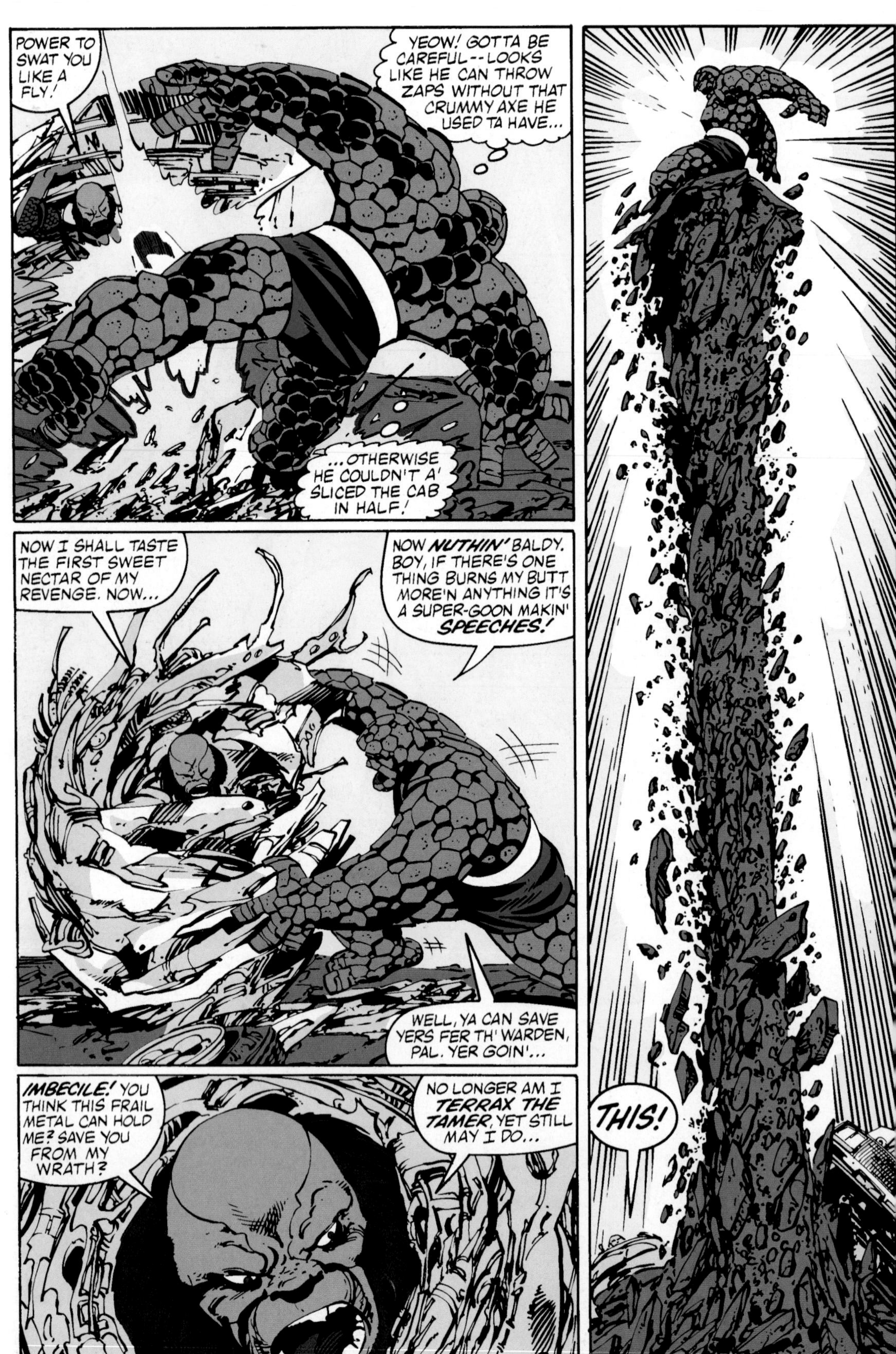
POWER TO SWAT YOU LIKE A FLY!
YEOW! GOTTA BE CAREFUL--LOOKS LIKE HE CAN THROW ZAPS WITHOUT THAT CRUMMY AXE HE USED TA HAVE...
...OTHERWISE HE COULDN'T A' SLICED THE CAB IN HALF!
NOW I SHALL TASTE THE FIRST SWEET NECTAR OF MY REVENGE. NOW...
NOW NUTHIN' BALDY. BOY, IF THERE'S ONE THING BURNS MY BUTT MORE'N ANYTHING IT'S A SUPER-GOON MAKIN' SPEECHES!
WELL, YA CAN SAVE YERS FER TH' WARDEN, PAL. YER GOIN'...
IMBECILE! YOU THINK THIS FRAIL METAL CAN HOLD ME? SAVE YOU FROM MY WRATH?
NO LONGER AM I TERRAX THE TAMER, YET STILL MAY I DO...
THIS!

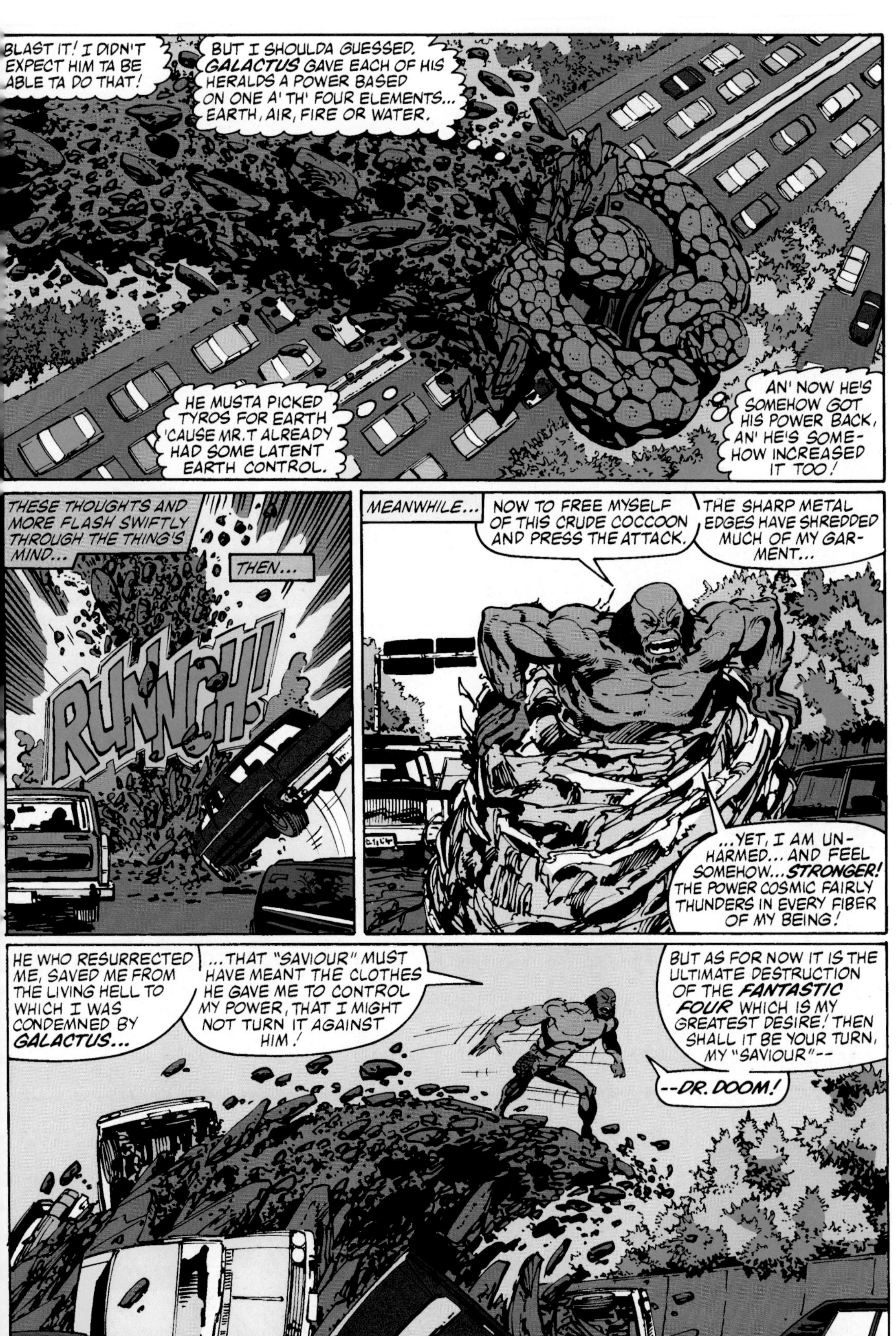
BLAST IT! I DIDN'T EXPECT HIM TA BE ABLE TA DO THAT!
BUT I SHOULDA GUESSED. GALACTUS GAVE EACH OF HIS HERALDS A POWER BASED ON ONE A' TH' FOUR ELEMENTS... EARTH, AIR, FIRE OR WATER.
HE MUSTA PICKED TYROS FOR EARTH 'CAUSE MR.T ALREADY HAD SOME LATENT EARTH CONTROL.
AN' NOW HE'S SOMEHOW GOT HIS POWER BACK, AN' HE'S SOME-HOW INCREASED IT TOO!
THESE THOUGHTS AND MORE FLASH SWIFTLY THROUGH THE THING'S MIND...
THEN...
RUNNCH!
MEANWHILE...
NOW TO FREE MYSELF OF THIS CRUDE COCCOON AND PRESS THE ATTACK.
THE SHARP METAL EDGES HAVE SHREDDED MUCH OF MY GAR-MENT...
...YET, I AM UN-HARMED... AND FEEL SOMEHOW... STRONGER! THE POWER COSMIC FAIRLY THUNDERS IN EVERY FIBER OF MY BEING!
HE WHO RESURRECTED ME, SAVED ME FROM THE LIVING HELL TO WHICH I WAS CONDEMNED BY GALACTUS...
...THAT "SAVIOUR" MUST HAVE MEANT THE CLOTHES HE GAVE ME TO CONTROL MY POWER, THAT I MIGHT NOT TURN IT AGAINST HIM!
BUT AS FOR NOW IT IS THE ULTIMATE DESTRUCTION OF THE FANTASTIC FOUR WHICH IS MY GREATEST DESIRE! THEN SHALL IT BE YOUR TURN, MY "SAVIOUR"--
--DR. DOOM!

NOT FAR AWAY...
MAN-O-MAN! JUST ABOUT... SHOOK HANDS... WITH TH' REAPER THAT TIME!
NOW, WHERE DID I GET DUMPED...?
AW, NO! RIGHT IN FRONT OF A SUPERMARKET!
SPECIAL HEAD LETTUCE

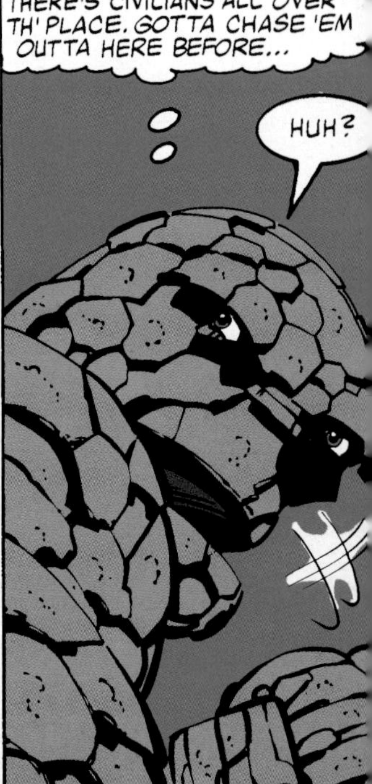
THERE'S CIVILIANS ALL OVER TH' PLACE. GOTTA CHASE 'EM OUTTA HERE BEFORE...
HUH?

IME HAS COME, BEN
M. THE MOMENT OF
ANNIHILATION IS
ST AT HAND!
BETTER MEN THAN YOU HAVE SAID THAT, BUNKY, AN' I'M STILL HERE.
DO YER WORST!
DAIRY
98¢ A DOZEN

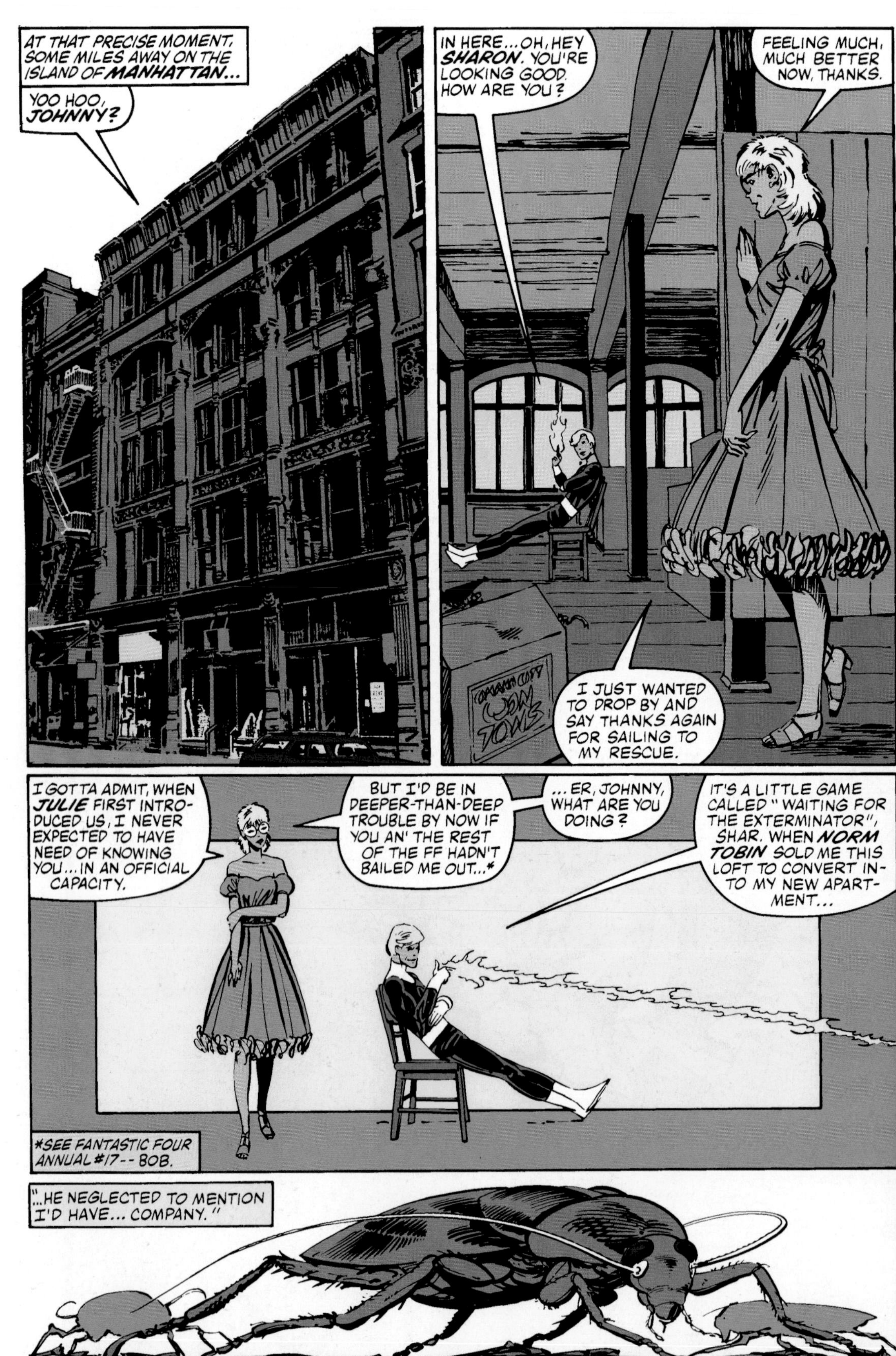
AT THAT PRECISE MOMENT, SOME MILES AWAY ON THE ISLAND OF MANHATTAN...
YOO HOO, JOHNNY?
IN HERE...OH, HEY SHARON. YOU'RE LOOKING GOOD. HOW ARE YOU?
FEELING MUCH, MUCH BETTER NOW, THANKS.
I JUST WANTED TO DROP BY AND SAY THANKS AGAIN FOR SAILING TO MY RESCUE.
I GOTTA ADMIT, WHEN JULIE FIRST INTRODUCED US, I NEVER EXPECTED TO HAVE NEED OF KNOWING YOU... IN AN OFFICIAL CAPACITY.
BUT I'D BE IN DEEPER-THAN-DEEP TROUBLE BY NOW IF YOU AN' THE REST OF THE FF HADN'T BAILED ME OUT...*
...ER, JOHNNY, WHAT ARE YOU DOING?
IT'S A LITTLE GAME CALLED "WAITING FOR THE EXTERMINATOR", SHAR. WHEN NORM TOBIN SOLD ME THIS LOFT TO CONVERT INTO MY NEW APARTMENT...
*SEE FANTASTIC FOUR ANNUAL #17--BOB.
"...HE NEGLECTED TO MENTION I'D HAVE... COMPANY."

USIN' YOUR POWER TO KILL ROACHES? THAT'S A BIT LIKE USIN' A NUKE TO KILL MICE, AIN'T IT?
JUST THINK OF IT AS MY LOWLY CONTRIBUTION TO A BATTLE THAT'S BEEN GOING ON FOR 300 MILLION YEARS.
BESIDES, IT'S FASTER, CLEANER, AND PROBABLY A LOT LESS CRUEL THAN USING POISONS...
...AND... AHEM ...MORE FUN, TOO.

ANYWAY, CAN I OFFER YOU A COKE OR SOMETHING? THE PREVIOUS TENANTS LEFT AN OLD BUT FUNCTIONAL ICE-BOX.
WELL, TO BE HONEST...

...I CAN THINK OF MUCH MORE ENJOYABLE WAYS TO SPEND AN AFTERNOON IN JUNE, CAN'T YOU?
SHAR-UMPH!

SH--SHARON! PLEASE! YOU'RE... A CUTE KID... BUT I'M NOT... I MEAN...
WELL, JULIE AND I... THAT IS...
DON'T WASTE YOUR TIME ON JULIE, JOHNNY. SHE'S...
HOLY...! THE FF EMERGENCY FLARE SIGNAL!

JOHNNY, WAIT! MAYBE IT ISN'T FOR YOU. I MEAN, MAYBE IT ISN'T A REAL EMERGENCY.
WE NEVER USE THAT FLARE UNLESS IT'S MAJOR-LEAGUE SERIOUS, SHARON.
I GOTTA GO!

FLAME ON!
JOHNNY!
OH... #%*&¢!

REED'S OVER AT AVENGERS MANSION, AND THAT LOOKS QUIET...
SUE'S HOUSE-HUNTING IN CONNECTICUT, SO IT MUST BE THE THING WHO'S SIGNALING.
BUT WHERE DID THAT FLARE...?

THERE!
THE RESIDUAL TRAIL OF THE SIGNAL IS ON THE QUEENS SIDE OF THE EAST RIVER.
A QUICK CHANGE OF DIRECTION AND THE HUMAN TORCH ACCELERATES OUT OF MANHATTAN TOWARDS...

HOLY COW!
WHAT IN BLAZES IS GOING ON HERE?

AT THAT MOMENT, SOME FIFTY MILES DUE NORTH AND BLISSFULLY IGNORANT OF THE DANGERS NOW CONFRONTING HER BROTHER AND HER DEAREST FRIEND...
I SHOULD BE BACK HOME... NO BACK TO THE BAXTER BUILDING... WITHIN TEN MINUTES AT THIS RATE.
I HOPE REED REMEMBERED TO POP THAT LASAGNA IN THE OVEN AS I ASKED HIM TO. I'M ABSOLUTELY FAMISHED!
BUT, AS DOMESTIC MATTERS OCCUPY HER THOUGHTS, SUSAN RICHARDS DOES NOT NOTICE THE CLOUD MASS BILLOWING OUT OF A CLEAR SKY BEHIND HER...
NOR DOES SHE SENSE THE GREAT, DARK SHIP HIDDEN WITHIN THE CLOUDS...
SILENT AS A GLIDING BIRD, THE LEVIATHAN DRAWS CLOSER, ITS STEALTH SO TOTAL THAT THE INVISIBLE GIRL REMAINS COMPLETELY UNAWARE...
...UNTIL IT IS TOO LATE...
WHAT IN THE NAME OF...?

ALTHOUGH SHE IS CAUGHT UNAWARES, SUE IS NOT UNPREPARED...
INSTINCTIVELY SHE WRAPS AN IMPENATRABLE, INVISIBLE FORCE-FIELD ABOUT HERSELF...
I RECOGNIZE THIS STYLE OF TECHNOLOGY.
ONLY ONE MAN COULD HAVE BUILT THIS SHIP!
SIMULTANEOUSLY SHE RENDERS HER STREET CLOTHES INVISIBLE, AND THE UNIFORM SHE WEARS BENEATH REVEALS ITSELF...
DOCTOR DOOM!
EXCELLENT, SUSAN. YOU ARE AS INTELLIGENT AS YOU ARE BEAUTIFUL.
IT WILL TROUBLE ME A LITTLE TO ANNIHILATE YOU ALONG WITH THE REST OF THE FANTASTIC FOUR.
SPARE ME YOUR HYPOCRISY, DOOM. THE INHIBITOR RAY YOU ONCE USED AGAINST US* HAS LONG SINCE WORN OFF.
THERE'S NOTHING NOW TO PREVENT ME FROM USING MY FORCE-FIELD TO CRACK OPEN YOUR ARMOR AND SQUASH YOU--IF IT REALLY IS YOU, AND NOT ONE OF YOUR ROBOT DOUBLES.
*SEE ISSUE #'S 246-247--BOB.

SUCH A GREETING! IS THAT HOW YOU ADDRESS YOUR BETTERS, WOMAN?
I HAD THOUGHT YOU A LADY. BUT IF YOU INSIST ON SPEAKING LIKE A KITCHEN WENCH...

...I'LL TREAT YOU AS ONE!
UNGH!

I... FELT THAT!
DOOM MUST BE USING SOME KIND OF CONCUSSIVE WEAPON THAT COUNTERS MY FORCE-FIELD.
FOR THE SAKE OF THE BABY I MUST FINISH THIS FIGHT BEFORE HE CAN KNOCK ME ABOUT TOO MUCH...
YET, WITH HIS STRANGE CODE OF HONOR I'M SHOCKED THAT HE WOULD STRIKE A WOMAN...

...KILL ONE, YES, BUT I THOUGHT HIM ABOVE SIMPLE BRUTALITY.
COSMIC-SPAWNED ENERGY IN HER CELLS SHAPES THE POWERS LOCKED WITHIN THEM, AND SUE LASHES OUT...

I KNEW IT! ANOTHER OF DOOM'S WRETCHED ROBOTS!
AND NOT A PARTICULARLY GOOD ONE, EITHER. MY FORCE-FIELD RAM TOOK ITS HEAD RIGHT OFF!

FORGIVE ME FOR NOT PERSONALLY WELCOMING YOU, SUSAN. THERE WERE MORE PRESSING MATTERS TO CONCERN ME.
REALLY, VON DOOM? YOU USED YOUR ROBOTS AGAINST US THE LAST TIME WE BATTLED. *
I'M INCLINED TO THINK YOU'VE SIMPLY BECOME AFRAID TO FACE ANY OF THE FANTASTIC FOUR YOURSELF.
*ISSUE # 246--BOB.

YOU KNOW ME BETTER THAN THAT, WOMAN. I SIMPLY FIND IT UNDIGNIFIED FOR A MONARCH TO ENGAGE IN SUCH MENIAL PHYSICALITY.
MY TRUE POWER LIES IN THE STRENGTH OF MY INTELLECT, AND HOW I USE IT TO GUIDE OTHERS.
A PRETTY SPEECH, DOOM, BUT LACKING CONVICTION. YOU STILL WON'T CONFRONT ME YOURSELF!
DO I HAVE TO COME AFTER YOU? DO I HAVE TO TAKE THIS WHOLE SHIP APART TO FIND YOU?

WONDERFUL! WONDERFUL! SUCH FIRE! SUCH UNGUESSED STRENGTH! I APPLAUD YOU, SUSAN RICHARDS. YOU HAVE BECOME A TRUE WARRIOR IN YOUR OWN RIGHT!
YOU COULD INDEED SMASH YOUR WAY THROUGH THIS VESSEL. YOU COULD CERTAINLY FIND YOUR WAY TO ME.
FOR THE FIRST TIME I AM EVEN COMPELLED TO CONSIDER THAT YOU, WHOM I ONCE THOUGHT WEAKEST OF THE FOUR, MIGHT ACTUALLY SURVIVE A BATTLE WITH VICTOR VON DOOM.
BUT, BEFORE WE TEST THAT HYPOTHESIS, LOOK BEHIND YOU.
WHAT KIND OF GAME ARE YOU PLAYING NOW, VON DOOM...?

...OH...
...NO...

BEHIND HER A BULKHEAD HAS SWUNG SILENTLY TO ONE SIDE. SUSAN STORM RICHARDS LOOKS OUT ON A SCENE MORE SUITED TO A WAR-ZONE.
TH-THAT'S JOHNNY DOWN THERE! AND BEN! BUT... WHO ARE THEY FIGHTING?
DOOM'S COLD, METALLIC VOICE IS ALMOST WITHOUT EMOTION NOW, YET IT SNAPS AGAINST HER LIKE A CAT-O'-NINE-TAILS. "FIGHTING? YOU MEAN WHO IS DESTROYING THEM, DO YOU NOT?
"LOOK CLOSELY, SUSAN. SURELY YOU RECOGNIZE AN OLD... FRIEND."
SHE SQUINTS THROUGH BILLOWING BLACK SMOKE, AND AN ICY CLAW SNATCHES AT HER HEART. "TYROS! TYROS! BUT HE'S DEAD!"
"NO, SUSAN. HE IS RESURRECTED, AND AT MY HAND. THE POWER COSMIC IS HIS ONCE MORE, THAT SAME POWER I ONCE STOLE FROM THE SILVER SURFER!
FISK'S POTATO CHIPS
"AND THIS TIME NOTHING WILL PREVENT TYROS, MY UNWITTING SLAVE, FROM DESTROYING THE FANTASTIC FOUR!"

AND SO, I CONFRONT YOU. IT IS THE TRUE VICTOR VON DOOM YOU SEE HERE NOW.
THE CHOICE THEN IS YOURS. ENGAGE ME NOW IN A BATTLE YOU MIGHT SURVIVE...
"...LEAVING YOUR LOVED ONES TO A BATTLE THEY CANNOT POSSIBLY SURVIVE...
"...OR GO NOW TO THEIR AID, REMEMBERING ALWAYS THAT TO DO SO IS TO FLEE DOOM, TO ACKNOWLEDGE HIM YOUR MASTER!"
HIS LOGIC IS FLAWED, WARPED BY HIS UNEQUALED EGO, YET THE CHOICE HE PRESENTS IS PLAIN AND TRUE...
...AND IN THE LAST ANALYSIS, NO CHOICE AT ALL...
CURSE YOU, DOOM!

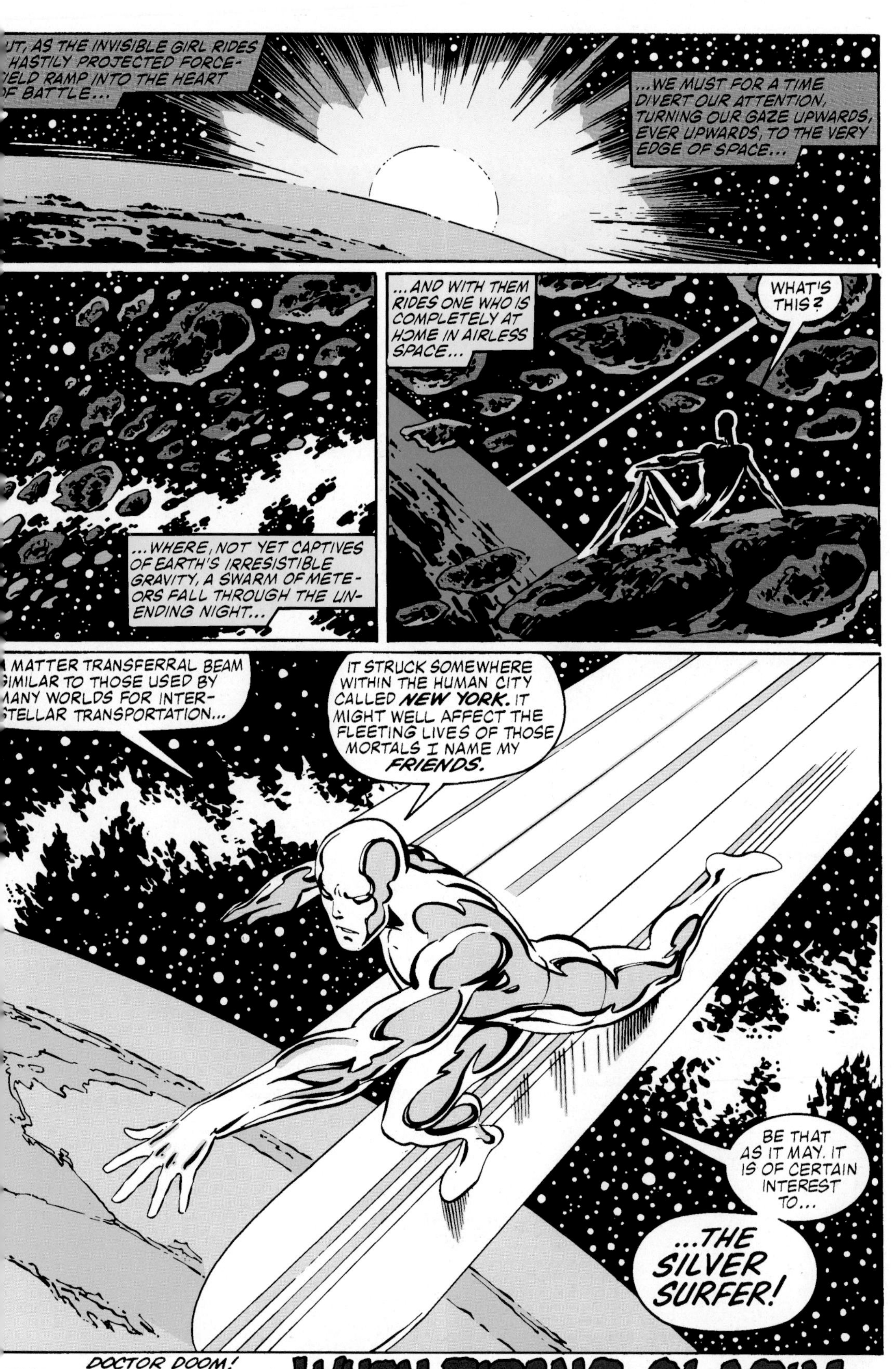

UT, AS THE INVISIBLE GIRL RIDES HASTILY PROJECTED FORCE-IELD RAMP INTO THE HEART OF BATTLE...
...WE MUST FOR A TIME DIVERT OUR ATTENTION, TURNING OUR GAZE UPWARDS, EVER UPWARDS, TO THE VERY EDGE OF SPACE...
...WHERE, NOT YET CAPTIVES OF EARTH'S IRRESISTIBLE GRAVITY, A SWARM OF METE-ORS FALL THROUGH THE UN-ENDING NIGHT...
...AND WITH THEM RIDES ONE WHO IS COMPLETELY AT HOME IN AIRLESS SPACE...
WHAT'S THIS?
MATTER TRANSFERRAL BEAM IMILAR TO THOSE USED BY ANY WORLDS FOR INTER-STELLAR TRANSPORTATION...
IT STRUCK SOMEWHERE WITHIN THE HUMAN CITY CALLED NEW YORK. IT MIGHT WELL AFFECT THE FLEETING LIVES OF THOSE MORTALS I NAME MY FRIENDS.
BE THAT AS IT MAY. IT IS OF CERTAIN INTEREST TO...
...THE SILVER SURFER!

NEXT SSUE: DOCTOR DOOM! TYROS THE TERRIBLE! THE SILVER SURFER! A STORY WE COULD ONLY CALL... **WHEN TITANS CLASH!** BE HERE!

fantastic four # 260

N O V E M B E R 1 9 8 3

BEFORE WE PICK UP WHERE WE LEFT OFF LAST ISSUE--
HIGH ABOVE THE ARCTIC WASTES OF FAR NORTHERN CANADA A REGAL FIGURE CLEAVES THE FRIGID AIR, HEEDLESS OF TEMPERATURES THAT WOULD FREEZE ANOTHER MAN TO DEATH IN MERE MINUTES.
HYBRID EYES, EQUALLY AT HOME IN THE HIGH STRATOSPHERE OR THE DEEPEST OCEANS, SCAN THE LANDS BELOW, SEEKING DETAIL IN THE UNIFORMITY OF THE ICE FLOES.
HE IS NAMOR, PRINCE OF ATLANTIS, THE MIGHTY, SAVAGE SUB-MARINER, AND THIS DAY HE IS FAR FROM HOME, SEARCHING...

FROM HERE I DETECT NOTHING OUT OF THE ORDINARY. THE WATER COLOR HAS NOT CHANGED, THE ICE FLOES FLOAT NEITHER HIGHER NOR LOWER.
YET SOMETHING IS SORELY AMISS IN THESE REGIONS, OR THE EVENTS OF THE LAST TWO DAYS WOULD NOT HAVE OCCURRED.
SO THINKING, THE MONARCH'S MIND PULLS BACK THE CURTAIN OF TIME, AND YESTERDAY COMES ALIVE FOR HIM AGAIN.
HE SEES ONCE MORE THE FRANTIC ARRIVAL OF AN ATLANTEAN BORDER GUARD AT A MORNING'S COUNCIL...
...HE STANDS AGAIN ALONE ON A DISTANT OUTPOST OF THE FABLED REALM, BEHOLDING WITH HIS OWN EYES THE APPROACH OF MANY HUNDREDS OF THE BARBARIANS OF THE NORTHERN REACHES.
NAMOR IS PREPARED FOR BATTLE...
...HE FINDS INSTEAD A PEOPLE SCARCELY RECOVERED FROM SOME TERRIBLE ORDEAL.
THE BARBARIANS HAVE COME NOT AS INVADERS, BUT AS SUPPLICANTS, BEGGING SANCTUARY IN THE NOBLE HALLS OF ATLANTIS.
THE BARBARIANS LACK THE WISDOM TO PROPERLY DESCRIBE WHAT HAS DRIVEN THEM FROM THEIR HOME WATERS--ABLE ONLY TO SAY THAT THOSE WATERS HAVE BECOME UNLIVABLE.
AND SO THE AVENGING SON SETS FORTH TO LEARN FOR HIMSELF WHAT HAS TRANSPIRED.
2

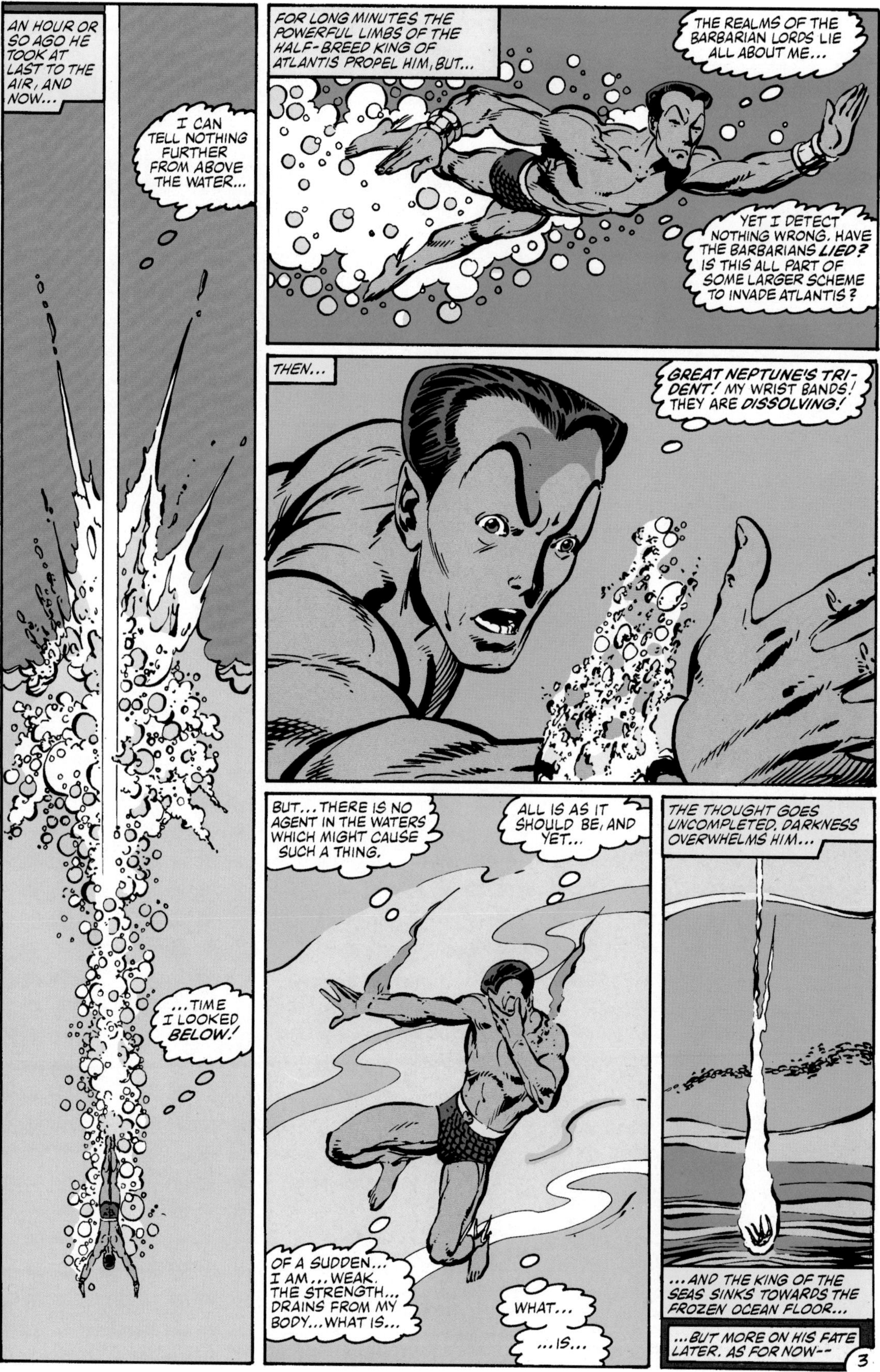
AN HOUR OR SO AGO HE TOOK AT LAST TO THE AIR, AND NOW...
I CAN TELL NOTHING FURTHER FROM ABOVE THE WATER...
...TIME I LOOKED BELOW!
FOR LONG MINUTES THE POWERFUL LIMBS OF THE HALF-BREED KING OF ATLANTIS PROPEL HIM, BUT...
THE REALMS OF THE BARBARIAN LORDS LIE ALL ABOUT ME...
YET I DETECT NOTHING WRONG. HAVE THE BARBARIANS LIED? IS THIS ALL PART OF SOME LARGER SCHEME TO INVADE ATLANTIS?
THEN...
GREAT NEPTUNE'S TRIDENT! MY WRIST BANDS! THEY ARE DISSOLVING!
BUT... THERE IS NO AGENT IN THE WATERS WHICH MIGHT CAUSE SUCH A THING.
ALL IS AS IT SHOULD BE, AND YET...
OF A SUDDEN... I AM... WEAK. THE STRENGTH... DRAINS FROM MY BODY... WHAT IS...
WHAT...
...IS...
THE THOUGHT GOES UNCOMPLETED. DARKNESS OVERWHELMS HIM...
...AND THE KING OF THE SEAS SINKS TOWARDS THE FROZEN OCEAN FLOOR...
...BUT MORE ON HIS FATE LATER. AS FOR NOW--
3

--STAN LEE PRESENTS A BATTLE OF TRULY COSMIC PROPORTIONS!
WHEN TITANS CLASH!
THE STORY SO FAR: DOCTOR DOOM HAS AT LAST SUCCEEDED IN RECREATING ARTIFICIALLY THE POWER COSMIC HE ONCE TRIED UNSUCCESSFULLY TO STEAL FROM THE SILVER SURFER. USING THAT POWER, DOOM HAS RESURRECTED TYROS THE TERRIBLE, FALLEN HERALD OF GALACTUS, AND DISPATCHED HIM ON A MISSION TO DESTROY THE FANTASTIC FOUR, AND MOST ESPECIALLY THEIR LEADER, REED RICHARDS, DOOM'S GREATEST FOE. WHAT TYROS DOES NOT KNOW IS THAT HE HAS ONLY HOURS OF LIFE LEFT BEFORE THE AWESOME POWER COSMIC CONSUMES HIM. AND WHAT DOOM AND THE REST OF THE F.F. DO NOT KNOW IS THAT REED HAS VANISHED!
FOOLS! CRETINS! YOU PIT YOUR PUNY POWERS AGAINST TYROS? AGAINST THE MASTER OF ROCK AND EARTH?
UNGH! HE'S TOO POWERFUL FOR ME ALONE! THING! DO SOMETHING!
WADDAYA THINK I'M DOIN', HOTSHOT? PICKIN' POSIES? HEY, CHROME DOME, LOOK OVER HERE!
TASTY POPS
JOHN BYRNE STORY AND ART | JIM NOVAK LETTERS | GLYNIS WEIN COLORS | BOB BUDIANSKY EDITOR | JIM SHOOTER TITAN
4

IT'S CLOBBERIN' TIME!
SUPER CLEEN
SUPER CLEEN

NOW JUST LIE THERE LIKE A GOOD L'IL SUPER-PUNK...
...AN' I'LL TRY TA MAKE THIS AS PAINLESS AS POSSIBLE!
IMBECILE! HAVE YOU NOT YET LEARNED THE EXTENT OF MY POWER? FOR AN INSTANT YOU MAY GAIN AN UPPER HAND, BUT IN THE END WILL TYROS TRIUMPH!!

BLAST IT, TH' SUCKER MIGHT BE RIGHT!
ME AN' TH' TORCH ARE AS TOUGH AS HIM ANY DAY, BUT HE CAN KEEP TOSSIN' ROCKS AT US UNTIL WE'RE TOO POOPED T' PANT...
...AN' DOIN' IT DON'T SEEM TA COST HIM BEANS IN ENERGY!

MAN-O-MAN. THIS IS ONE DAY I SHOULD HAVE TAKEN MY VITAMINS.
BUT I CAN'T JUST LIE HERE DOING MY IMPRESSION OF POTTING SOIL. BEN NEEDS MY HELP.
5.

AND EVEN THOUGH I DON'T NEED TO SAY IT SINCE I'M ALREADY ABLAZE, I CAN USE THE EGO-BOOST OF MY BATTLE-CRY...
FLAME ON!
WHAT? THE STRIPLING AGAIN? WHY DO YOU NOT JUST LAY DOWN AND DIE!
DAIRY

IT WILL SAVE YOU A GREAT DEAL OF PAIN!
NOT AGAIN!

THE THING IS BURIED FOR THE NONCE. I CAN AFFORD A MOMENT TO DESTROY THE HUMAN TORCH!
BUT I DO NOT NEED TO USE MY EARTHEN POWER FOR THAT. I NEED ONLY MY STRENGTH...

...MY STRENGTH, AND THIS WATER PIPE UNCOVERED BY OUR BATTLE.
DROWN, FLAMING ONE!
DROWN!

BUT...
WHAT? SOMETHING STOPS THE WATER STREAM...?

NOT SOMETHING, TYROS. SOMEONE. NAMELY ME.
THE INVISIBLE GIRL! BUT...I DID NOT KNOW YOU COULD FLY...?

NOT FLIGHT, TYROS. JUST RIDING ONE OF MY INVISIBLE FORCE-FIELDS. YOU REMEMBER THEM, DON'T YOU? THEY WORK SOMETHING LIKE THIS!
A... BUBBLE... FORMING AROUND MY HEAD...CUTTING OFF MY AIR...
I CAN'T BREATHE... BUT I CAN DO...

...THIS!
RUMBLE
NO!
7

HA HA HA HA! FOOLS! FOOLS AND WEAKLINGS! THIS IS ALMOST TOO EASY!
WELL, IT AIN'T GONNA BE FER LONG, BUTTERCUP! I'D BE HAPPY TA PLAY WITH YA ALL DAY...

...BUT WE'VE ALREADY WRECKED A SUPER-MARKET, AN' IT'S JUST DUMB LUCK NO CIVILIANS GOT KILLED.
SO I GOTTA END THIS FIGHT FAST!
WHAT IN...?!

WAY TO GO BENJAMIN!
NOW LET'S PUT TYROS IN LA-LA LAND BEFORE ANY OF OUR AUDIENCE GETS TOO CLOSE.
I HEAR YA TALKIN', KIDDO!

IT'S NO USE! EVEN WITH THEIR COMBINED POWERS ALL JOHNNY AND BEN CAN DO IS PROLONG THE BATTLE.

WE MUST BRING IT TO AN END!
WE NEED REED!

SECONDS LATER, A FAMILIAR FLARE SIGNAL LIGHTS THE AFTERNOON SKY OVER QUEENS.

AND, IN A GREAT SHIP, HIDDEN BY ROLLING CLOUDS, FAR ABOVE THE BURSTING FLARE...
EXCELLENT. EXCELLENT. ALL GOES EXACTLY ACCORDING TO PLAN. MY INSTRUMENTS SHOW TYROS HAS LESS THAN FORTY-EIGHT MINUTES BEFORE THE POWER COSMIC WILL BEGIN TO OVERWHELM HIM.
GIVEN THE PRESENT CONFIGURATIONS OF THE BATTLE, BY THAT TIME HE SHOULD HAVE SUBJUGATED THESE THREE MEMBERS OF THE ACCURSED FOURSOME, JUST IN TIME FOR REED RICHARDS TO ARRIVE.
THEN DOCTOR DOOM WILL TAKE A HAND, AND MY OLD AND HATED ENEMY WILL BE FOREVER DESTROYED!
BUT AS LONG MINUTES TICK AGONIZINGLY BY...
WHERE IS RICHARDS? HE MUST COME! HE MUST SEE THE HUMILIATION AND DESTRUCTION OF HIS LOVED ONES BEFORE HE, HIMSELF, PERISHES.
SOMETHING HAS GONE WRONG. HE IS NOT COMING.
SECONDS LATER ON THE STREET BELOW...
HOLY COW, IT'S DOCTOR DOOM!
LOOK OUT, MAN! I'M GONE!
THE FF HAVE HAD IT FER SURE NOW!
NAH, THEY'LL BEAT HIM EASY!
ONE SIDE, PEASANTS! NONE MAY BLOCK THE PASSAGE OF THE LORD OF LATVERIA!
IT'S DOC DOOM! HE'S BEHIND ALL THIS!
WHO'S HE THINK HE IS, ORDERIN' US AROUND?
IT'S DOOM!
YOU GONNA ARGUE WITH HIM, PAL?
SHOP-RITE
FOXY LADY
9.

HOLD, TYROS! THE BATTLE IS ENDED! WE WILL NOT DESTROY THE FANTASTIC FOUR WITHOUT REED RICHARDS PRESENT!
DO NOT ORDER ME, HUMAN. TYROS IS NOT YOURS TO COMMAND!

THEN TYROS IS DEAD!
YEOW!

YOU DARE! YOU DARE ATTACK TYROS THE TERRIBLE? YOU DARE ATTACK A WIELDER OF THE POWER COSMIC?!
YOU ARE A FOOL, DOOM! A GREATER FOOL THAN I HAD EVEN IMAGINED. THE GREATEST FOOL IN ALL THE WORLD!

AND THE TIME HAS COME FOR YOU TO PAY FOR YOUR FOLLY!

DOOM'S IN ON THIS, TOO? WHAT IS THIS, NATIONAL TROMP THE FF WEEK?
THIS WHOLE ATTACK WAS DOOM'S PLAN, BEN. HE'S THE ONE WHO BROUGHT TYROS BACK!
YEAH? WELL THEM TWO DON'T LOOK NONE TOO BUDDY-BUDDY TA ME!

INDEED, DOOM IS UNLEASHING THE FULL MIGHT OF HIS ARMORED BATTLE SUIT AGAINST HIS ERSTWHILE "PARTNER".
IGNORANT ALIEN SAVAGE! I AM DOOM! THIS IS MY PLAN! MY VICTORY! WITHOUT THE DEGRADATION OF REED RICHARDS IT WOULD MEAN NOTHING!
UNFH!

NO, DOOM, THIS BATTLE DOES NOT BELONG TO YOU. THIS TRIUMPH IS NOT YOURS TO TAKE OR LEAVE AT WILL. THE FANTASTIC FOUR BETRAYED ME!*
THEIR LIVES ARE MINE TO GRIND AWAY TO DUST!
*SEE ISSUE #'S 242, 243, AND 244 --BOB.

MINE!
YEARRGH!
11.

HA HA HA HA! YOU ARE FINISHED, DOOM! THE POWER COSMIC HAS FUSED YOUR ARMOR, AND THUS SHALL YOU REMAIN, A MONUMENT TO YOUR OWN STUPIDITY, UNTIL IT PLEASES ME TO GRANT YOU THE RELEASE OF DEATH!
AND NOW SHALL I FINISH WITH THE FANTASTIC FOUR, FOR THERE REMAINS NO ONE IN ALL THE WORLD WHO CAN STOP ME!
NO ONE, FELLOW HERALD?
THEN "NO ONE" RIDES A SHINING SILVER BOARD!
THE AIR SCREAMS ABOUT HIS ARGENT FORM, AS HE FLASHES DOWN FROM THE VERY EDGE OF SPACE.
TO THE UNHUMAN EYES OF TYROS THE POWER COSMIC FAIRLY BRISTLES AROUND HIM, AND THE WOULD-BE DESTROYER FEELS A SINGLE DROP OF ACID FEAR SPLASH AGAINST HIS HEART.
THE SILVER SURFER!*
*THE SURFER'S ATTENTION WAS DRAWN TO NEW YORK CITY WHEN HE SAW, FROM HIS VANTAGE POINT AT THE EDGE OF THE EARTH'S ATMOSPHERE, A MATTER TRANSFERRAL BEAM HEADING TOWARD THAT LOCALE LAST ISSUE-- BOB.
12

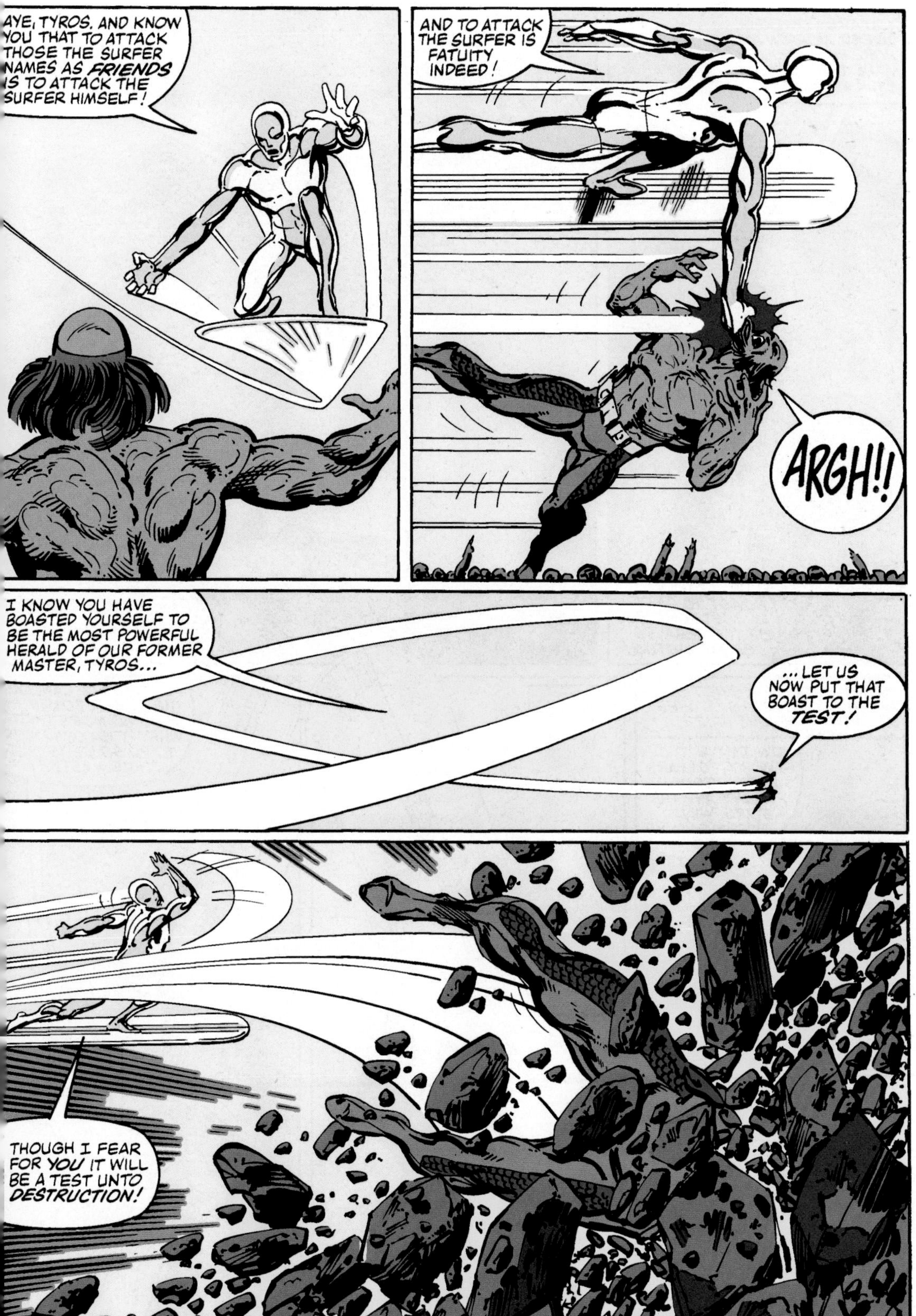
AYE, TYROS, AND KNOW YOU THAT TO ATTACK THOSE THE SURFER NAMES AS FRIENDS IS TO ATTACK THE SURFER HIMSELF!
AND TO ATTACK THE SURFER IS FATUITY INDEED!
ARGH!!
I KNOW YOU HAVE BOASTED YOURSELF TO BE THE MOST POWERFUL HERALD OF OUR FORMER MASTER, TYROS...
...LET US NOW PUT THAT BOAST TO THE TEST!
THOUGH I FEAR FOR YOU IT WILL BE A TEST UNTO DESTRUCTION!
13.

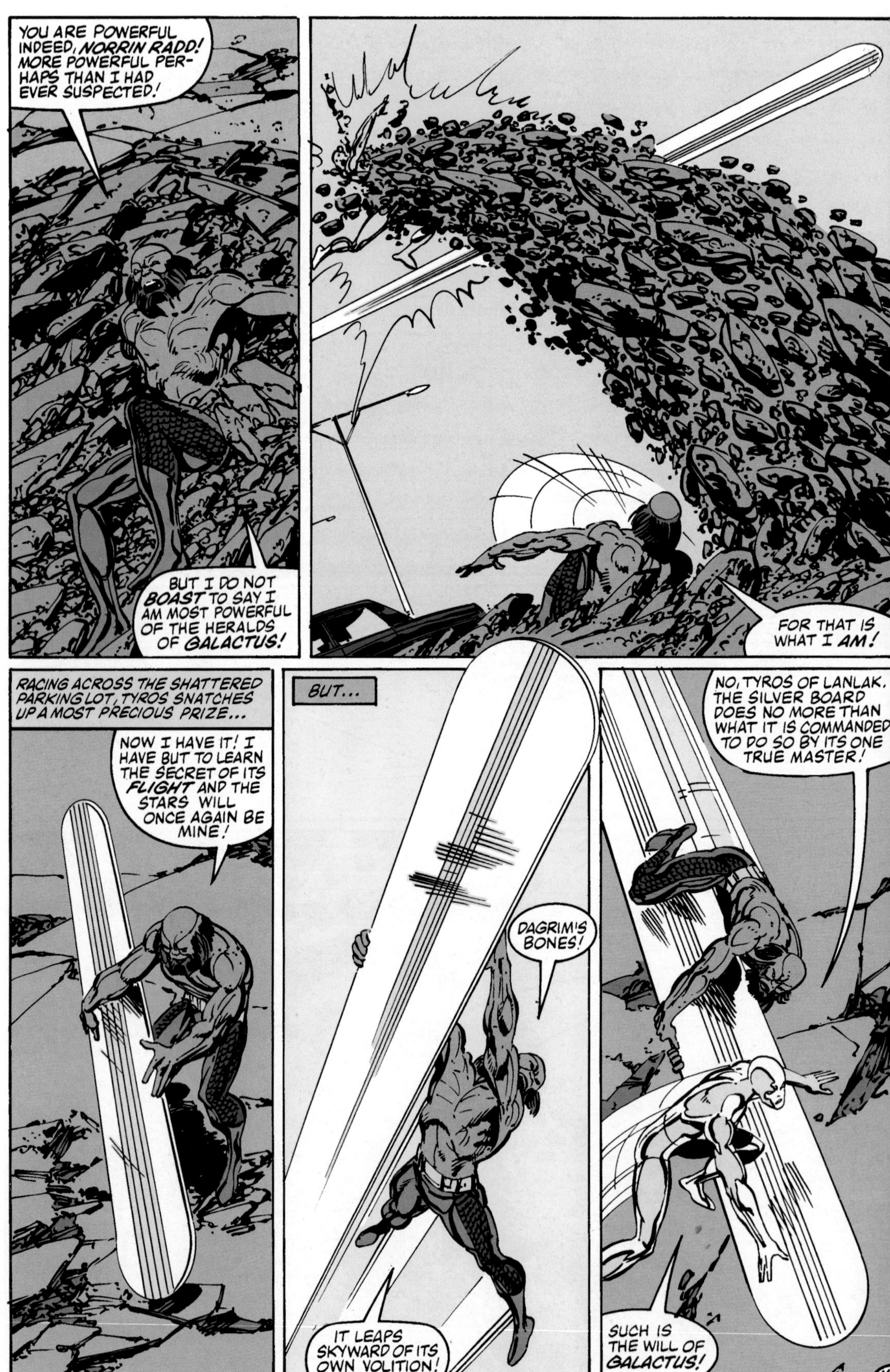
YOU ARE POWERFUL INDEED, NORRIN RADD! MORE POWERFUL PERHAPS THAN I HAD EVER SUSPECTED!
BUT I DO NOT BOAST TO SAY I AM MOST POWERFUL OF THE HERALDS OF GALACTUS!
FOR THAT IS WHAT I AM!
RACING ACROSS THE SHATTERED PARKING LOT, TYROS SNATCHES UP A MOST PRECIOUS PRIZE...
NOW I HAVE IT! I HAVE BUT TO LEARN THE SECRET OF ITS FLIGHT AND THE STARS WILL ONCE AGAIN BE MINE!
BUT...
DAGRIM'S BONES!
IT LEAPS SKYWARD OF ITS OWN VOLITION!
NO, TYROS OF LANLAK. THE SILVER BOARD DOES NO MORE THAN WHAT IT IS COMMANDED TO DO SO BY ITS ONE TRUE MASTER!
SUCH IS THE WILL OF GALACTUS!
14

AND, AS THE BATTLE CLIMBS ONCE AGAIN TOWARDS THE CLOUDS...
THIS IS A CONTINGENCY I HAD NOT CALCULATED.
IT WAS STUPID OF ME TO CONFRONT TYROS MYSELF, INSTEAD OF USING A ROBOT.
NOW, WITH MY ARMOR FUSED, I AM UNABLE TO ACTIVATE MY ESCAPE MECHANISMS.
BUT I CANNOT SIMPLY STAND HERE. EVEN IN THIS CONDITION DOCTOR DOOM IS NOT HELPLESS.
THERE MUST BE A WAY TO EXTRICATE MYSELF FROM THIS PREDICAMENT.
AND THERE IS! BUT IT IS SOMETHING I HAVE NOT ATTEMPTED FOR MANY YEARS.
THE CONDITIONS ARE FAR FROM IDEAL, BUT IT IS MY ONE CHANCE! I MUST ATTEMPT IT!
AND AS VICTOR VON DOOM TURNS HIS AWESOME INTELLECT ALONG STRANGE PATHS...
WHY IS IT TAKING THE FANTASTIC FOUR SO LONG TO STOP THESE AWFUL PEOPLE? FROM ALL I'VE READ I WOULD HAVE THOUGHT THEY WERE POWERFUL ENOUGH...
WHY, THEY'VE BEATEN THAT NASTY DOCTOR DOOM DOZENS OF TIMES BEFORE. I...
BE SILENT, OLD WOMAN! I HAVE NO TIME TO LISTEN TO YOUR RIDICULOUS PRATTLING!
HEY, DOWNER! WHAT SET HIM OFF, GRANNY?
I DONT THINK ANYTHING "SET HIM OFF." I THINK IT'S JUST ANOTHER SIGN OF THE AWFUL MANNERS YOUNG PEOPLE HAVE NOWADAYS!
IF MY NEPHEW WERE HERE, HE'D GIVE HIM A PIECE OF HIS MIND!
AND I AM NOT YOUR GRANNY!
15.

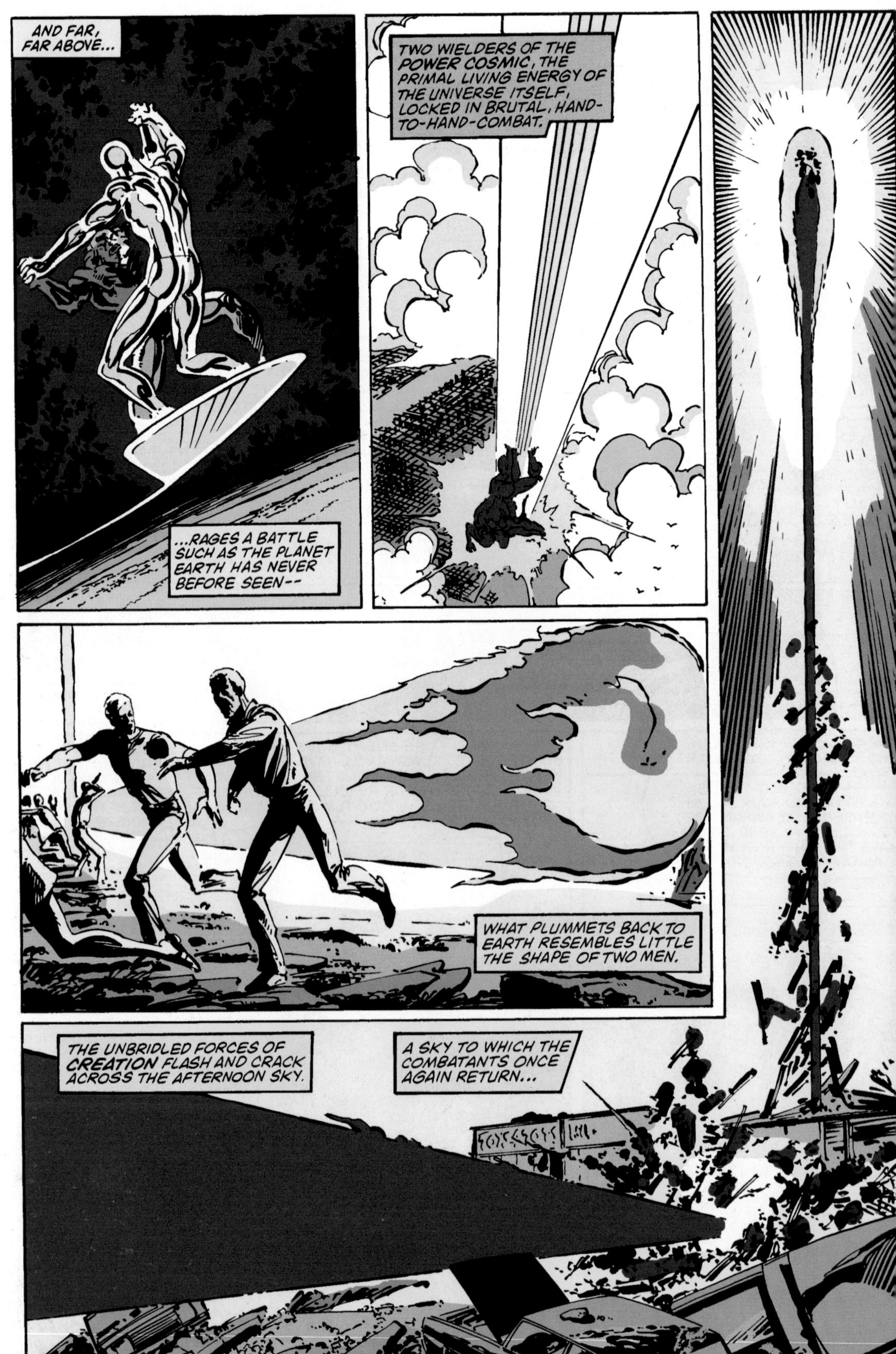
AND FAR, FAR ABOVE...
...RAGES A BATTLE SUCH AS THE PLANET EARTH HAS NEVER BEFORE SEEN--
TWO WIELDERS OF THE POWER COSMIC, THE PRIMAL LIVING ENERGY OF THE UNIVERSE ITSELF, LOCKED IN BRUTAL, HAND-TO-HAND-COMBAT.
WHAT PLUMMETS BACK TO EARTH RESEMBLES LITTLE THE SHAPE OF TWO MEN.
THE UNBRIDLED FORCES OF CREATION FLASH AND CRACK ACROSS THE AFTERNOON SKY.
A SKY TO WHICH THE COMBATANTS ONCE AGAIN RETURN...

AND AT THE HEART OF THAT UNIVERSAL FIRE...
TYROS!
BUT EVEN AS THE STARTLED SURFER GASPS HIS OPPONENT'S NAME HE REALIZES TYROS IS NO LONGER TRULY THERE...

WHAT GRAPPLES WITH WITH HIM NOW IS A LIVING EXTENSION OF THE POWER COSMIC...
BUT LIVING NOT FOR LONG, AS THE FIREBALL PLUNGES EARTHWARD ONCE AGAIN...

AND THE MORTAL FORM OF THE CREATURE ONCE CALLED TYROS BOILS AWAY.
AND AN ARMORED FIGURE SCREAMS...

17.

HOLY CATS! I AIN'T NEVER SEEN AN EXPLOSION LIKE THIS BEFORE.
IT'S LIKE IT'S ALMOST ALIVE!
GET CLEAR, BOTH OF YOU!
I'VE SURROUNDED IT WITH AN INVISIBLE FORCE FIELD, BUT IT'S SO POWERFUL...
PUSHING ME BACK...
SIS...?

SUZIE!

PROPELLED BY THE PRESSURE OF THE BLAST AGAINST HER FORCE-FIELD, SUSAN STORM RICHARDS FAIRLY FLIES ACROSS THE PARKING LOT.
EVEN TAKEN THUS BY SURPRISE, HER LITHE FORM IS GRACEFUL IN MOTION.
THE SAME CANNOT BE SAID FOR HER STOPPING...

SIS! SIS, ARE YOU OKAY?
THE BABY...?
WE'RE FINE, JOHNNY.

BUT...
...WHAT ABOUT THE SILVER SURFER?

I DUNNO, SUE. IT DON'T LOOK LIKE ANYBODY'S COMIN' UP OUTTA THIS MESS...

WAIT A SEC...
STRUGGLING, STRAINING, THE BATTERED FIGURE RISES FROM THE BUBBLING CAULDRON.

IT... WOULD SEEM... I HAVE ...WON...

WOW, GLINTY, AM I EVER GLAD TA SEE YOU ALL IN ONE PIECE. BUT, TYROS...?
AN' DOOM??
OF DOOM I CANNOT SAY. BUT TYROS IS GONE, ULTIMATELY CONSUMED BY THE POWER COSMIC.
AND AS FOR DOCTOR DOOM...
SIS, BE CAREFUL!

DON'T WORRY, JOHNNY. I DON'T THINK I HAVE ANYTHING TO FEAR FROM DOOM ANYMORE!
I DON'T THINK ANY OF US NEED FEAR HIM EVER AGAIN!

DOOM'S MASK! THE BLAST MUST HAVE BLOWN IT RIGHT OFF!
AND IF THE BLAST COULD SHATTER HIS ARMOR THEN... DOOM COULD NOT HAVE SURVIVED. THE GREATEST EVIL THE WORLD HAS EVER FACED IS... DEAD!
AN' GOOD RIDDANCE, SEZ I. LET'S BLOW THIS JOINT!
19.

LEAVING WILL NOT PROVE QUITE SO EASY, THE CONSEQUENCES OF A MAJOR BATTLE IN THE MIDDLE OF A HIGHLY POPULATED AREA BEING MANY. THERE ARE ACCOUNTS BOTH ECONOMIC AND EMOTIONAL THAT WILL TAKE YEARS TO SETTLE. WE NEED NOT CONCERN OURSELVES WITH SUCH MATTERS FOR THE PRESENT, HOWEVER.
4

WE TURN OUR ATTENTION INSTEAD A FEW HOURS INTO THE FUTURE...
...AS DUSK CREEPS INTO THE GLEAMING CANYONS OF THE WORLD'S GREATEST CITY, AND SUNSET PINKS THE TOPS OF THE MIGHTY SKYSCRAPERS.

AND, ON THE THIRTY-SECOND FLOOR OF THE FANTASTIC FOUR'S FAR-FAMED BAXTER BUILDING HEADQUARTERS...
TAKE IT EASY NOW, NORRIN RADD. YOU'RE STILL VERY WEAK.
DO NOT DISTRESS YOURSELF, SUSAN. I SHALL... RECOVER.
I'M SURE YOU WILL, BUT THAT DOESN'T MEAN YOU SHOULDN'T REST AFTER YOUR BATTLE.

WAIT HERE IN THE INFIRMARY, AND I'LL SEE IF REED IS BACK FROM AVENGERS MANSION.

BUT AS THE BEAUTIFUL INVISIBLE GIRL MOVES QUICKLY THROUGH THE MANY LEVELS OF THE TOWER COMPLEX A STRANGE EMPTINESS TOUCHES HER...
THIS IS VERY ODD.
I WISH JOHNNY AND BEN HADN'T GONE OFF TO TAKE CARE OF THEIR OWN AFFAIRS.
4
I CAN'T SHAKE THE FEELING SOMETHING IS ABOUT TO HAPPEN. SOMETHING AWFUL!

FINALLY, ON THE THIRTY-FIRST STORY RESIDENTIAL LEVEL...
I DON'T LIKE THE FEEL OF THIS AT ALL.

REED WASN'T IN ANY OF THE LABS UPSTAIRS. IN FACT THE EXPERIMENTS HE WAS WORKING ON WHEN I WENT OUT THIS MORNING...
...LOOK EXACTLY AS THEY DID THEN. HE SAID HE WAS GOING OVER TO AVENGERS MANSION AT TEN...

...BUT HE WAS CERTAIN HE'D BE BACK IN TIME TO START DINNER COOKING AT THREE.
I'M SURE HE DIDN'T FORGET. EVEN IF HE GOT TIED UP AT THE MANSION...

...HE'D HAVE WHIPPED UP SOME WIDGET TO COME AND TURN ON THE OVEN.
BUT, NO, THE LASAGNA I LEFT IS STONE COLD.
I'D BETTER GIVE THE AVENGERS A QUICK CALL...

BUT BEFORE A PHONE CAN BE REACHED...
S... SUSAN...
OH MY!
21.

NAMOR!
SUSAN RICHARDS... I HAVE NEED OF YOU!
TO BE CONTINUED! BUT NOT IN THE PAGES OF THE FANTASTIC FOUR! DON'T MISS ALPHA FLIGHT #4, NOW ON SALE!
NEXT ISSUE: A MYSTERY UNRAVELS, A TERRIBLE TRUTH IS REVEALED!
THE SEARCH FOR REED RICHARDS!

AND READY FOR NEXT YEAR, SUE... ER, SUSAN? WHERE ARE YOU?
ASTOUND ME! HOW COULD YOU DO SOM THING... SO... SO PRACTICAL?
BUT SURELY THIS IS BETTER THAN CELEBRATING THE SEASON OF LIFE BY KILLING A TREE?
E THIS DISCUSSION CAN ESS FURTHER, HOWEVER...
VOOOOSH
WHAT IN...?
PEED HONED BY YEARS OF CE MISTER FANTASTIC HIS PLIABLE BODY TO INTER- HE SMALL MISSILE.
WHILE THE INVISIBLE GIRL TENDS TO THEIR SON...
THAT WAS VERY NAUGHTY, FRANKLIN. YOU KNOW YOU'RE NOT SUPPOSED TO PLAY WITH SUCH TOYS IN THE HOUSE!
I'M AFRAID THERE'S MORE TO IT THAN THAT, SUE.
LOOK AT THIS!
THIS IS NOT A FLYING TOY
OH, MY!

alpha flight # 4

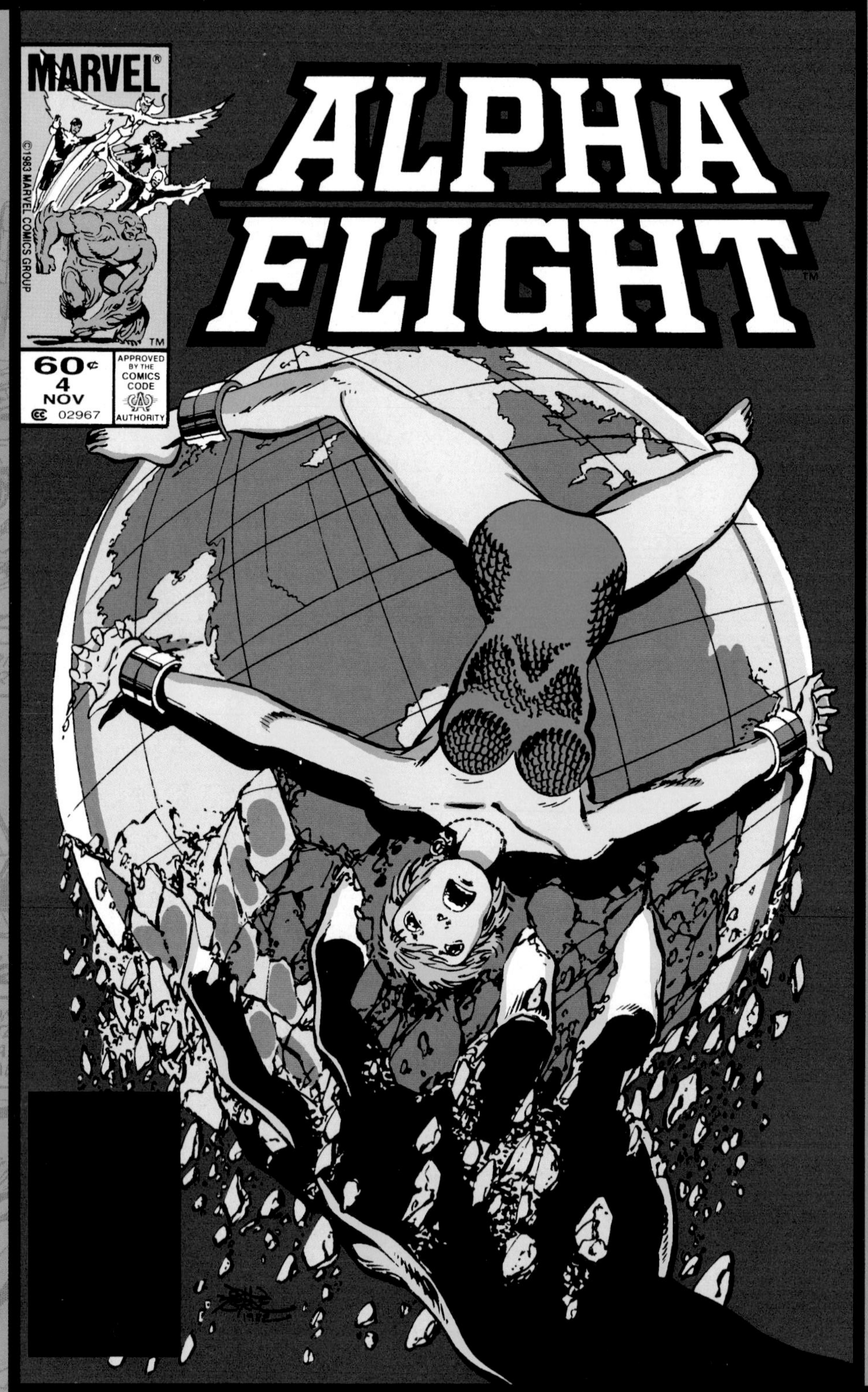

NOVEMBER 1983

RESOLUTIONS!

Stan Lee PRESENTS: JOHN BYRNE WRITER - ARTIST * RICK PARKER LETTERER * ANDY YANCHUS COLORIST * DENNY O'NEIL EDITOR * JIM SHOOTER RESOLVED

EXPLAIN IT TO ME AGAIN, NAMOR.
WHY AM I CHASING ALL OVER THE NORTH POLE WITH YOU WHEN I SHOULD BE HOME TRYING TO CONTACT MY HUSBAND, AND TENDING TO THE SILVER SURFER?
ICY WINDS WHIP PAST HER AT MORE THAN FORTY MILES AN HOUR. IT IS SUMMER IN THE ARCTIC, BUT EVEN THROUGH HER INSULATED COSTUME THE COLD STABS AT SUSAN STORM RICHARDS, THE INVISIBLE GIRL.*
* NO, READERS, JOHN HASN'T CONFUSED ALPHA FLIGHT WITH THE FANTASTIC FOUR. BEAR WITH US -- Denny.

YOU ARE HERE FOR THE SIMPLE REASON THAT I ASKED YOU TO BE HERE, SUSAN.
AND YOU KNOW THAT THE SUB-MARINER DOES NOT CRAVE THE AID OF ANY HUMAN-- NOT EVEN YOU-- UNLESS THE NEED IS DIRE INDEED.
NOW, BE ALERT. WE ARE NEARING THE AREA OF ICE-CAP OVER THOSE WATERS I FOUND MOST INHOSPITABLE...
ARE YOU CERTAIN, NAMOR? HOW INFALLIBLE IS YOUR NAVIGATION SENSE WHEN YOU ARE OUT OF WATER?
ENOUGH THAT I AM CERTAIN WHATEVER EVILS DROVE SOUTH THE BARBARIAN HORDES* LIE NEAR HERE, SOMEWHERE IN THE ICE.
I'LL TAKE YOUR WORD FOR IT. BUT HOW CAN YOU TELL ONE PATCH OF ICE FROM ANOTHER?
WAIT! YOU'RE RIGHT, NAMOR! MY FANTASTICAR'S SENSORS ARE PICKING UP SOMETHING BENEATH THE ICE-CAP.
SOMETHING INCREDIBLE!
* SEE FANTASTIC FOUR #260 -- D.O'NEIL.

...BUT SOMETHING I CAN'T SEEM TO GET A CLEAR FIX ON. OH... IF ONLY REED WERE HERE. HE'D BE ABLE TO MODIFY THE SCANNER, GET PERFECT RESOLUTION...
BUT YOUR HUSBAND IS NOT WITH US. DO THE BEST YOU CAN, SUSAN.
YOUR BEST HAS EVER BEEN MORE THAN SUFFICIENT.

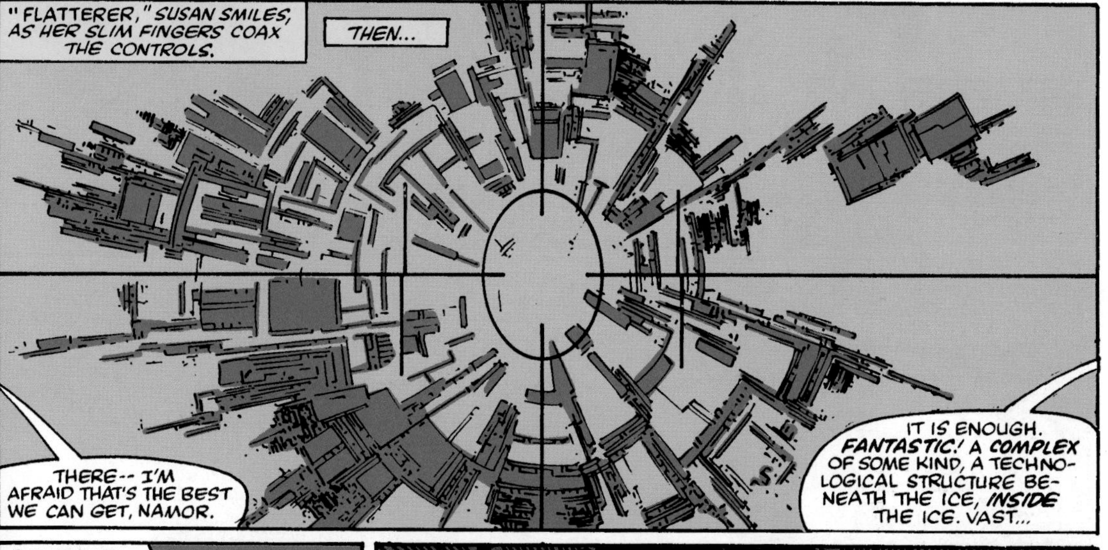
"FLATTERER," SUSAN SMILES, AS HER SLIM FINGERS COAX THE CONTROLS.
THEN...
THERE-- I'M AFRAID THAT'S THE BEST WE CAN GET, NAMOR.
IT IS ENOUGH. FANTASTIC! A COMPLEX OF SOME KIND, A TECHNOLOGICAL STRUCTURE BENEATH THE ICE, INSIDE THE ICE. VAST...

BUT, WHY DO THE EDGES SEEM TO BLUR, AS IF THERE IS NO SHARP DEFINITION BETWEEN METAL AND ICE?
THAT MAY BE JUST THE LACK OF CLEAR... WAIT. WAIT A MOMENT...
ENERGY READING...!

THREE AND ONE HALF MILES AWAY, AT JUST THAT MOMENT...
RRR?
THE GREAT WHITE BEAR TURNS TOWARD THE BLAST, AND UN-EXPECTED INTEL-LIGENCE SHINES IN ITS CLEAR EYES.

IT STANDS BEFORE GIANT, BROKEN DOORS, BURIED IN THE ICE AND SNOW, AND ITS ANI-MAL SENSES, KEENER FAR THAN HUMAN, SCAN THE AREA.
IT WONDERS, IN ITS SLOW, BEAR WAY, IF THIS DISTANT EXPLOSION IS IN SOME WAY CONNECTED TO THE WRECKAGE IT FOUND EARLIER.
WHEN IT WAS NOT A BEAR.

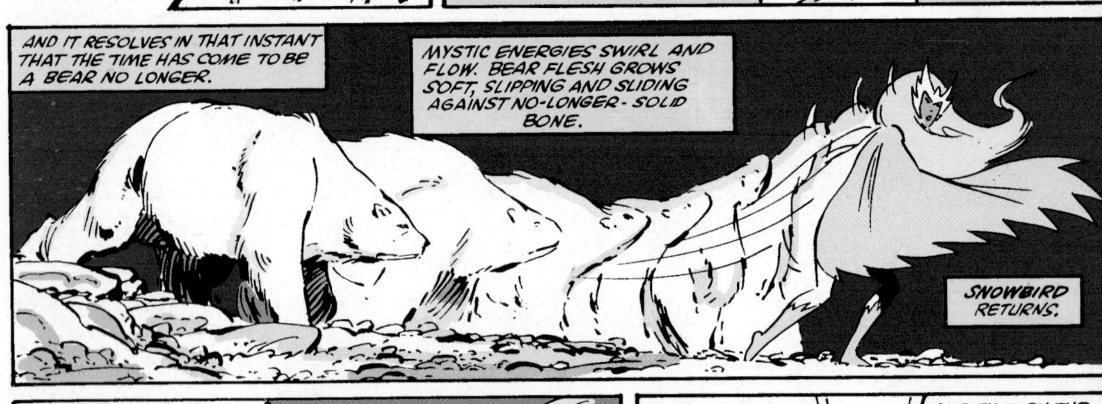
AND IT RESOLVES IN THAT INSTANT THAT THE TIME HAS COME TO BE A BEAR NO LONGER.
MYSTIC ENERGIES SWIRL AND FLOW. BEAR FLESH GROWS SOFT, SLIPPING AND SLIDING AGAINST NO-LONGER-SOLID BONE.
SNOWBIRD RETURNS.

THERE IS MUCH WRONG HERE--GREAT EVIL IN THIS PLACE. ANCIENT EVIL.
THAT EXPLOSION OCCURRED NOT FAR FROM THE WRECKED ALPHA FLIGHT SKY-SHIP I FOUND NOT AN HOUR AGO... IT IS LOGICAL TO ASSUME THE TWO EVENTS ARE IN SOME WAY CONNECTED. BUT IT IS NOT NOW THE TIME TO INVESTIGATE EITHER.

I SENSE MY FELLOW MEMBERS OF ALPHA ARE SOMEWHERE AHEAD.
AND THOUGH THE EVIL IN THIS PLACE THREATENS TO SMO-THER MY MYSTICAL SENSES AND OVER-WHELM ME...
...I MUST JOIN THEM.

SEVERAL LEVELS BELOW...
I THINK EXPLANATIONS ARE IN ORDER, JIMMY-BOY. WHAT DO YOU MEAN AURORA HAS RETREATED INTO HER JEANNE-MARIE PERSONA?
AREN'T THEY THE SAME PERSONA?
NOT EXACTLY, SASQUATCH. BUT WE'VE NO TIME TO WASTE TALKING...
THEN MAKE TIME. WE'RE NOT GOING ANYWHERE UNTIL I UNDERSTAND MORE FULLY WHAT'S WRONG HERE.

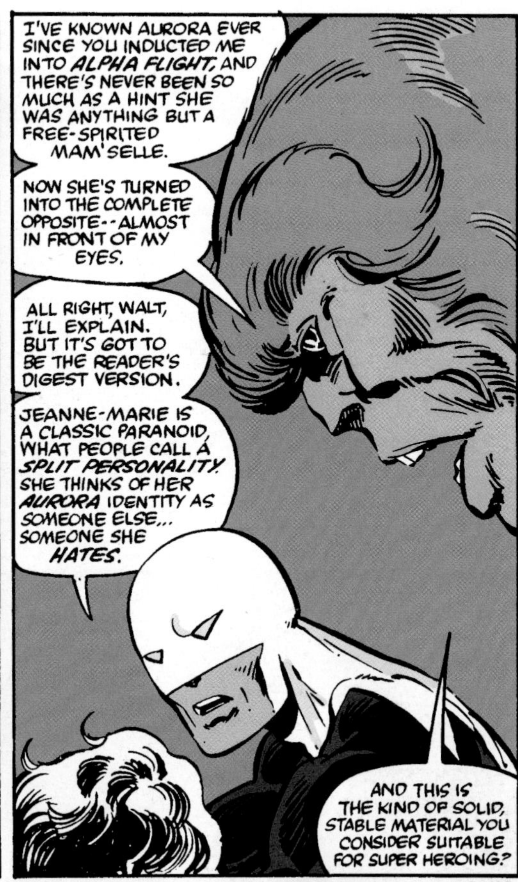
I'VE KNOWN AURORA EVER SINCE YOU INDUCTED ME INTO ALPHA FLIGHT, AND THERE'S NEVER BEEN SO MUCH AS A HINT SHE WAS ANYTHING BUT A FREE-SPIRITED MAM'SELLE.
NOW SHE'S TURNED INTO THE COMPLETE OPPOSITE--ALMOST IN FRONT OF MY EYES.
ALL RIGHT, WALT, I'LL EXPLAIN. BUT IT'S GOT TO BE THE READER'S DIGEST VERSION.
JEANNE-MARIE IS A CLASSIC PARANOID, WHAT PEOPLE CALL A SPLIT PERSONALITY. SHE THINKS OF HER AURORA IDENTITY AS SOMEONE ELSE... SOMEONE SHE HATES.
AND THIS IS THE KIND OF SOLID, STABLE MATERIAL YOU CONSIDER SUITABLE FOR SUPER HEROING?

NO. WHEN I FIRST MET HER SHE WAS IN HER AURORA PERSONA. I DIDN'T LEARN THE OTHER SIDE OF HER UNTIL IT WAS TOO LATE.
NOW THE TRAP WE JUST RESCUED HER FROM SEEMS TO HAVE FORCED SOME KIND OF SPONTANEOUS REGRESSION, AND JEANNE-MARIE IS DOMINANT AGAIN!
OOOH-- MA TÊTE! WHAT... IS... 'APPEN?

EASY, EASY. YOU'RE SAFE NOW, AURORA. YOU CAN...
AURORA! DO NOT CALL ME ZAT NAME! TAKE YOUR FILTHY PAWS OFF!
I MUS' GET AWAY! AWAY FROM AURORA!

OH, BLAST! JEANNE-MARIE!
I'M SORRY!
WAIT!

IDIOT! IDIOT! IDIOT! EVEN AFTER EXPLAINING HER PROBLEM TO YOU I INSTINCTIVELY CALLED HER "AURORA". EXACTLY THE ***WRONG*** THING TO DO.

I'VE GOT TO GET AFTER HER AND...

NO...

YOU SAID HER BROTHER ***NORTHSTAR*** COULD BRING HER OUT OF IT. YOU LOOK FOR HIM!

I'VE... KNOWN HER BETTER THAN YOU.

WAIT... OH, WALT, YOU DON'T MEAN...

ASK ME NO QUESTIONS, AND I'LL TELL YOU NO LIES, JIMMY. JUST GET AFTER NORTHSTAR.

THUS, WITH A TROUBLED BACKWARD GLANCE, THE MAN CALLED ***GUARDIAN*** LAUNCHES HIMSELF DEEPER INTO THE SURROUNDING COMPLEX...
...AS THE MAN-MONSTER KNOWN AS SASQUATCH HEADS OFF IN THE OPPOSITE DIRECTION.

AND AS HE MOVES HIS LONG, LOPING GAIT CHANGES, BALANCE SHIFTING, PROPORTIONS ALTERING...
I MAY BE ABLE TO REACH THROUGH JEANNE-MARIE TO AURORA...

UNTIL...
BUT I THINK I'LL FARE BETTER AS PLAIN OL' ***WALTER LANGOWSKI***.
ASSUMING I CAN ***FIND*** HER WITHOUT MY BLASTED ***GLASSES!***

AND, JUST TO MAKE MATTERS WORSE, THESE CORRIDORS AREN'T CONSTANT. SOMEHOW, THEY KEEP SHIFTING, ALTERING DIRECTION, SIZE--EVERYTHING.
AS IF THIS WHOLE PLACE IS SOME KIND OF LIVING ORGANISM.
AND IF I DON'T FIND AURORA IN SHORT ORDER, WE'LL BOTH BE HOPELESSLY LOST!

AH, THERE YOU ARE! DON'T BE AFRAID, JEANNE MARIE, YOU REMEMBER ME, DON'T YOU? I'D NEVER HURT YOU, WOULD I?
ZAT IS NOT FOR ME TO SAY, M'SIEUR. I AM NOT IN ZE 'ABIT OF ASSOCIATING WIZ NAKED MEN!
INCREDIBLE! A TOTALLY SEPARATE PERSONALITY! EVEN HER ACCENT HAS CHANGED, AS IF SHE'S HAVING TROUBLE WITH ENGLISH.

I'M HARDLY NAKED, JEANNE-MARIE, IN FACT THERE ARE BEACHES IN THIS COUNTRY WHERE I'D BE CONSIDERED OVERDRESSED. NOW PLEASE COME WITH ME. WE MUST GET BACK TO THE OTHERS!
DO NOT TOUCH ME. I DON' WANT TO SEE ZE "OTHEIRS." I WANT TO KNOW WAIR I AM--AND WHY I AM 'ERE.

JEANNE-MARIE... PLEASE, YOU MUST LISTEN TO ME...
HIS WORDS ARE CALM, HIS DEEP VOICE SLOW AND SOOTHING. WHEN HE REACHES OUT HIS HAND HIS TOUCH IS GENTLE, HARDLY THREATENING.

HE SPEAKS OF MOMENTS THEY HAVE SHARED--A NIGHT IN NEW YORK, WEEKS BEFORE.
HE SPEAKS OF INTIMACY, TWO PEOPLE SHARING SOMETHING MORE THAN FRIENDSHIP, IF NOT ENTIRELY LOVE.
HIS WORDS ARE KIND, CALMING, EVOKING IN HER NOT AT ALL THE DISGUST SHE WOULD HAVE EXPECTED OF HERSELF.
SLOWLY, O-SO-SLOWLY, SHE REMEMBERS...
7

BUT SHE REMEMBERS AS JEANNE-MARIE.

ANIMAL!

BLAST!

OBVIOUSLY, THIS ISN'T GOING TO BE AS EASY AS I'D HOPED.

MEANWHILE...

THIS IS POINTLESS.

I HAVE RACED THROUGH WHAT MUST BE FIVE HUNDRED MILES OF CORRIDORS WITHOUT A SIGN OF AURORA.*

*THEY WERE SEPARATED LAST ISSUE -- DEN.

AND THESE WRETCHED HALLS NEVER LOOK THE SAME TWICE. EVEN THOUGH I'M SURE I'VE RETRACED MY PATH SEVERAL TIMES.
FACE FACTS, JEAN-PAUL, YOU ARE VERY, VERY LOST...

WELCOME, NORTHSTAR. I WAS BEGINNING TO THINK YOU'D NEVER GET HERE.
GUARDIAN! YOU FOLLOWED ME HERE? C'EST IMPOSSIBLE!
NOT ENTIRELY. I CHEATED.

I USED THE CYBERNETIC CIRCUITRY IN MY SUPER-SUIT TO TAP INTO THE INTERNAL SYSTEMS OF THIS COMPLEX. IT "SPEAKS" SOME INCOMPREHENSIBLE GOBBLEDEEGOOK, BUT I WAS ABLE TO PINPOINT ALL OUR LOCATIONS, AND FIND YOU.
ALL OF US? THEN YOU KNOW WHERE MY SISTER IS? YOU CAN HELP ME FIND HER?

I COULD, BUT I THINK THERE ARE MORE PRESSING MATTERS FOR US TO ATTEND TO JUST NOW, NORTHSTAR.
AURORA IS SAFE WITH SASQUATCH RIGHT NOW, BUT UNLESS WE ACT SHE WON'T BE SAFE FOR LONG. NONE OF US WILL UNLESS WE MOVE QUICKLY.
YOU SPEAK IN RIDDLES, GUARDIAN. WHAT ARE YOU TALKING ABOUT?
I'M TALKING ABOUT WHAT I THINK I'VE DISCOVERED TO BE THE PURPOSE OF THIS COMPLEX. AND, UNLESS WE SHUT IT DOWN...
...IT WILL MEAN THE EXTERMINATION OF ALL LIFE ON EARTH!

SEVERAL MINUTES EARLIER...
THAT WAS ALMOST TOO CLOSE, SUE...
DON'T QUIBBLE ABOUT TIMING, NAMOR. THAT RAY MAY HAVE DESTROYED THE FANTASTICAR...

...BUT I WAS ABLE TO THROW AN INVISIBLE FORCE FIELD AROUND US, AND SHIELD US FROM THE BLAST.
INDEED. DROP THE FIELD NOW, SUSAN, SO THAT WE MAY LAND PROPERLY.

HMM. IT IS AS I THOUGHT. THE EVIL THAT HAS INFECTED THE WATERS OF THIS REGION ALSO CORRUPTS THE ICE AND SNOW.
YOU'RE RIGHT. I CAN... FEEL SOMETHING WRONG. SOMETHING MISSING IN THE ICE...
WE MUST DISCOVER WHAT IT IS. STAND BACK, SUSAN. AS AERIAL APPROACH DID US NO GOOD, WE MUST GET...

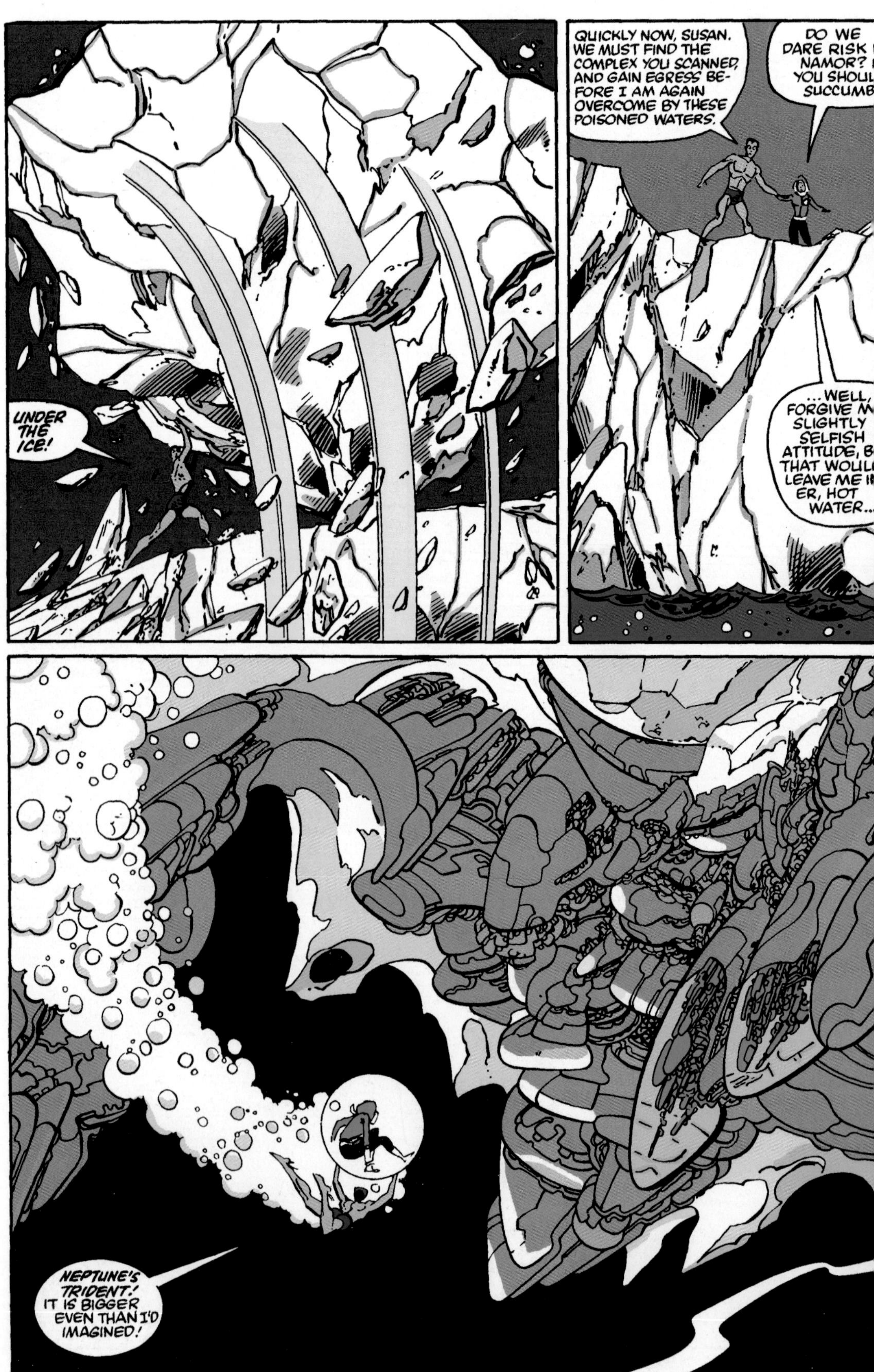
UNDER THE ICE!
QUICKLY NOW, SUSAN. WE MUST FIND THE COMPLEX YOU SCANNED, AND GAIN EGRESS BEFORE I AM AGAIN OVERCOME BY THESE POISONED WATERS.
DO WE DARE RISK NAMOR? YOU SHOUL SUCCUMB
...WELL, FORGIVE M SLIGHTLY SELFISH ATTITUDE, B THAT WOUL LEAVE ME I ER, HOT WATER...
NEPTUNE'S TRIDENT! IT IS BIGGER EVEN THAN I'D IMAGINED!

THEN, IF YOU WORSHIP ANY GODS, SUSAN, I SUGGEST YOU OFFER UP A PRAYER TO THEM.
WE ARE COMMITTED.

FOR SEVERAL LONG MINUTES, THE TWO TRAVEL THROUGH ICY DARKNESS, LIKE EXPLORERS, IN SOME UNGUESSED DEPTH OF STARLESS SPACE...
THEN...
I... GROW STEADILY WEAKER, SUSAN. I FEAR I... MAY HAVE... FAILED YOU...
NAMOR, NO! LOOK!

WITHIN SECONDS...
FANTASTIC! THIS COMPLEX MUST SOMEHOW BE FEEDING ON THE WATERS, DRAWING VITAL ELEMENTS OUT OF THEM, RENDERING THEM DEADLY TO MEMBERS OF MY RACE.
I THINK YOU MAY BE RIGHT, NAMOR. EVERYTHING ABOUT THIS PLACE SUGGESTS A LIVING THING-- A GROWING THING.
WE'VE GOT TO DISCOVER WHO'S BEHIND THIS PLACE, AND WHAT ITS PURPOSE IS...

THUS...
NOT SO FAST, IF YOU PLEASE, SUSAN. IT IS MOST... UNNERVING TO BE RENDERED INVISIBLE!
TRY NOT TO THINK ABOUT IT, NAMOR. JUST MOVE NATURALLY. THAT'S WHAT I DO.
WE NEED MY INVISIBILITY POWER TO GET INTO THIS COMPLEX WITHOUT -- I HOPE -- BEING DETECTED.

AND, SOME FORTY MINUTES LATER...
YOU CONTINUE TO RESIST THE PROBES, LITTLE MARRINA. EVEN THOUGH I HAVE TOLD YOU TO DO SO IS USELESS.
WHY... WHY DO YOU TORTURE ME? YOU TOLD ME THIS SHIP DID THE SAME TO YOU, FORTY THOUSAND YEARS AGO...
WHY DO YOU INFLICT SUCH AGONY ON ANOTHER LIVING BEING?
" SHIP...?"

MARRINA, I HAVE TOLD YOU WHO I AM, HOW I CAME TO BE MASTER OF THIS, YOUR SHIP.
WHY DO YOU INSIST ON PRETENDING NOT TO KNOW THE PURPOSE OF THIS PLACE? LET ME DEMONSTRATE THE FUTILITY OF THIS
LET ME PROVE TO YOU I ALREADY KNOW WHAT YOU SEEK TO KEEP CONCEALED FROM ME

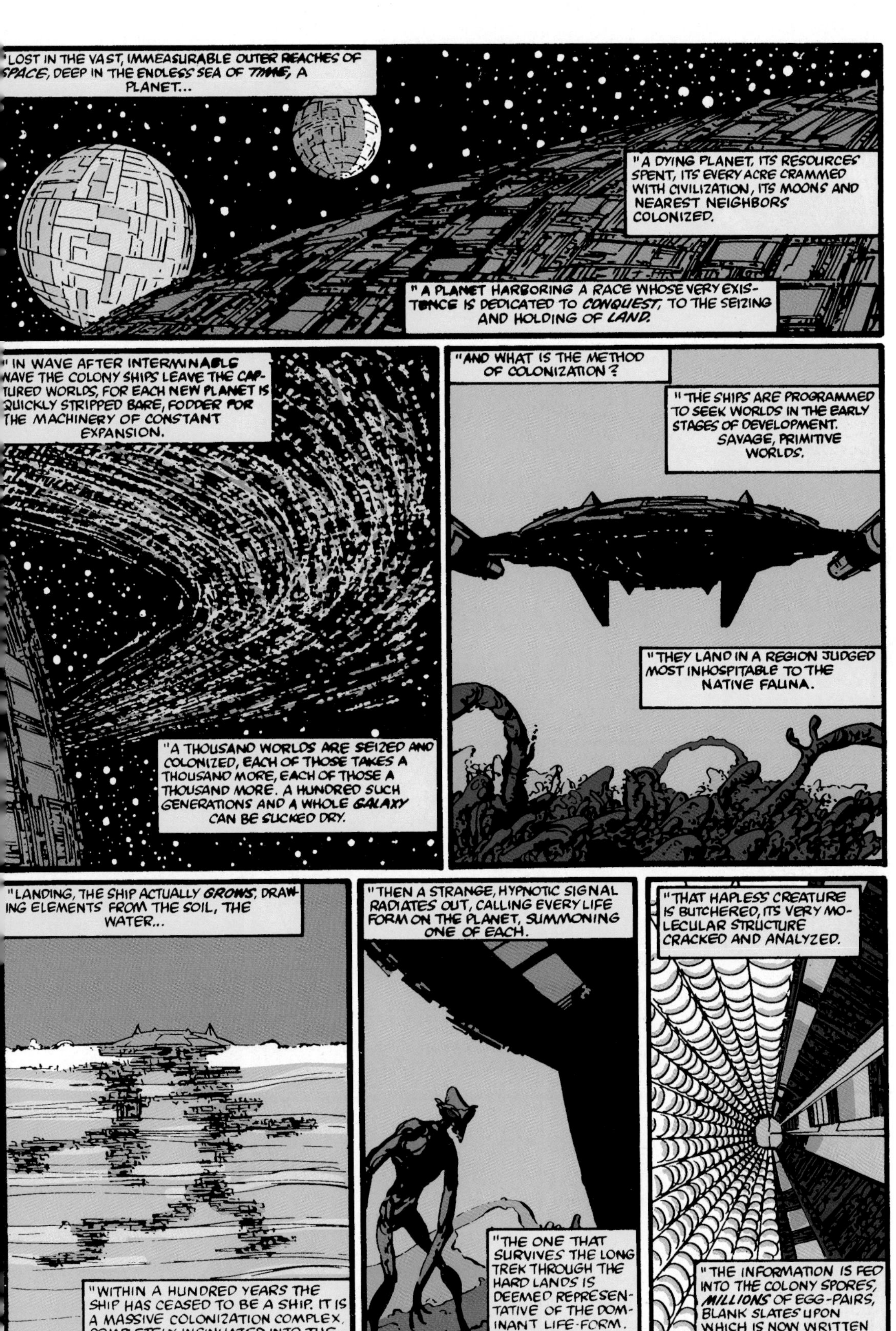
"LOST IN THE VAST, IMMEASURABLE OUTER REACHES OF SPACE, DEEP IN THE ENDLESS SEA OF TIME, A PLANET...
"A DYING PLANET, ITS RESOURCES SPENT, ITS EVERY ACRE CRAMMED WITH CIVILIZATION, ITS MOONS AND NEAREST NEIGHBORS COLONIZED.
"A PLANET HARBORING A RACE WHOSE VERY EXISTENCE IS DEDICATED TO CONQUEST, TO THE SEIZING AND HOLDING OF LAND.
"IN WAVE AFTER INTERMINABLE WAVE THE COLONY SHIPS LEAVE THE CAPTURED WORLDS, FOR EACH NEW PLANET IS QUICKLY STRIPPED BARE, FODDER FOR THE MACHINERY OF CONSTANT EXPANSION.
"A THOUSAND WORLDS ARE SEIZED AND COLONIZED, EACH OF THOSE TAKES A THOUSAND MORE, EACH OF THOSE A THOUSAND MORE. A HUNDRED SUCH GENERATIONS AND A WHOLE GALAXY CAN BE SUCKED DRY.
"AND WHAT IS THE METHOD OF COLONIZATION?
"THE SHIPS ARE PROGRAMMED TO SEEK WORLDS IN THE EARLY STAGES OF DEVELOPMENT. SAVAGE, PRIMITIVE WORLDS.
"THEY LAND IN A REGION JUDGED MOST INHOSPITABLE TO THE NATIVE FAUNA.
"LANDING, THE SHIP ACTUALLY GROWS, DRAWING ELEMENTS FROM THE SOIL, THE WATER...
"WITHIN A HUNDRED YEARS THE SHIP HAS CEASED TO BE A SHIP. IT IS A MASSIVE COLONIZATION COMPLEX, COMPLETELY INSINUATED INTO THE PLANET'S FIBER.
"THEN A STRANGE, HYPNOTIC SIGNAL RADIATES OUT, CALLING EVERY LIFE FORM ON THE PLANET, SUMMONING ONE OF EACH.
"THE ONE THAT SURVIVES THE LONG TREK THROUGH THE HARD LANDS IS DEEMED REPRESENTATIVE OF THE DOMINANT LIFE-FORM.
"THAT HAPLESS CREATURE IS BUTCHERED, ITS VERY MOLECULAR STRUCTURE CRACKED AND ANALYZED.
"THE INFORMATION IS FED INTO THE COLONY SPORES, MILLIONS OF EGG-PAIRS, BLANK SLATES UPON WHICH IS NOW WRITTEN THE GENETIC CODE OF THE DOMINANT LIFE.
13

"THUS CONDITIONED, THE INDESTRUCTIBLE EGG-PAIRS ARE EJECTED, FIRED ON BALLISTIC PATHS THAT WILL CARRY THEM TO EVERY CORNER OF THE DOOMED PLANET.
"NOT ALL WILL SURVIVE THEIR HATCHING. NOT ALL WILL FIND THEIR MATE AND BE ABLE TO BREED. BUT THERE ARE MILLIONS...!

"AND ON AS MANY DIFFERENT WORLDS THEY HAVE SUCCESSFULLY ADAPTED TO COUNTLESS LIFE FORMS, ASSUMING THUS THE DOMINATION OF THE PLANETS.

"THAT WOULD HAVE HAPPENED HERE, BUT FOR AN INEXPLICABLE FLAW IN THE COLONY SHIP.
"AFTER TEN THOUSAND YEARS IN SPACE ONE OF ITS DRIVE UNITS EXPLODED.
"IT DID NOT LAND ON THIS EARTH OF OURS. IT CRASHED.

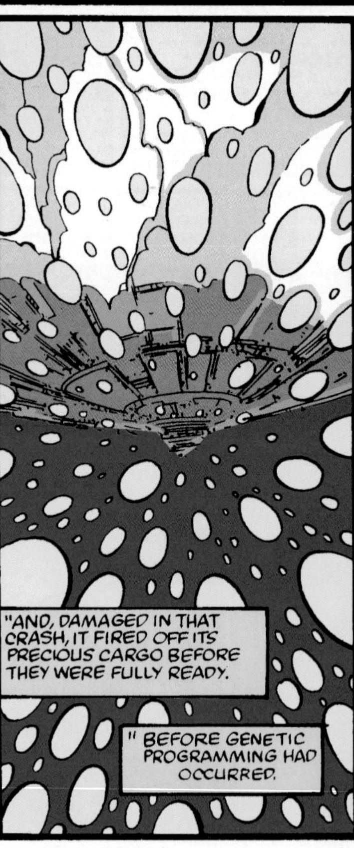
"AND, DAMAGED IN THAT CRASH, IT FIRED OFF ITS PRECIOUS CARGO BEFORE THEY WERE FULLY READY.
" BEFORE GENETIC PROGRAMMING HAD OCCURRED.

"THUS THE CREATURE OCCUPYING THE EGG FORCED OPEN BY GLADYS SMALLWOOD WAS STILL PRIMED FOR CONDITIONING. *
*SEE ISSUE #2 --Denny.

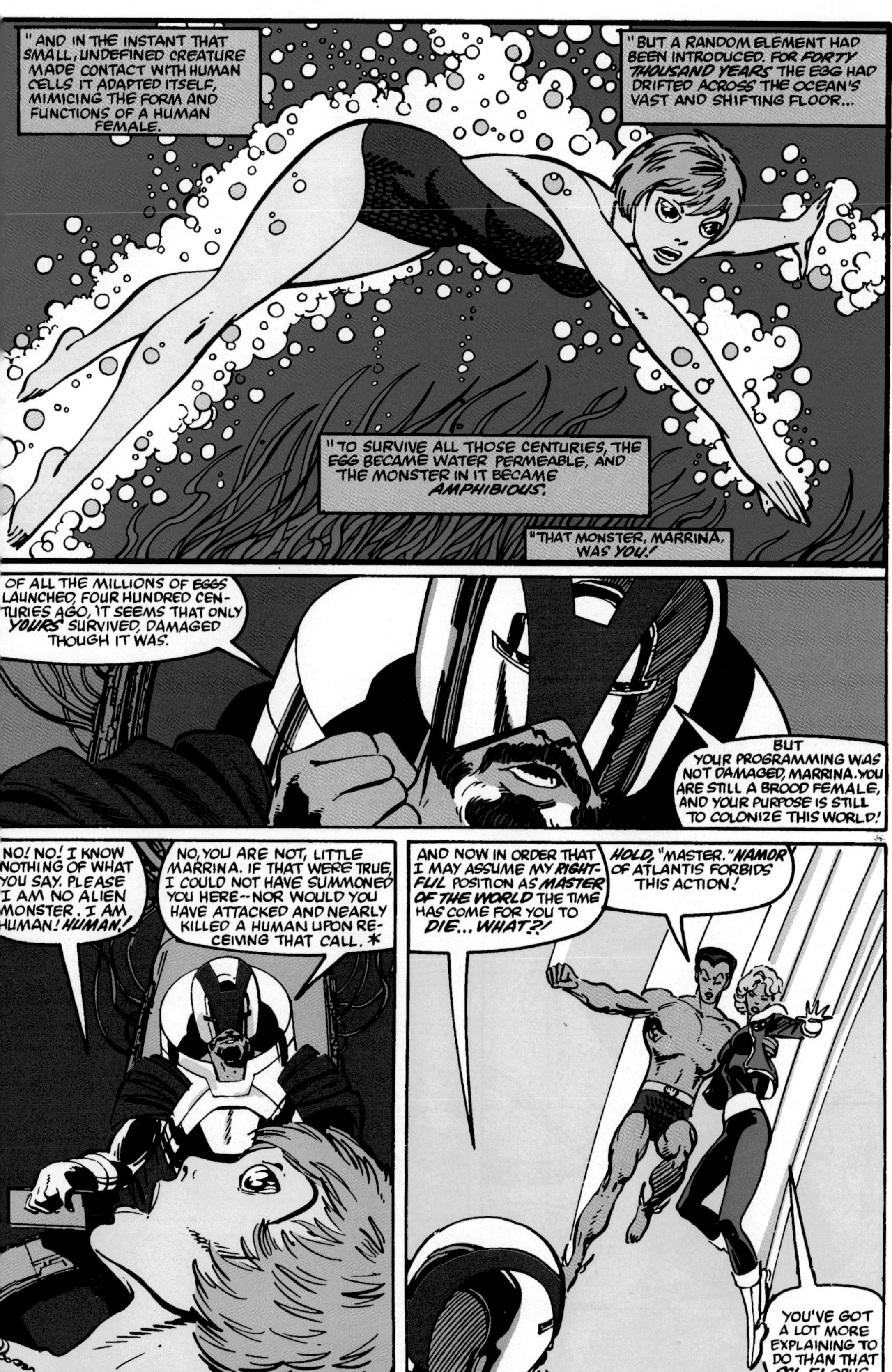
"AND IN THE INSTANT THAT SMALL, UNDEFINED CREATURE MADE CONTACT WITH HUMAN CELLS IT ADAPTED ITSELF, MIMICING THE FORM AND FUNCTIONS OF A HUMAN FEMALE.
"BUT A RANDOM ELEMENT HAD BEEN INTRODUCED. FOR FORTY THOUSAND YEARS THE EGG HAD DRIFTED ACROSS THE OCEAN'S VAST AND SHIFTING FLOOR...
"TO SURVIVE ALL THOSE CENTURIES, THE EGG BECAME WATER PERMEABLE, AND THE MONSTER IN IT BECAME AMPHIBIOUS.
"THAT MONSTER, MARRINA, WAS YOU!
OF ALL THE MILLIONS OF EGGS LAUNCHED, FOUR HUNDRED CENTURIES AGO, IT SEEMS THAT ONLY YOURS SURVIVED, DAMAGED THOUGH IT WAS.
BUT YOUR PROGRAMMING WAS NOT DAMAGED, MARRINA. YOU ARE STILL A BROOD FEMALE, AND YOUR PURPOSE IS STILL TO COLONIZE THIS WORLD!
NO! NO! I KNOW NOTHING OF WHAT YOU SAY. PLEASE I AM NO ALIEN MONSTER. I AM HUMAN! HUMAN!
NO, YOU ARE NOT, LITTLE MARRINA. IF THAT WERE TRUE, I COULD NOT HAVE SUMMONED YOU HERE--NOR WOULD YOU HAVE ATTACKED AND NEARLY KILLED A HUMAN UPON RECEIVING THAT CALL. *
* ALSO ISSUE #2--Denny.
AND NOW IN ORDER THAT I MAY ASSUME MY RIGHTFUL POSITION AS MASTER OF THE WORLD THE TIME HAS COME FOR YOU TO DIE... WHAT?!
HOLD, "MASTER." NAMOR OF ATLANTIS FORBIDS THIS ACTION!
YOU'VE GOT A LOT MORE EXPLAINING TO DO THAN THAT SCI-FI OPUS. A LOT MORE.

SUB-MARINER AND THE INVISIBLE GIRL! I HAD NOT EXPECTED SO SOON TO COME INTO CONTENTION WITH THE LIKES OF YOU. BUT YOU WILL FIND THE MASTER IS NOT UNPREPARED!
MECHANICAL GRABBERS!
THEY SEEMED TO GROW RIGHT OUT OF THE WALLS!
OF COURSE! REMEMBER WHAT HE SAID, SUSAN! THIS SHIP IS LIKE SOME HIGH-ORDER ORGANISM, ABLE TO GROW AT HIS COMMAND.
YOU'RE BEGINNING TO SOUND LIKE REED, NAMOR. DON'T WASTE ENERGY ON EXPLANATIONS.
MY FORCE-FIELD SEEMS TO BE CONFUSING THESE TENTACLES...
BUT WE MUST STOP THE MASTER HIMSELF!
AS IF ON CUE...
THE TIME HAS COME TO RETREAT AND REGROUP.
SO FAR EVERYTHING IS GOING EXACTLY ACCORDING TO PLAN!
BUT I MUST GIVE THESE HEROES THE ILLUSION THEY CONTROL THEIR OWN DESTINY OR ALL IS LOST.
FAREWELL, LITTLE MARRINA. KNOW THAT WHAT NOW OCCURS...
"...IS FOR THE GOOD OF ALL MANKIND!"
NO! NO! HELP ME!
I'M BEING TORN APART!
AT THAT MOMENT...
FROM A NEARBY CIRCULATION DUCT...

THE MOSQUITOES SWARM, BUZZING ACROSS THE GREAT CHAMBER...
THEN, MIRACULOUSLY...

FEAR NOT, MARRINA.
SASQUATCH IS NOT THE ONLY ONE WITH STRENGTH...
SNOWBIRD!

SNOWBIRD! THEN ALPHA-FLIGHT IS INVOLVED IN THIS!

SUSAN RICHARDS! AND PRINCE NAMOR! YOU TAKE ME QUITE BY SURPRISE!
INDEED, MY FELLOW ALPHAS ARE INVOLVED. ARE THE REST OF THE FANTASTIC FOUR WITH YOU?

"QUESTIONS LATER," SUE RESPONDS. "HELP US SMASH THESE GRABBERS. WE HAVE TO GO AFTER THE MASTER."
AND, NEARLY TEN MILES AWAY...
ALL SYSTEMS ARE RESPONDING AS EXPECTED. EVEN NOW GUARDIAN AND NORTHSTAR ARE BEING SUBTLY GUIDED.
WITHIN MINUTES THEY SHOULD REACH THE PRIME POWER COMPLEX...

NOW!
IT BEGINS!
THOOM!

AT THAT MOMENT...
SAPRISTI! GUARDIAN, I THINK PERHAPS WE BROKE TOO MUCH OF THIS PLACE!
NOT AT ALL, NORTHSTAR.
WE HAD TO DO MAXIMUM DAMAGE TO ENSURE WE WERE KNOCKING OUT VITAL SYSTEMS.
I'M STILL IN CYBERNETIC LINK WITH THE COMPLEX, AND WHOLE AREAS ARE BLANKING OUT, GOING DARK.
SASQUATCH! I THOUGHT WE'D FIND YOU ALONG HERE.
I WON'T ASK HOW YOU DEDUCED THAT IN THIS FUN HOUSE, JIMMY. ARE YOU TWO RESPONSIBLE FOR THE PRESENT DISTURBANCE?
THAT WE ARE, 'SQUATCH. I...
AURORE! LET HER GO, LANGKOWSKI!

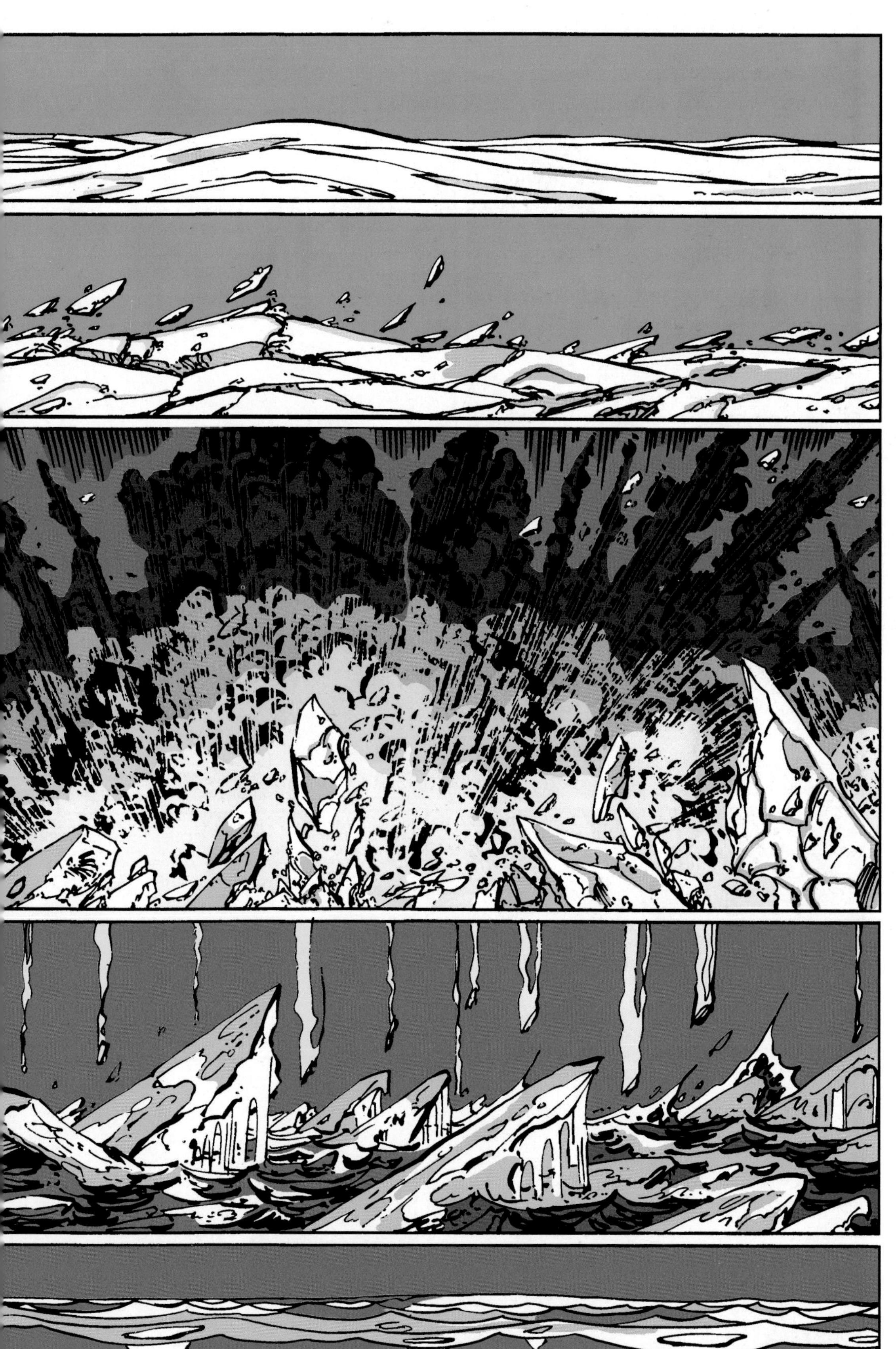

SUNNUVAGUN! WE MADE IT!
SUSAN, QUICKLY, OPEN YOUR FORCE-FIELD BUBBLE...

DONE, NAMOR, BUT...
THE MASTER, SUSAN! THERE IS A CHANCE HE SURVIVED, AS WE DID. I MUST SEARCH FOR A TRACE OF HIM...
SUB-MARINER WAIT! LET ME COME WITH YOU!

TWENTY TENSE MINUTES LATER...
NOTHING! NO SIGN OF HIM AT ALL!
AND NO SIGN OF THE COMPLEX. NOT EVEN WRECKAGE.
IT IS AS IF IT DISSOLVED INTO THE OCEAN WATERS!

THEN OUR TASK HERE IS DONE!
I MUST RETURN TO MY CIVILIAN GUISE. FAREWELL, ALPHA FLIGHT!
TAKE CARE, SNOWBIRD. KEEP IN TOUCH.
SHE'S A COLD ONE, ISN'T SHE? SO COOL AND DISMISSING.

I... THINK WE SHOULD BE GOING NOW, TOO, DON'T YOU, PRINCE NAMOR?
"GOING"...? YOUR HIGHNESS, WHAT...?
THERE ARE MANY QUESTIONS YET SURROUNDING MARRINA, GUARDIAN. MY PEOPLE ARE BEST SUITED, I THINK, TO SOLVE THEM.
I HAVE INVITED MARRINA TO COME AND DWELL FOR A TIME IN ATLANTIS, AND SHE HAS AGREED.

WELL, IF THAT'S ALL AGREED ON, BEFORE WE GO OUR SEPARATE WAYS I NEED A LIFT BACK TO NEW YORK. THAT ISN'T OUT OF YOUR WAY, IS IT NAMOR?
NOT AT ALL, SUE. LET THE REST OF ALPHA FLIGHT DEPART, THEN YOU CAN DISPENSE WITH THIS FORCE FIELD RAFT, AND WE'LL BE ON OUR WAY.
GOOD LUCK, MARRINA. WE'LL MISS YOU.

SO-- ANOTHER DAY, ANOTHER SUPER-VILLAIN SENT TO HIS JUST REWARD. I THINK WE CAN SAFELY MARK THIS ONE AS CLOSED.
I WOULDN'T BE SO QUICK TO WRITE OFF THE MASTER, WALT.

AND DON'T CLOSE THIS CASE JUST YET. I'VE GOT ONE UNENVIABLE TASK TO TAKE CARE OF BEFORE WE HEAD HOME.
THE TWINS ARC TOWARDS LA BELLE PROVINCE. GUARDIAN'S COURSE CONTINUES EASTWARD...

UNTIL, ON THE RUGGED, ROCKY COAST OF CANADA'S YOUNGEST PROVINCE, NEWFOUNDLAND...

DAN SMALLWOOD!

HMM?

OH, DOCTOR HUDSON! GOOD TO SEE YOU AGAIN, SIR. IS... IS MARRINA WITH YOU?

THE YOUNGER MAN'S ENTHUSIASM BUBBLES IN HIS CLEAR GREEN EYES. HE HAS FUNCTIONED FOR MANY YEARS AS A KIND OF BROTHER TO THE ADOPTED MARRINA.
BUT JAMES HUDSON RECOGNIZED THE FIRST TIME HE MET DAN SMALLWOOD THAT HIS LOVE FOR MARRINA WAS SOMETHING MORE THAN FRATERNAL.
GUARDIAN WOULD GIVE MUCH TO AVOID THE WORDS HE MUST NOW SPEAK, BUT THEY ARE NOT TO BE ESCAPED.

HE TELLS HIM. QUICKLY, QUIETLY, WITH AS LITTLE PAIN AS POSSIBLE.
BUT THE ANGUISH THAT FLOODS DAN SMALLWOOD'S FACE SPEAKS VOLUMES.
TODAY ALPHA FLIGHT MAY WELL HAVE SAVED THE WHOLE WORLD.
BUT JUST NOW THE WORLD OF ONE YOUNG MAN IS ENDING...

JOHNNY, WE NEED A QUICK AERIAL RECONNAISSANCE. YOU KNOW WHAT TO DO.
ON MY WAY, BROTHER-IN-LAW. FLAME ON!
WOW! THIS PLACE IS INCREDIBLE. AND THE AIR IS BREATHABLE.
NORMALLY, I COULDN'T FLY ABOVE THE RIM OF THE CRATER SYSTEM THAT HOLDS THE ATMOSPHERE IN THE BLUE AREA. BUT NOW I CAN FLY
AND THAT'S JUST WHAT I'M GONNA DO. I'VE GOT TO GET A BETTER LOOK AT...

fantastic four # 261

DECEMBER 1983

THE SEARCH FOR REED RICHARDS

STAN LEE PRESENTS
JOHN BYRNE STORY & ART
GLYNIS WEIN COLORS
JIM NOVAK LETTERS
BOB BUDIANSKY EDITING
JIM SHOOTER SEARCHING

WELL, THAT WAS INTERESTING. YOU CERTAINLY HAVEN'T LOST YOUR... TOUCH, NAMOR.
A REMINDER, SUSAN. A REMINDER OF SOMETHING WHICH NEVER TRULY WAS, BUT MIGHT HAVE BEEN, IN ANOTHER WORLD, ANOTHER TIME.
THIS IS FANTASTIC! I'M HERE--IN NEW YORK--AT THE BAXTER BUILDING--WITH THE SUB-MARINER AND THE INVISIBLE GIRL!
*CHRONOLOGICAL NOTE: THIS SCENE TAKES PLACE A FEW HOURS AFTER THE END OF ALPHA FLIGHT #4-- BOB.

NOW, COME ALONG, MARRINA. IT IS TIME WE RETURNED TO OUR NATURAL HABITAT-- THE SEA!
OF COURSE, YOUR MAJESTY.
IT WAS... WONDERFUL MEETING YOU, MRS. RICHARDS.
CALL ME SUE, MARRINA. TAKE CARE NOW.

DEFYING ALL KNOWN PHYSICAL LAWS, THE TINY WINGS ON HIS ANKLES BEAT, AND THE MIGHTY SUB-MARINER TAKES TO THE AIR!
WE WILL FLY AS FAR AS THE OCEAN ITSELF. I HAVE NO WISH TO PLUNGE US INTO EITHER OF THIS CITY'S POLLUTED RIVERWAYS.
AS YOU WISH, PRINCE NAMOR. I JUST CAN'T WAIT TO SEE ATLANTIS!

AND AS THE TWO DWINDLE TO A TINY SPECK AGAINST THE CITY-BRIGHT HAZE, SUSAN RICHARDS TURNS HER THOUGHTS ELSEWHERE...
NO ONE COULD ACCUSE ME OF LOAFING FOR THE PAST DAY OR SO.

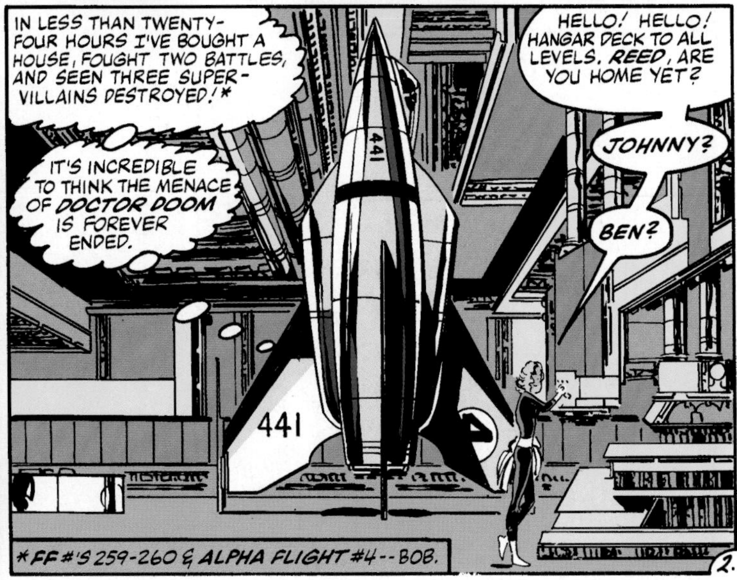
IN LESS THAN TWENTY-FOUR HOURS I'VE BOUGHT A HOUSE, FOUGHT TWO BATTLES, AND SEEN THREE SUPER-VILLAINS DESTROYED!*
IT'S INCREDIBLE TO THINK THE MENACE OF DOCTOR DOOM IS FOREVER ENDED.
HELLO! HELLO! HANGAR DECK TO ALL LEVELS. REED, ARE YOU HOME YET?
JOHNNY?
BEN?
441
*FF #'S 259-260 & ALPHA FLIGHT #4--BOB.
2.

ONLY ECHOES ANSWER.
A FEW HOURS AGO SUSAN CAME BACK FROM CONNECTICUT TO FIND HER HUSBAND HAD NOT RETURNED FROM AVENGERS' MANSION.

THE UNEXPECTED ARRIVAL OF THE SUB-MARINER HAD DIVERTED HER FROM A REAL SEARCH...
...NOW SHE FEELS ANXIETY WELLING WITHIN HER ONCE MORE.

WHERE CAN HE BE? NOW THAT I THINK ABOUT IT HE FAILED TO RESPOND TO MY FLARE SIGNAL, TOO.*
NOTHING COULD PREVENT REED FROM RESPONDING IF HE SAW THAT FLARE...
ONLY ONE THING TO DO. I'LL HAVE TO CALL...
*LAST ISSUE. NOW YOU'RE ALL CAUGHT UP--BOB.

...AVENGERS' MANSION. JARVIS THE BUTLER SPEAKING. OH, GOOD EVENING, MRS. RICHARDS. NO, NO I'M AFRAID NONE OF THE AVENGERS ARE AVAILABLE AT THE MOMENT.
WELL, AS I UNDERSTAND IT THEY'VE GONE OFF TO THE S.H.I.E.L.D. SPACE STATION, TO GET HELP TRACKING A MYSTERIOUS BEAM THAT BREACHED THE MANSION EARLIER.
NO, I'M AFRAID I DON'T KNOW IF YOUR HUSBAND IS WITH THEM.

ALL RIGHT, THANK YOU, JARVIS. IF MY HUSBAND SHOULD TURN UP THERE, PLEASE ASK HIM TO CALL ME RIGHT AWAY. BYE.
NOW THAT DOESN'T SOUND AT ALL LIKE REED. CHARGING OFF WITH THE AVENGERS WITHOUT LEAVING WORD FOR ME?
IS THERE SOMETHING I CAN HELP YOU WITH, SUSAN?

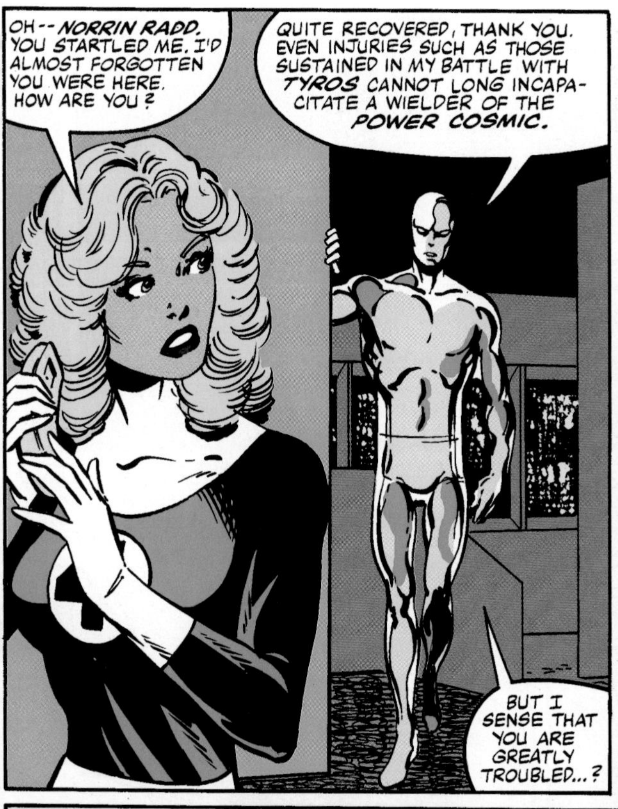
OH--NORRIN RADD. YOU STARTLED ME. I'D ALMOST FORGOTTEN YOU WERE HERE. HOW ARE YOU?
QUITE RECOVERED, THANK YOU. EVEN INJURIES SUCH AS THOSE SUSTAINED IN MY BATTLE WITH TYROS CANNOT LONG INCAPACITATE A WIELDER OF THE POWER COSMIC.
BUT I SENSE THAT YOU ARE GREATLY TROUBLED...?

QUICKLY SUSAN EXPLAINS TO HER GLEAMING GUEST...
A BEAM? IT WAS A MATTER TRANSFERRAL BEAM, STRIKING FROM SPACE, WHICH DREW ME TO THIS CITY EARLIER TODAY.
I CARE LITTLE FOR THE SOUND OF THIS, SUSAN. IF YOUR HUSBAND WAS IN ANY WAY AFFECTED, IT BEHOOVES ME TO OFFER MY AID TO HIM--AND YOU.
BUT FIRST...

AND AS THE SILVER SURFER SPEAKS...
...IN WHAT WAS ONCE THE PARKING LOT OF WHAT WAS ONCE A SUPERMARKET IN QUEENS...
THAT'S THE SPOT, GEORGE.

RIGHT HERE DOC DOOM GOT ZAPPED INTA FAIRY-DUST BY TH' SILVER SURFER.
YOU SURE HE'S DEAD HARRY? LOOKS TO ME LIKE THERE'S SOMETHIN'...

...HAPPENIN'!!!
4.

SCANT SECONDS LATER...
THAT BOARD OF YOURS NEVER CEASES TO ASTOUND ME.
IT PASSED RIGHT THROUGH THAT WALL WITHOUT EVEN LEAVING A HOLE.

SUCH IS THE WILL OF GALACTUS, SUSAN. IT WAS HE WHO CREATED MY SHINING BOARD, AND IMPARTED TO IT A FRACTION OF HIS OWN COSMIC POWER.
NOW, COME QUICKLY. WE MUST DISCOVER THE WHEREABOUTS OF REED RICHARDS.
JUST SECURING MY HAIR, SURFER.

IF WE'RE GOING FLYING I DON'T WANT IT BLOWING IN MY EYES.

SILENTLY, THE BIZARRE TRANSPORT FLASHES ACROSS THE TOWERS OF MANHATTAN, PASSING ALONGSIDE THE DARK, GREEN SPRAWL OF CENTRAL PARK UNTIL...
THERE'S AVENGERS MANSION. CIRCLE IT QUICKLY, SURFER. LET'S SEE IF WE CAN SPOT ANY DAMAGE.
AS YOU WISH...

THERE!
WOW!
JARVIS WASN'T KIDDING WHEN HE SAID THE MANSION HAD BEEN BREECHED.
AND IF I REMEMBER THE LAYOUT, THAT SHOULD BE...
POLICE NYPD

... THE MEDICAL FACILITIES... WANDA! JARVIS TOLD ME ALL THE AVENGERS WERE OUT.
SUSAN...!
THE OTHERS ARE OUT, BUT I REMAINED BEHIND TO WATCH OVER MY HUSBAND, THE VISION. I TOLD JARVIS I DID NOT WISH TO BE DISTURBED.

THAT MUST HAVE BEEN WHAT HE MEANT. HOW IS THE VISION?
NO CHANGE... BUT SURELY YOU'RE MORE CONCERNED ABOUT WHAT HAPPENED TO REED?
WHAT DO YOU MEAN? ISN'T HE WITH THE REST OF THE AVENGERS?

N-NO. SUSAN, I WISH I WAS NOT THE ONE TO HAVE TO TELL YOU THIS, BUT REED WAS CHECKING OUT THE CONDITION OF THE VISION... IT TOOK LONGER THAN HE'D ANTICI-PATED, SO I WENT TO MAKE SOME TEA...
THAT WAS WHEN THE INTRUDER ALERT SOUNDED. I RACED BACK HERE TO FIND THIS GREAT HOLE HAD BEEN SLICED THROUGH THE WALL...
...AND... REED...?

I... I TRIED TO REACH YOU. HE'S GONE, SUSAN.
VANISHED WITHOUT A TRACE!
6.

WITHOUT A TRACE? I CAN'T BELIEVE THAT! NOT WITH ALL THE SPECIALIZED SCANNING EQUIPMENT HERE IN THE MANSION-- EQUIPMENT REED HIMSELF HELPED TONY STARK DESIGN.
THERE HAS TO BE SOME INDICATION-- SOME SIGN!
DO NOT DISTRESS YOURSELF, SUSAN. THERE IS LITTLE THAT CAN TRULY BE HIDDEN FROM ONE WHO HAS RIDDEN THE COSMIC WINDS.

LOOK AWAY NOW MY FRIENDS! WHAT FOLLOWS NOW IS NOT FOR MORTAL EYES TO BEHOLD...
N-NORRIN RADD...?

THE INDESCRIBABLE POWER COSMIC PEELS AWAY THE FABRIC OF THE UNIVERSE ITSELF, ROLLING BACK THE HOURS FOR A LOOK INTO THE PAST...
...UNTIL...
YES...

IT IS AS I FEARED, SUSAN. THE BEAM I SAW FROM SPACE DID INDEED STRIKE THIS BUILDING, WHISKING AWAY YOUR HUSBAND TO A PLACE BEYOND THE DETECTION OF THE INSTRUMENTS WITHIN THESE WALLS.
I KNOW WHERE HE HAS GONE, AND IT IS BEYOND MY POWER TO TAKE YOU TO HIM, FOR BY THE WILL AND THE POWER OF GALACTUS IS THE SILVER SURFER EVER DENIED TO RIDE AGAIN THE BOUNDLESS COSMOS.
AND THAT IS WHERE THE QUEST FOR YOUR HUSBAND MUST SURELY TAKE YOU, FOR THE MAN CALLED MISTER FANTASTIC IS NO LONGER ON EARTH!
7

EAVING THE SCARLET WITCH
ND THE SILVER SURFER, THE
NVISIBLE GIRL RACES BACK TO
HE BAXTER BUILDING...

...WHERE LESS THAN HALF AN HOUR LATER, AFTER A FAMILIAR FLARE HAS BRIGHTENED THE MANHATTAN SKY...
YA MEAN TA SAY SOME SLIMEY ALIENS JUST SCOOPED UP REED AN' TOOK OFF WITH HIM?
THAT'S HOW IT LOOKS, BEN. AND WE MUST NOT WASTE A MINUTE GETTING AFTER HIM!
THAT'S A TALL ORDER, SUE. WITHOUT THE SILVER SURFER TO HELP US LOOK... WELL A NEEDLE IN A HAYSTACK WOULD BE EASIER.

I'M WELL AWARE OF THE MMENSITY OF THE TASK, JOHNNY. IN FACT I'VE LREADY TAKEN STEPS TOWARD CONTACTING SOMEONE ELSE WHO MIGHT HELP US.
BUT, ENOUGH TALK. IT'S TIME WE WERE ON OUR WAY.
"WE?" NOW HOLD ON JUST A SECOND, LITTLE LADY. DID I DREAM IT, OR DID YOU ANNOUNCE A COUPLA DAYS AGO THAT YER GONNA HAVE ANOTHER BABY?

BEN'S RIGHT, SIS. YOU JUST CAN'T POSSIBLY GO CHASING ALL OVER THE GALAXY. NOT IN YOUR CONDITION. YOU'D BETTER LEAVE THIS TO US.
I'M NOT INVITING A DEBATE, GENTLEMEN.

WITH REED MISSING, I AM THE ACTING LEADER OF THE FANTASTIC FOUR. WE WILL DO WHAT I SAY.
I DO NOT HAVE TO REMIND YOU THAT REED IS THE MAN I LOVE, AND THE FATHER OF THE CHILD I'M CARRYING.
NOTHING AND NO-ONE IS GOING TO STOP ME FROM FINDING HIM!
8.

MINUTES LATER, SPECIAL BAFFLES DAMPEN THE ROAR OF ROCKET ENGINES AS A UNIQUE SPACECRAFT LEAPS FROM ITS SILO ATOP THE BAXTER BUILDING.
ZERO PLUS TWENTY-EIGHT SECONDS. ALL SYSTEMS NOMINAL.
BEN, STAND BY TO ACTIVATE SECONDARY THRUSTERS.
WAY AHEAD OF YA, SUZIE. OUT OF ATMOSPHERE IN TWELVE SECONDS...
...AN' INTA THE COSMIC RAY BELT AGAIN...
UNBIDDEN, THE MIND OF BEN GRIMM TURNS BACK, TO ANOTHER ROCKET, ANOTHER LAUNCH...
PRIMARY CIRCUITS AT MAXIMUM FUNCTION. ALL SYSTEMS SHOW GREEN FOR FIRST STAGE JETTISON.
SHE'S BEHAVING LIKE A BABY. EVERY-THING IS PERFECT.
YEAH, EXCEPT FOR THE COSMIC RAYS. NO ONE KNOWS WHAT THEY'LL DO.
FOUR PEOPLE, FOUR FRIENDS, EMBARKING ON A BOLD VENTURE INTO THE UNKNOWN, REACHING FOR THE STARS, GUESSING NOT AT ALL WHAT FATE TRULY HELD IN STORE FOR THEM...
WE'RE ENTERING THE COSMIC STORM AREA! HANG ON!
HEAR THAT? IT'S THE COSMIC RAYS! THEY'RE PENETRATING THE SHIP!

AND AS THE UBIQUITOUS RAYS PIERCE THE HULL PLATES...
MY HEAD... POUNDING AS THOUGH IT'S ABOUT TO BURST!
BEN WAS RIGHT. WE SHOULD HAVE WAITED.
SHOULD HAVE GOTTEN HEAVIER SHIELDING...
JOHNNY...WHAT'S HAPPENING TO YOU?
I DON'T KNOW, SUE!
MY BODY FEELS HOT--LIKE I'M ON FIRE!
SOMEONE ELSE TAKE THE CONTROLS. MY ARMS ARE TOO HEAVY...
TOO HEAVY. GOTTA LIE DOWN...
CAN'T MOVE...
BEN!
ONLY THE SHIP'S SOPHISTICATED AUTOPILOT PREVENTS ULTIMATE TRAGEDY.
THE GLORIOUS MISSION TO THE STARS ENDS IGNOMINIOUSLY IN A WOODED AREA NORTH OF ITHACA, NEW YORK.
BUT THE TALE DOES NOT END THERE.
EXPOSED TO A POTENTIALLY LETHAL DOSE OF RADIATION, THE FOUR ADVENTURERS FIND THEMSELVES NOT DYING, BUT TRANSFORMED!
THEY HAVE BECOME...
MISTER FANTASTIC!
THE THING!
THE INVISIBLE GIRL!
THE HUMAN TORCH!
10

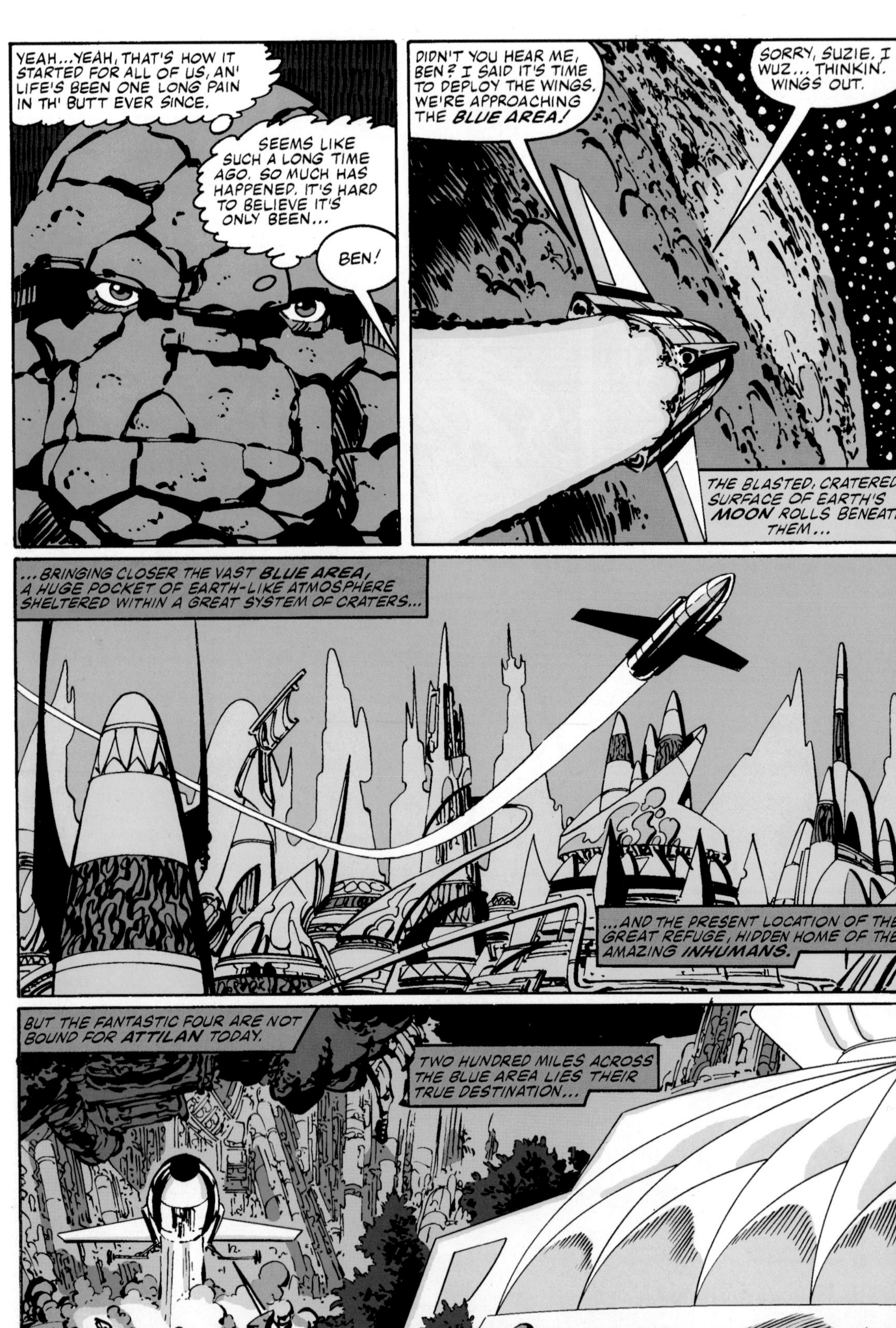
YEAH...YEAH, THAT'S HOW IT STARTED FOR ALL OF US, AN' LIFE'S BEEN ONE LONG PAIN IN TH' BUTT EVER SINCE.
SEEMS LIKE SUCH A LONG TIME AGO. SO MUCH HAS HAPPENED. IT'S HARD TO BELIEVE IT'S ONLY BEEN...
BEN!
DIDN'T YOU HEAR ME, BEN? I SAID IT'S TIME TO DEPLOY THE WINGS. WE'RE APPROACHING THE BLUE AREA!
SORRY, SUZIE. I WUZ... THINKIN'. WINGS OUT.
THE BLASTED, CRATERED SURFACE OF EARTH'S MOON ROLLS BENEATH THEM...
...BRINGING CLOSER THE VAST BLUE AREA, A HUGE POCKET OF EARTH-LIKE ATMOSPHERE SHELTERED WITHIN A GREAT SYSTEM OF CRATERS...
...AND THE PRESENT LOCATION OF THE GREAT REFUGE, HIDDEN HOME OF THE AMAZING INHUMANS.
BUT THE FANTASTIC FOUR ARE NOT BOUND FOR ATTILAN TODAY.
TWO HUNDRED MILES ACROSS THE BLUE AREA LIES THEIR TRUE DESTINATION...
THERE IT IS! THE HOME OF... THE WATCHER!

TH' WATCHER, HUH? YEAH, IF ANYONE CAN HELP US FIND YOUR HUBBINS, IT'S HIM. HE MAKES REED LOOK LIKE A KINDERGARTEN DROP-OUT.
BUT HOW DO WE GET INTO HIS HOUSE? I DON'T SEE ANY SIGN OF A DOOR...?
FOR SHAME, JOHNNY! HAVE YOU FORGOTTEN ALREADY? THE WAY TO ENTER...

...IS SIMPLY TO STEP THROUGH THE WALL!

MAN-O-MAN, I'D FORGOTTEN HOW SPOOKY THIS PLACE IS. THE WHOLE HOUSE MAKES ME FEEL LIKE I LEFT MY 3-D GLASSES AT HOME...
REED SAYS THAT'S BECAUSE SO MUCH OF THE HOUSE ACTUALLY EXISTS OUTSIDE OUR CONVENTIONAL THREE DIMENSIONS.
YEAH, WELL IT'LL TAKE FOREVER TO FIND THE WATCHER ON FOOT. FLAME ON!

BUT...
HMM. SUDDENLY I DON'T THINK THIS WAS SUCH A GRAND IDEA AFTER ALL.
IT'S ONLY A COUPLE OF SECONDS SINCE I LEFT BEN AND SUE--BUT I'M NOT SURE I CAN FIND MY WAY BACK TO THEM...

BLAST! I WISH THE TORCH HADN'T FLOWN OFF LIKE THAT! I CONTACTED THE WATCHER BY SUB-ETHER WAVEBAND EARLIER, AND HE SAID HE'D BE HERE TO MEET US!
AND AS MY WORD IS GIVEN, SO IS IT KEPT, SUSAN RICHARDS.
EEP!
12.

SILENCE SEEMS TO FLOOD THE VAST CHAMBER, A PALPABLE SILENCE, GIFTED ALMOST WITH A LIFE-FORCE OF ITS OWN.
AND, INTO THE GREAT CALM CENTER OF THAT SILENCE THE BEING KNOWN AS THE WATCHER STRIDES FORWARD. OLDER THAN OUR PLANET, OLDER PERHAPS THAN OUR GALAXY ITSELF, HE RADIATES THE WISDOM OF INFINITY IN HIS UNFATHOMABLE GAZE.
GREETINGS, EARTHLINGS! WELCOME TO MY HOME!
YOU GOT A FUNNY WAY OF SAY-IN' HOWDY, BALDY.
YOU ALMOST SCARED THE TRUNKS OFF ME.
BEN, BE QUIET PLEASE. WATCHER, YOU KNOW OUR DILEMMA. HAVE YOU DECIDED YET WHETHER TO HELP US, OR NOT?
IT IS NOT THE NATURE OF MY RACE TO ASSIST THOSE WE OBSERVE, SUSAN. YET I HAVE BEEN IN CONTACT WITH THE HOMEWORLD.
THEY ARE AWARE OF WHAT HAS TRANS-PIRED, AND BELIEVE INVOLVEMENT WOULD NOT BREAK OUR OATH.
THE MATTERS THAT CON-CERN THE FATE OF YOUR HUSBAND MAY WELL AFFECT THE UNIVERSE, AND ALL THAT DWELL IN IT.
COME, THERE IS A GREAT DISTANCE TO BE TRAVELED.
WAIT...
JOHNNY...? WHERE IS THE TORCH?
FEAR NOT, SUSAN RICHARDS. THOUGH HE VENTURED FAR INTO MY HOUSE, YOUR BROTHER IS UNHARMED.
I RETURN HIM NOW TO YOU...
HOLY--!
WHERE WAS I? IT FELT LIKE... LIKE...
I DON'T KNOW WHAT IT FELT LIKE!

YOU HAVE NO WORDS, JOHN STORM, TO DESCRIBE THE INDESCRIBABLE. TO SAVE YOU FROM THE DANGERS OF MY HOUSE...
...I SIMPLY REMOVED YOU FROM IT...REMOVED YOU FOR A MOMENT FROM THIS VERY PLANE OF REALITY.
THAT'S FANCY TALK, WATCHER. BUT WHEN ARE WE GETTIN' GOIN'?
AS FOR THAT, BEN GRIMM...

...WE ARE ALREADY ON OUR WAY...

AROUND THEM THE UNIVERSE SEEMS TO FOLD IN UPON ITSELF.
TIME AND SPACE SEEM SUDDENLY MEANINGLESS, MERELY THE FRAGILE CONCEPTS OF SMALL MINDS STRIVING HOPE-LESSLY TO COMPREHEND THEIR PLACE IN INFINITY.

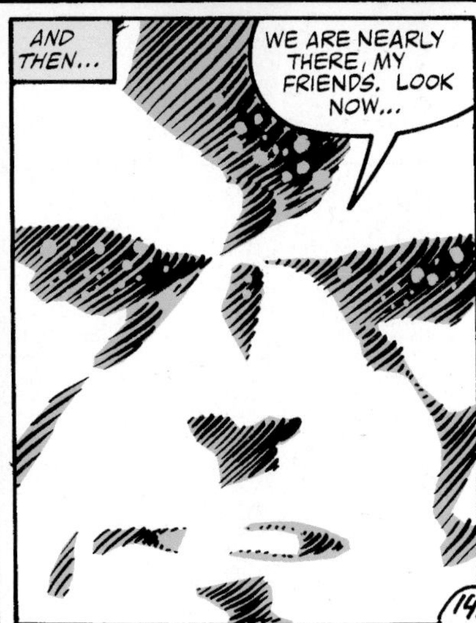
AND THEN...
WE ARE NEARLY THERE, MY FRIENDS. LOOK NOW...
14.

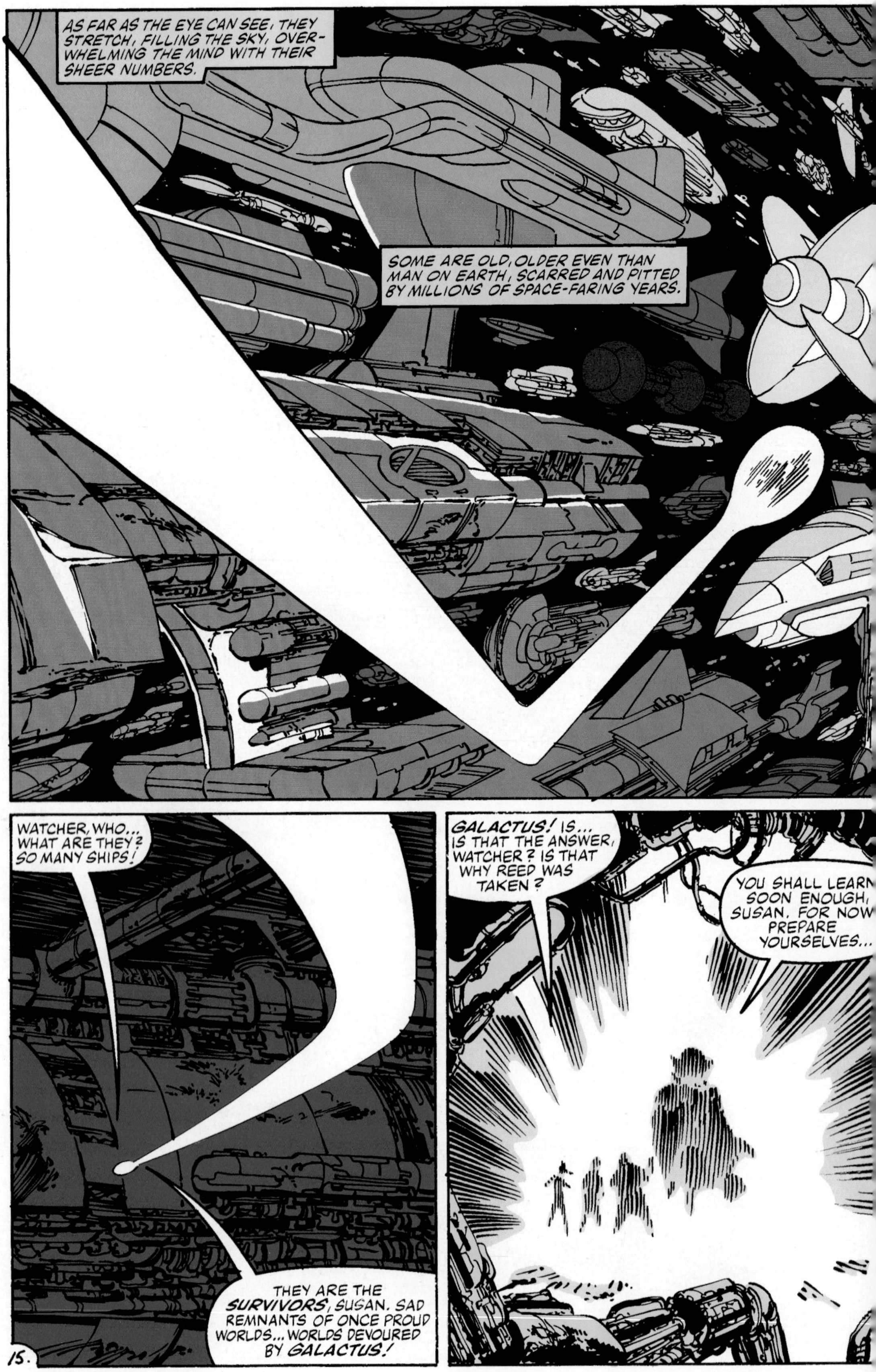

AS FAR AS THE EYE CAN SEE, THEY STRETCH, FILLING THE SKY, OVERWHELMING THE MIND WITH THEIR SHEER NUMBERS.

SOME ARE OLD, OLDER EVEN THAN MAN ON EARTH, SCARRED AND PITTED BY MILLIONS OF SPACE-FARING YEARS.

WATCHER, WHO... WHAT ARE THEY? SO MANY SHIPS!
THEY ARE THE *SURVIVORS*, SUSAN. SAD REMNANTS OF ONCE PROUD WORLDS... WORLDS DEVOURED BY *GALACTUS!*
15.

GALACTUS! IS... IS THAT THE ANSWER, WATCHER? IS THAT WHY REED WAS TAKEN?
YOU SHALL LEARN SOON ENOUGH, SUSAN. FOR NOW PREPARE YOURSELVES...

OTHERS ARE NEWER, GLEAMING SILVER SPINDLES, ALL SMOOTH LINES AND GRACEFUL CURVES, NOT YET MARRED BY THE ENDLESS STREAM OF MICRO-METEORITES THAT SCRIBE THEIR WAY THROUGH SPACE.

STILL OTHERS ARE ALMOST COMICAL CONTRAPTIONS, BITS AND PIECES OF A HUNDRED OTHER CRAFT, FRAGMENTS OF VESSELS, BOLTED AND STRAPPED TOGETHER.

OUR JOURNEY IS AT AN END.
THIS SHIP... IT'S SO HUGE, SO OLD! I CAN ALMOST FEEL ITS AGE, LIKE A GREAT WEIGHT.
IT'S LIKE THAT SHIP WE ENCOUNTERED IN THE NEGATIVE ZONE -- THE ONE THAT HAD BEEN ON A TEN THOUSAND-YEAR QUEST...*
YEAH, WELL THIS AIN'T THE TIME FER NOSTALGIA, HOTSHOT! WE GOT COMPANY!
*SEE FF#252--BOB.
16.

I AM XXAN XXAR, LEADER OF THE DELEGATE COUNCIL. I BID GREETINGS TO THE FANTASTIC FOUR*.
YOU... KNOW WHO WE ARE?
WATCH IT, SUZIE. DON'T GET TOO CLOSE TO 'EM UNTIL WE KNOW WHAT'S UP.
*TRANSLATED BY THE FF'S UNIVERSAL TRANSLATORS.

OF COURSE WE KNOW YOU. THE FANTASTIC FOUR OF PLANET EARTH ARE LEGEND THROUGHOUT THE GALAXY.

IN THAT CASE PERHAPS YOU'D BE SO KIND AS TO TELL ME WHAT YOU'VE DONE WITH MY HUSBAND?

CERTAINLY. IF YOU WILL ALL FOLLOW ME, I WILL TAKE YOU TO HIM.

STILL VERY MUCH ON THEIR GUARD, THE FF, ALONG WITH THE WATCHER, ALLOW THEMSELVES TO BE LED THROUGH THE STRANGE, ANCIENT VESSEL.

LOOKIT THIS PLACE! LOOKS LIKE A CASTIN' CALL FOR E.T. II.

HOW MUCH FURTHER, XXAN XXAR?

NOT MUCH NOW, SUSAN RICHARDS.

THERE IS THE ONE YOU SEEK...
HOLY!
R-REED!

S-SUE? WHAT... ARE YOU ... DOING HERE? YOU MUST... GET AWAY...

REED! OH MY DEAR LORD! WHAT ARE YOU DOING TO HIM?

DOING, SUSAN RICHARDS? WE ARE *EXECUTING* HIM!

WHAT? YA MEAN YER GONNA KILL REED, JUST BECAUSE GALACTUS ACED THEM STINKIN' SKRULLS? YA OUGHTA GIVE HIM A MEDAL!
GUARDS!!

YEOW!

BEN! WHY THOSE MISERABLE...!
JOHNNY, NO! WE CAN'T FIGHT OUR WAY OUT OF THIS ONE! REED DID THE RIGHT THING, SAVING GALACTUS! SOMEHOW WE'VE GOT TO MAKE THESE PEOPLE REALIZE THAT!
LOOK... I UNDERSTAND HOW YOU MUST ALL HATE AND FEAR GALACTUS, BUT DON'T YOU SEE REED HAD NO CHOICE BUT TO SAVE HIM? WE MAY HAVE FOUGHT GALACTUS, BUT IN THE END WE HAD NO RIGHT, AS NO ONE HAS THE RIGHT, TO SIMPLY STAND BY AND LET HIM DIE.
WHAT BLINDLY ALTRUISTIC CREATURES YOU EARTHLINGS ARE!

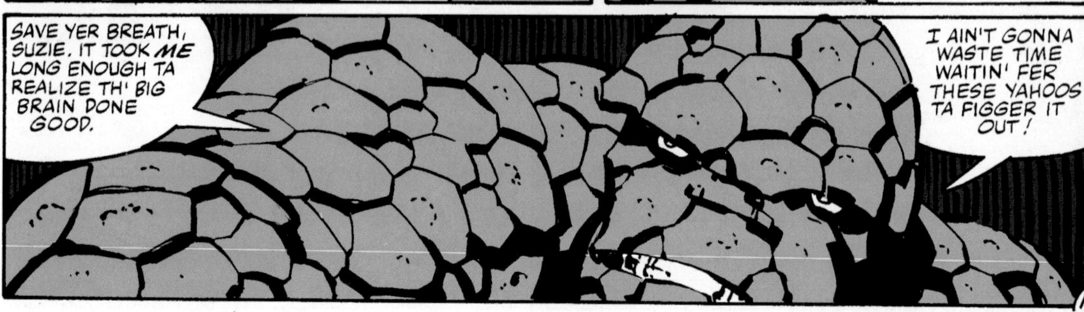
SAVE YER BREATH, SUZIE. IT TOOK ME LONG ENOUGH TA REALIZE TH' BIG BRAIN DONE GOOD.
I AIN'T GONNA WASTE TIME WAITIN' FER THESE YAHOOS TA FIGGER IT OUT!

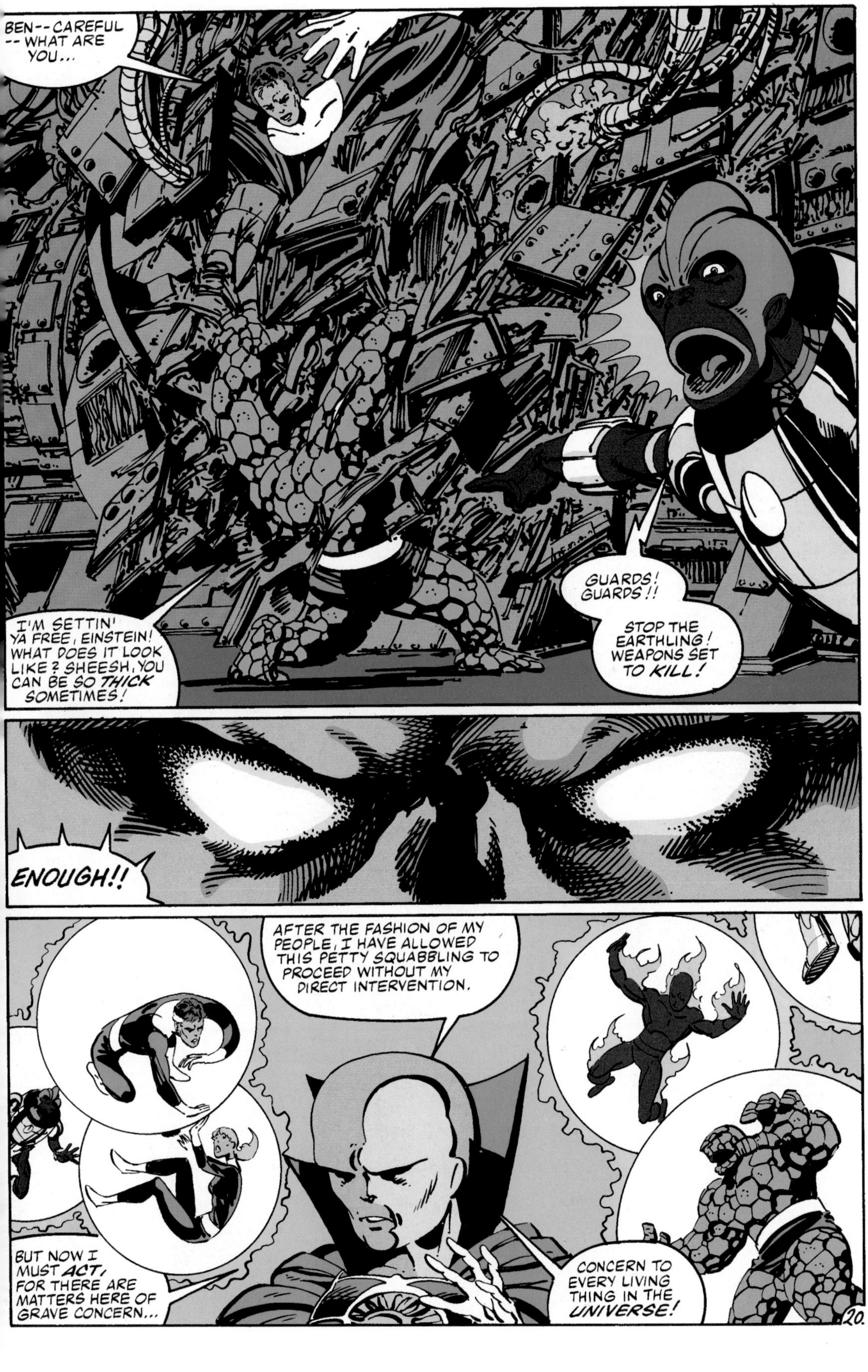

BEN--CAREFUL --WHAT ARE YOU...
I'M SETTIN' YA FREE, EINSTEIN! WHAT DOES IT LOOK LIKE? SHEESH, YOU CAN BE SO THICK SOMETIMES!
GUARDS! GUARDS!!
STOP THE EARTHLING! WEAPONS SET TO KILL!

ENOUGH!!

AFTER THE FASHION OF MY PEOPLE, I HAVE ALLOWED THIS PETTY SQUABBLING TO PROCEED WITHOUT MY DIRECT INTERVENTION.
BUT NOW I MUST ACT, FOR THERE ARE MATTERS HERE OF GRAVE CONCERN...
CONCERN TO EVERY LIVING THING IN THE UNIVERSE!
20.

WITHIN MINUTES, IN A GREAT COUNCIL HALL ABOARD ONE OF THE NEWER SHIPS...
THIS BOARD IS IN AGREEMENT THAT WE PERHAPS ACTED TOO HASTILY IN OUR DECISION TO EXECUTE THE EARTHLING.
HOWEVER, WE STILL FEEL THAT REED RICHARDS MUST BE HELD RESPONSIBLE FOR THE DESTRUCTION OF THE SKRULL HOMEWORLD.
FOR, IF HE HAD NOT CONVINCED HIS FELLOW HUMANS TO ACT TO SAVE GALACTUS, THE RAVAGER OF WORLDS WOULD HAVE PERISHED MANY CYCLES PAST, AND SEVEN BILLION SKRULLS WOULD STILL BE ALIVE. WHAT DO YOU SAY TO THIS, REED RICHARDS?

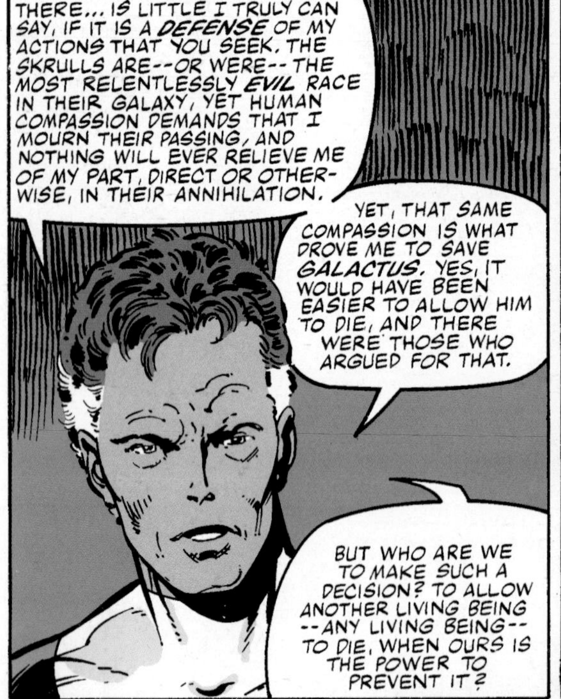

THERE... IS LITTLE I TRULY CAN SAY, IF IT IS A DEFENSE OF MY ACTIONS THAT YOU SEEK. THE SKRULLS ARE--OR WERE--THE MOST RELENTLESSLY EVIL RACE IN THEIR GALAXY, YET HUMAN COMPASSION DEMANDS THAT I MOURN THEIR PASSING, AND NOTHING WILL EVER RELIEVE ME OF MY PART, DIRECT OR OTHERWISE, IN THEIR ANNIHILATION.
YET, THAT SAME COMPASSION IS WHAT DROVE ME TO SAVE GALACTUS. YES, IT WOULD HAVE BEEN EASIER TO ALLOW HIM TO DIE, AND THERE WERE THOSE WHO ARGUED FOR THAT.
BUT WHO ARE WE TO MAKE SUCH A DECISION? TO ALLOW ANOTHER LIVING BEING --ANY LIVING BEING-- TO DIE, WHEN OURS IS THE POWER TO PREVENT IT?

UNDERSTAND ALSO, GENTLEMEN, THAT THERE IS ABOUT GALACTUS MUCH, MUCH MORE THAN MERE MORTAL MINDS CAN EVER COMPREHEND. MY RACE HAS KNOWN OF HIM SINCE HIS VERY BEGINNINGS, YET WE UNDERSTAND ONLY A TINY FRACTION OF HIS OVERWHELMING POWER AND PURPOSE.
AND DO NOT DOUBT THAT GALACTUS HAS A PURPOSE. THERE IS AN ORDER OF THINGS IN THIS UNIVERSE. ONE SUCH AS HE WOULD NOT BE PERMITTED TO EXIST UNLESS HE HAD A PLACE IN IT.

THERE IS MUCH TO CONTEMPLATE. GALACTUS DESTROYED OUR WORLDS, KILLED HUNDREDS OF BILLIONS OF OUR PEOPLE.
YET, DO WE NOT ALSO DESTROY LIFE WHEN WE FEED? EVEN THOSE OF US WHO EAT ONLY PLANTS...
WE MUST, I THINK, RECONSIDER OUR POSITION...
NO!!

WE ARE LILANDRA, MAJESTRIX SHI'AR. WE HAVE BEEN INFORMED OF YOUR CRIME.
WE HAVE ALREADY GIVEN WARNING TO THE EARTHLINGS ONCE THAT THE CONSEQUENCES OF THEIR ACTIONS WOULD NOT GO UNPUNISHED.
FOR HIS UNSPEAKABLE CRIME AGAINST ALL THINGS THAT LIVE...
REED RICHARDS MUST DIE!

fantastic four # 262

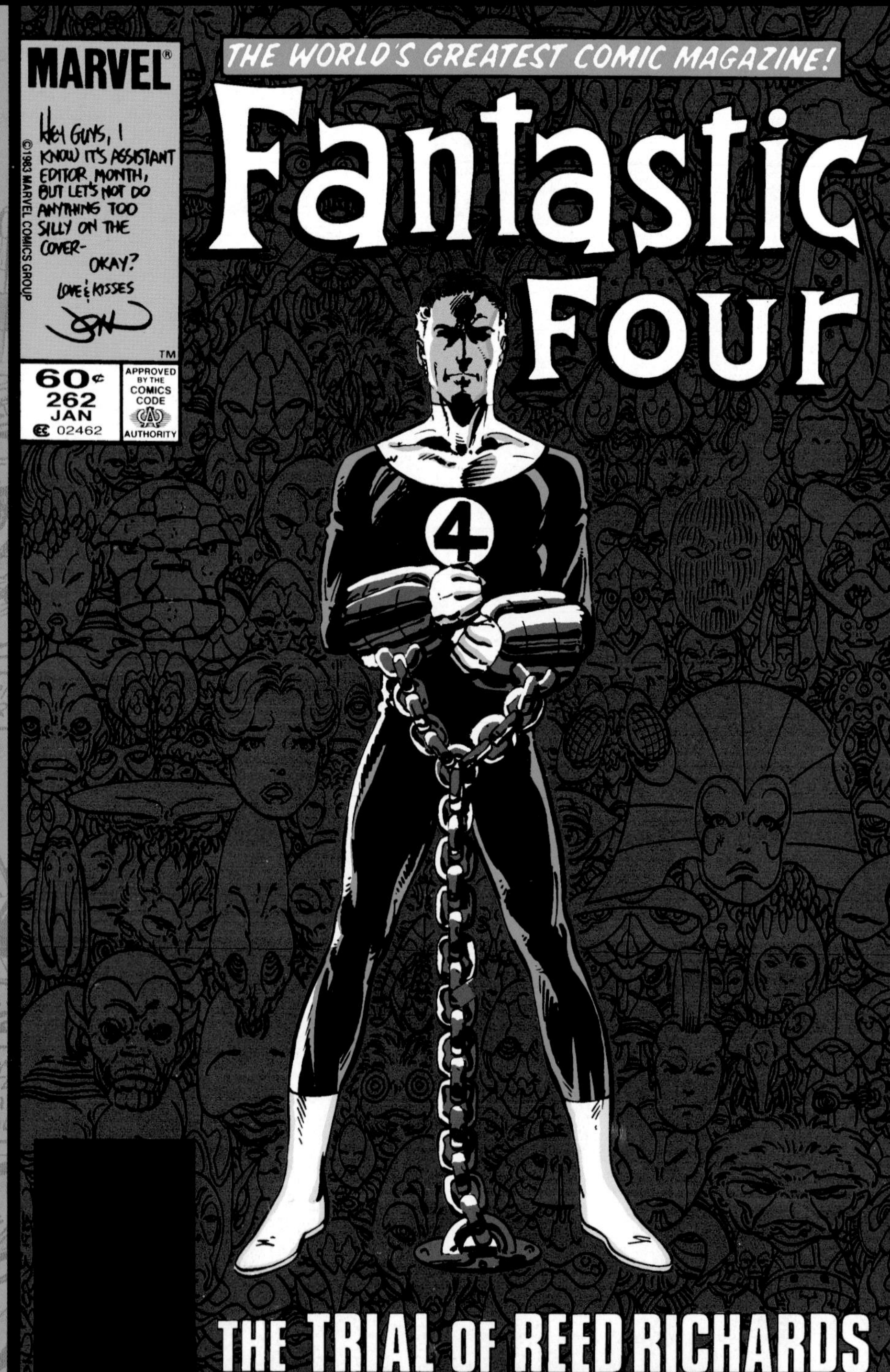

JANUARY 1984

NEW YORK, N.Y. 9:17 AM.
LOOK, JOHN, I KNOW YOU'RE REAL BUSY, BUT THE NEXT ISSUE OF THE FANTASTIC FOUR IS ALMOST TERMINALLY LATE. NOW, NEITHER OF US WANT TO PRODUCE AN FF ISSUE THAT'S STAN LEE PRESENTS TWENTY-TWO BLANK PAGES AND SOME ADS.
EVANSTON, IL. 8:17 AM.
MIKE, I APPRECIATE YOUR POSITION, BELIEVE ME. BUT I JUST DON'T HAVE THE STORY FOR THIS ISSUE. I'VE BEEN CALLING AND CALLING ALL WEEK, BUT ALL I GET FROM THE BAXTER BUILDING IS THE FF'S ROBOT RECEPTIONIST MAKING POLITE APOLOGIES.
WELL, WE'VE GOTTA DO SOMETHING, JOHN. I'VE GOT JIM NOVAK STANDING BY, READY TO LETTER IT, GLYNIS WEIN ALL READY TO COLOR IT. WHAT DO I TELL THEM?
TELL 'EM I'M SORRY, BUT I'M NOT ABOUT TO RISK MAKING UP A STORY. YOU KNOW HOW THE FF HATE IT WHEN WE DO THAT... ESPECIALLY THE THING!
BUT I DON'T REALLY SEE ANY ALTERNATIVE, JOHN, DO YOU? JIM SHOOTER LEFT ME IN CHARGE OF THE FF'S BOOK. I DON'T WANT MY OFFICIAL CREDIT TO BE MIKE HIGGINS, REPRINT EDITOR.
ALRIGHT, ALRIGHT! GIVE ME ANOTHER TWENTY-FOUR HOURS, OKAY? I'LL TRY THE FANTASTIC FOUR'S HEADQUARTERS AGAIN, AND IF I DON'T GET SATISFACTION I'LL INVENT A STORY.
FINE -- TWENTY-FOUR HOURS. BUT DON'T FAIL ME, JOHN. YOU'VE NEVER MISSED A DEADLINE YET -- BUT THIS IS REAL CLOSE!
IN
OUT
1 AUG.

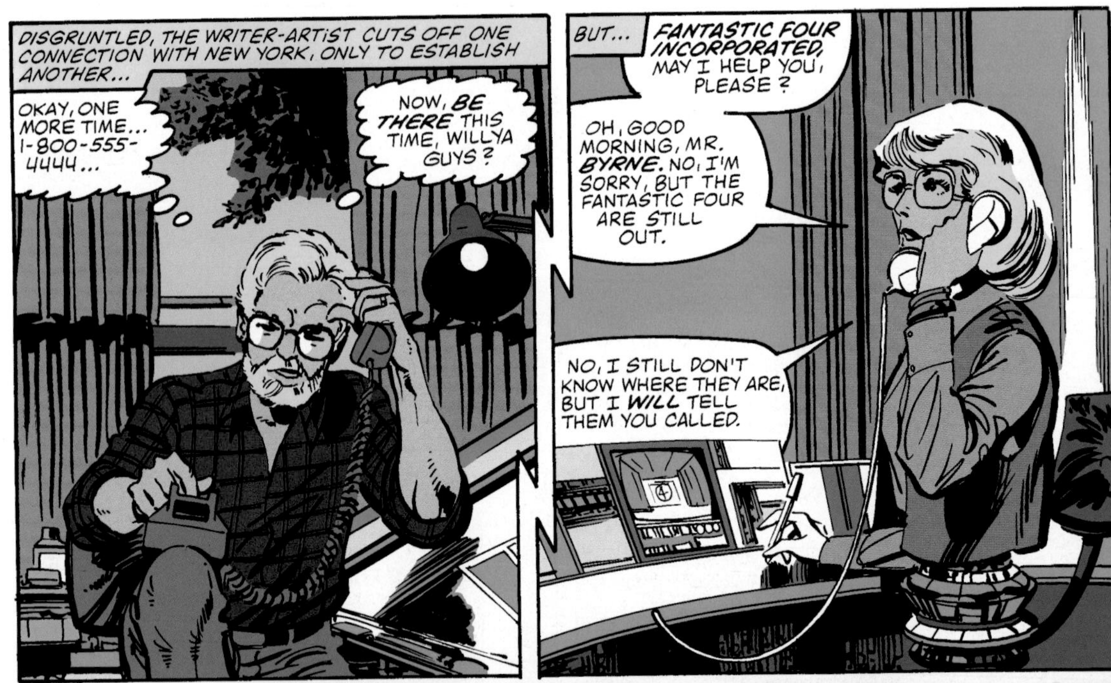

DISGRUNTLED, THE WRITER-ARTIST CUTS OFF ONE CONNECTION WITH NEW YORK, ONLY TO ESTABLISH ANOTHER...
OKAY, ONE MORE TIME... 1-800-555-4444...
NOW, BE THERE THIS TIME, WILLYA GUYS?
BUT...
FANTASTIC FOUR INCORPORATED, MAY I HELP YOU, PLEASE?
OH, GOOD MORNING, MR. BYRNE. NO, I'M SORRY, BUT THE FANTASTIC FOUR ARE STILL OUT.
NO, I STILL DON'T KNOW WHERE THEY ARE, BUT I WILL TELL THEM YOU CALLED.

WELL... FEH!! AT THIS RATE, I WILL HAVE TO MAKE UP SOME DUMB...
EH?
JOHN BYRNE!!

JOHN BYRNE, I HAVE COME FOR YOU!

THE WATCHER!

JUST THEN...
OKAY, HONEY, I'M OFF TO THAT WESTINGHOUSE SHOOT. I'LL BE BACK AROUND SIX...
JOHN?

JOHN...?!
BUT ANDREA BRAUN BYRNE'S HUSBAND NO LONGER EXISTS IN MORTAL TERMS...

FOR, IN A PLACE OUT OF SPACE AND TIME...
?...WATCHER...?
FEAR NOT, EARTH-MAN. NO HARM CAN BEFALL YOU HERE. WE ARE BEYOND THE PHYSICAL PLANE.
YOU ARE NOW BEING SHOWN SIGHTS THAT FEW HUMAN EYES HAVE EVER BEHELD.

I...I APPRECIATE THAT, SIR, BUT... WHY ME?
BECAUSE YOU ARE THE CHRONICLER, JOHN BYRNE. BECAUSE TO YOU HAS FALLEN THE TASK OF RECORDING THE EXPLOITS OF THE FANTASTIC FOUR.
AND EVEN AS WE SPEAK EVENTS UNFOLD WHICH MAY HERALD THE LAST ADVENTURE OF THAT HEROIC FOURSOME. SO MUST YOU REPORT UPON...
3.

THE TRIAL OF
I CAN'T BELIEVE ALL THIS! I WISH THE WATCHER HAD LET ME TAKE TIME TO GRAB A CAMERA--OR AT LEAST MY SKETCHBOOK!
MRS. RICHARDS -- WHAT IS THIS? WHAT'S HAPPENING?
HUH? WHAT THE HECK ARE YOU DOING HERE, BYRNE?
HUMPH! MAYBE HE'S COME TA TRY AN' GET TH' STORY RIGHT THIS TIME!
4.

REED RICHARDS
AH? WELL, I THINK 'RE TALKING ABOUT METHING MORE ORTANT THAN A OMIC BOOK STORY!
APPARENTLY THE WATCHER DISAGREES WITH YOU, KID. SUE...?
OH, JOHN, IT'S JUST TERRIBLE! YOU REMEMBER WHEN REED HELPED SAVE THE LIFE OF GALACTUS, ALL THOSE MONTHS AGO? WELL, NOW ALL THE SURVIVORS OF WORLDS GALACTUS HAS CONSUMED WANT TO KILL REED!
YEAH, AN' WE ALMOST HAD 'EM CONVINCED BIG BRAIN DONE TH' RIGHT THING SAVIN' THE BIG G...
5.

"THEN THAT BLASTED BIRD LADY TURNED UP AN' QUEERED THE WHOLE DEAL!"
"'BIRD LADY'?" BYRNE WONDERS ALOUD.
"OMIGOSH! THAT'S PRINCESS LILANDRA!!"

LILANDRA IS THE NAME, ALRIGHT, JOHN. BUT THESE DAYS SHE'S CALLING HERSELF "MAJESTRIX SHI'AR"-- WHATEVER THAT MEANS.
WE FIRST ENCOUNTERED HER SOME MONTHS AGO... OUR TIME.

"ON THE NIGHT BEFORE WE ENTERED THE NEGATIVE ZONE...*"
GALACTUS IS THE ENEMY OF ALL THAT LIVES-- FOR HE DESTROYS THOSE MOST RARE AND PRECIOUS OF RESOURCES, PLANETS CAPABLE OF SUPPORTING LIFE--AND BY SAVING HIM YOU HAVE BRANDED YOURSELVES HIS ALLIES.
SHOULD HE CONSUME ANY WORLD KNOWN TO US YOU WILL BE IN PART RESPONSIBLE... AND WILL BE HELD RESPONSIBLE FOR IT... TO THE FULL EXTENT OF SHI'AR LAW!**
*SEE FF ISSUES 251-256. **SEE X-MEN #167--MIKE.

WHY THAT ARROGANT WITCH! I ALWAYS HAD THE IMPRESSION SHE WAS TOO FULL OF HER OWN IMPORTANCE, BUT TO ACTUALLY THREATEN THE FANTASTIC FOUR....!

BUT THE OUTRAGED TIRADE IS CUT SHORT, AS...
WE ARE LILANDRA, MAJESTRIX SHI'AR, AND APPOINTED PROSECUTOR.
LET THE TRIAL BEGIN! OUR FIRST WITNESS: KARANT KIAR...
...SKRULL PRELATE OF THE SEVENTH QUADRANT.

WHAT TH'--! WHERE DOES SHE GET OFF STARTIN' TH' TRIAL? WE AIN'T EVEN PICKED TH' JURY YET!
BY HIS OWN CHOICE REED RICHARDS IS TO BE TRIED BY M'NDAVIAN PROCEDURES, BEN GRIMM--THE MOST PERFECT LEGAL SYSTEM IN THE GALAXY.
6.

SEE THE GREAT GLOW GLOBES THAT DEPEND FROM THE VAULT OF THE COURT? NOTE HOW THEIR COLORS FLICKER AND CHANGE CONSTANTLY?
THEY MONITOR THE EMOTIONS, THE JUDGEMENTS OF ALL PRESENT. THUS ALL-- ACCUSED, WITNESSES, PROSECUTION, DEFENSE--ALL ARE JUDGE AND JURY. AND SHOULD ALL THE GLOBES TURN WHITE AT ANY TIME, THEN IS THE VERDICT NOT GUILTY, AND THE TRIAL IS AT AN END.
HUH!

"NOW ATTEND, BEN GRIMM. THE WITNESS SPEAKS..."
I AM KARANT KIAR. I AM PRELATE OF THE SEVENTH QUADRANT OF THE SKRULL EMPIRE.
HEAR MY WORDS, O YOU GATHERED RACES, SURVIVORS OF THE HUNGER OF GALACTUS.
HEAR MY WORDS, AND SHARE MY ANGUISH AND MY RAGE AT THE DEATH OF A WORLD!

"SIXTEEN SPANS PAST, THE HERALD OF GALACTUS APPROACHED OUR HOMEWORLD.
"EVERY AVAILABLE SHIP WAS SENT TO STOP HER, BUT THE ONE-TIME EARTHLING SMASHED THEM ALL!

"THUS DID GALACTUS COME AT LAST.

"FOR TIME OUT OF MEMORY WE SKRULLS HAVE FEARED GALACTUS, AND HIDDEN OUR ENERGIES FROM HIM.
NOW THERE WAS NO HIDING...

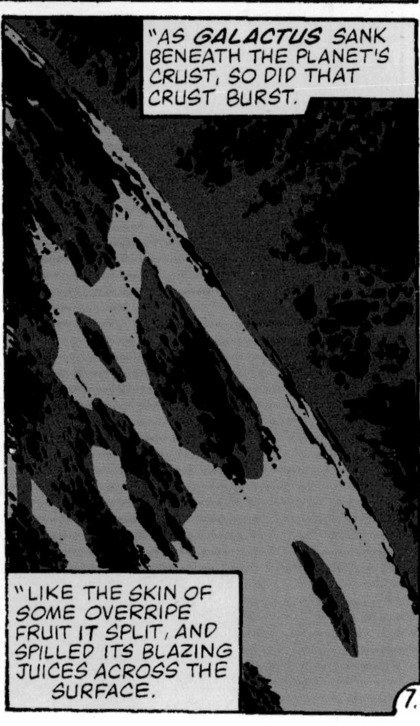
"AS GALACTUS SANK BENEATH THE PLANET'S CRUST, SO DID THAT CRUST BURST.
"LIKE THE SKIN OF SOME OVERRIPE FRUIT IT SPLIT, AND SPILLED ITS BLAZING JUICES ACROSS THE SURFACE.
7.

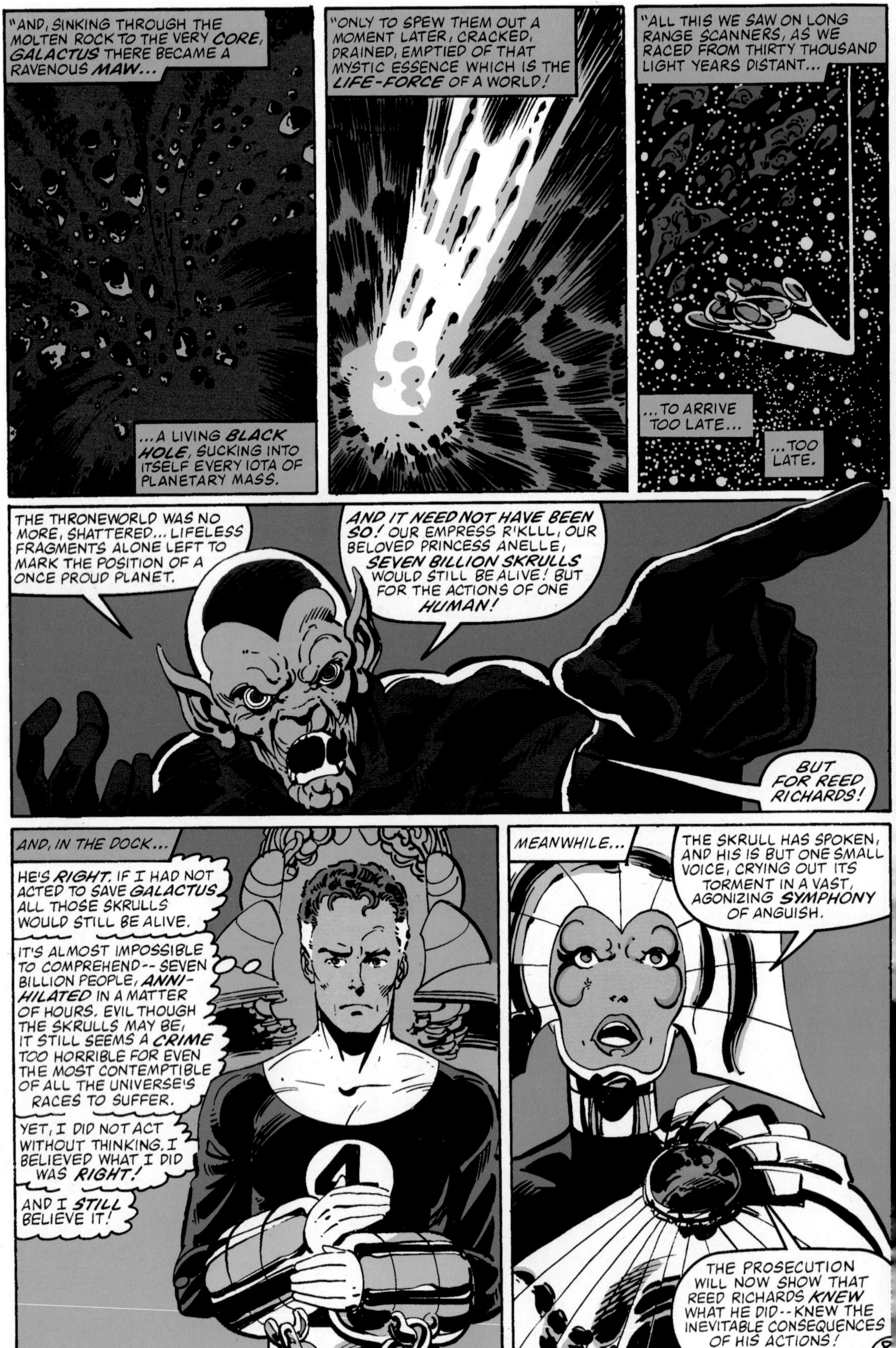

"AND, SINKING THROUGH THE MOLTEN ROCK TO THE VERY *CORE*, *GALACTUS* THERE BECAME A RAVENOUS *MAW*...

...A LIVING *BLACK HOLE*, SUCKING INTO ITSELF EVERY IOTA OF PLANETARY MASS.

"ONLY TO SPEW THEM OUT A MOMENT LATER, CRACKED, DRAINED, EMPTIED OF THAT MYSTIC ESSENCE WHICH IS THE *LIFE-FORCE* OF A WORLD!

"ALL THIS WE SAW ON LONG RANGE SCANNERS, AS WE RACED FROM THIRTY THOUSAND LIGHT YEARS DISTANT...

...TO ARRIVE TOO LATE...

...TOO LATE.

THE THRONEWORLD WAS NO MORE, SHATTERED... LIFELESS FRAGMENTS ALONE LEFT TO MARK THE POSITION OF A ONCE PROUD PLANET.

AND IT NEED NOT HAVE BEEN SO! OUR EMPRESS R'KLLL, OUR BELOVED PRINCESS ANELLE, *SEVEN BILLION SKRULLS* WOULD STILL BE ALIVE! BUT FOR THE ACTIONS OF ONE *HUMAN!*

BUT FOR REED RICHARDS!

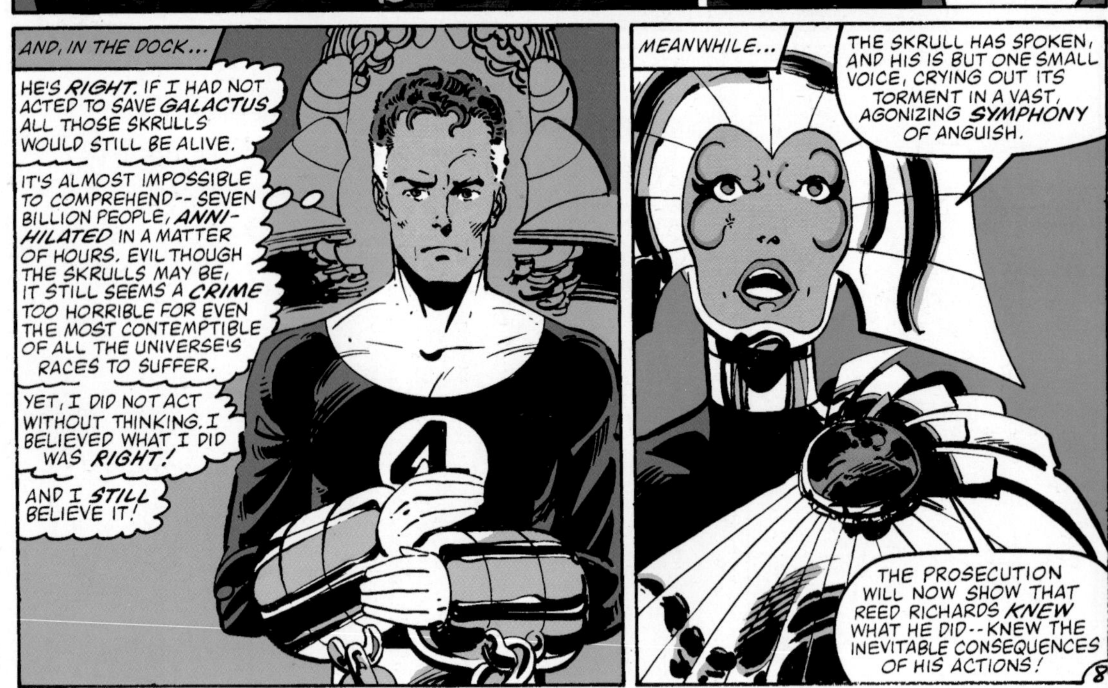

AND, IN THE DOCK...
HE'S *RIGHT*. IF I HAD NOT ACTED TO SAVE *GALACTUS* ALL THOSE SKRULLS WOULD STILL BE ALIVE.
IT'S ALMOST IMPOSSIBLE TO COMPREHEND-- SEVEN BILLION PEOPLE, *ANNI-HILATED* IN A MATTER OF HOURS. EVIL THOUGH THE SKRULLS MAY BE, IT STILL SEEMS A *CRIME* TOO HORRIBLE FOR EVEN THE MOST CONTEMPTIBLE OF ALL THE UNIVERSE'S RACES TO SUFFER.
YET, I DID NOT ACT WITHOUT THINKING. I BELIEVED WHAT I DID WAS *RIGHT!*
AND I *STILL* BELIEVE IT!
MEANWHILE...
THE SKRULL HAS SPOKEN, AND HIS IS BUT ONE SMALL VOICE, CRYING OUT ITS TORMENT IN A VAST, AGONIZING *SYMPHONY* OF ANGUISH.
THE PROSECUTION WILL NOW SHOW THAT REED RICHARDS *KNEW* WHAT HE DID--KNEW THE INEVITABLE CONSEQUENCES OF HIS ACTIONS!
8

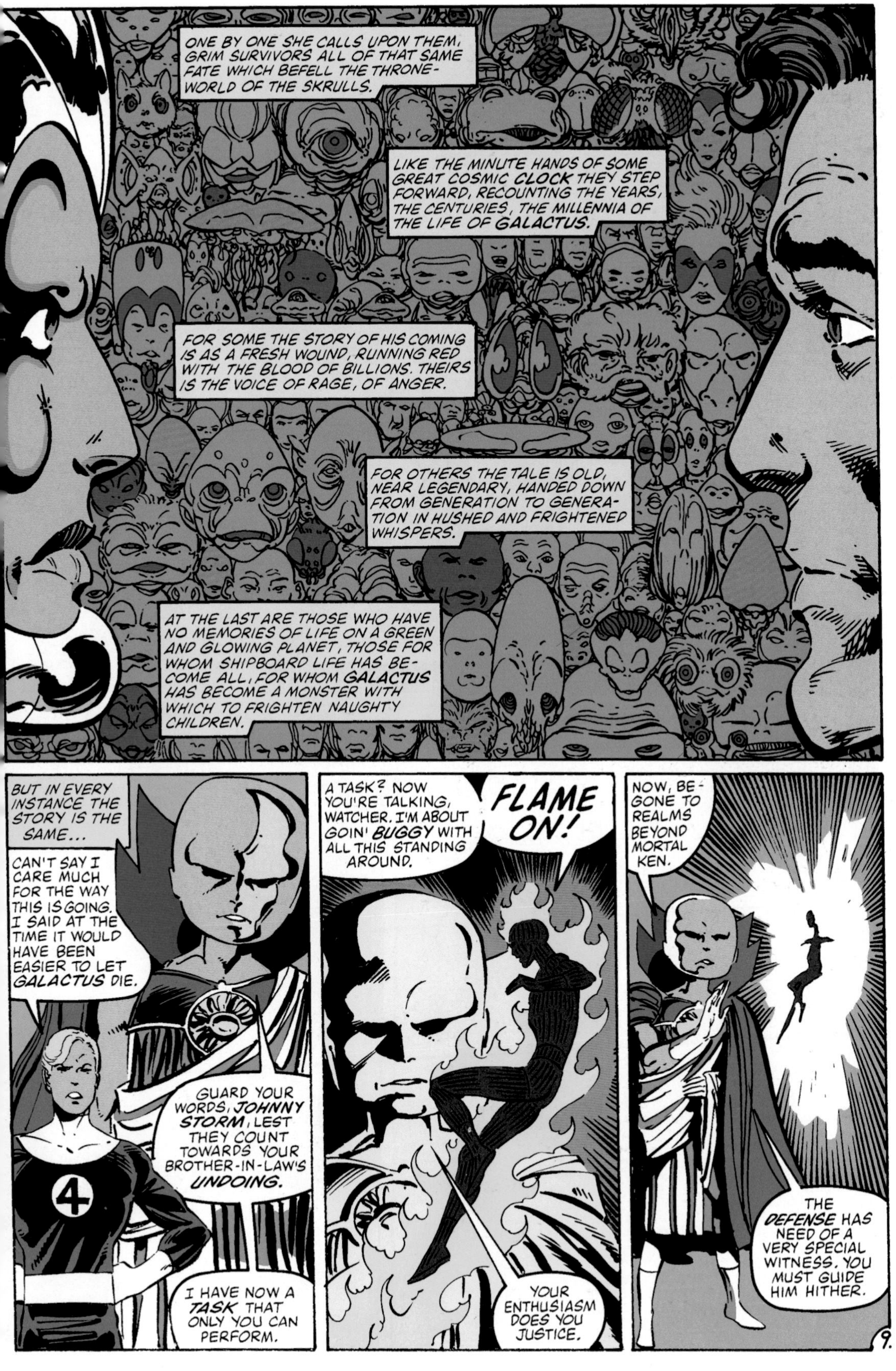

ONE BY ONE SHE CALLS UPON THEM: GRIM SURVIVORS ALL OF THAT SAME FATE WHICH BEFELL THE THRONE-WORLD OF THE SKRULLS.

LIKE THE MINUTE HANDS OF SOME GREAT COSMIC CLOCK THEY STEP FORWARD, RECOUNTING THE YEARS, THE CENTURIES, THE MILLENNIA OF THE LIFE OF GALACTUS.

FOR SOME THE STORY OF HIS COMING IS AS A FRESH WOUND, RUNNING RED WITH THE BLOOD OF BILLIONS. THEIRS IS THE VOICE OF RAGE, OF ANGER.

FOR OTHERS THE TALE IS OLD, NEAR LEGENDARY, HANDED DOWN FROM GENERATION TO GENERATION IN HUSHED AND FRIGHTENED WHISPERS.

AT THE LAST ARE THOSE WHO HAVE NO MEMORIES OF LIFE ON A GREEN AND GLOWING PLANET, THOSE FOR WHOM SHIPBOARD LIFE HAS BECOME ALL, FOR WHOM GALACTUS HAS BECOME A MONSTER WITH WHICH TO FRIGHTEN NAUGHTY CHILDREN.

BUT IN EVERY INSTANCE THE STORY IS THE SAME...
CAN'T SAY I CARE MUCH FOR THE WAY THIS IS GOING. I SAID AT THE TIME IT WOULD HAVE BEEN EASIER TO LET GALACTUS DIE.
GUARD YOUR WORDS, JOHNNY STORM, LEST THEY COUNT TOWARDS YOUR BROTHER-IN-LAW'S UNDOING.
I HAVE NOW A TASK THAT ONLY YOU CAN PERFORM.

A TASK? NOW YOU'RE TALKING, WATCHER. I'M ABOUT GOIN' BUGGY WITH ALL THIS STANDING AROUND.
FLAME ON!
YOUR ENTHUSIASM DOES YOU JUSTICE.

NOW, BEGONE TO REALMS BEYOND MORTAL KEN.
THE DEFENSE HAS NEED OF A VERY SPECIAL WITNESS. YOU MUST GUIDE HIM HITHER.
9.

THEN, AS THE HUMAN TORCH WINKS FROM SIGHT...
WATCHER... WAIT... THE TORCH... WHAT... I MEAN, WHERE HAVE YOU...?
CALM YOURSELF, JOHN BYRNE...
HAVE I NOT PROMISED THAT ALL THINGS SHALL BE MADE KNOWN TO YOU IN TIME?
TAKE NOW YOUR PLACE WITH THE REST OF THE FANTASTIC FOUR. IT IS TIME TO BEGIN THE DEFENSE!

HUH? YOU MEAN THE WATCHER IS GOING TO BE MISTER FANTASTIC'S DEFENSE COUNCIL? DOESN'T THAT VIOLATE HIS RACE'S CODE OF NON-INTERFERENCE?
THE WATCHER SAYS NOT, JOHN. HE SAYS THAT MORE THAN JUST REED IS ON TRIAL HERE. HE SAYS IT IS GALACTUS HIM-SELF WHO IS BEING JUDGED.
AND THAT MAKES THIS TRIAL SO IMPORTANT THAT ITS EVENTUAL OUTCOME WILL EFFECT EVEN THE WATCHER'S OWN RACE!

AS THE BEAUTIFUL INVISIBLE GIRL CONCLUDES...
HEAR ME NOW, SURVIVORS. I AM UATU, OF THE RACE OF THE WATCHERS. MINE IS A PEOPLE OLDER THAN ALL YOUR HISTORIES COMBINED. OURS WAS A PLANET OF THE FIRST TO FORM FROM THE COSMIC FIRES THAT BIRTHED THE UNIVERSE.
LONG HAS THE BEING CALLED GALACTUS BEEN KNOWN TO US, AND LONG HAVE WE SOUGHT TO COM-PREHEND HIM.
REED RICHARDS' ACT WAS BASED UPON HIS OWN SMALL COMPREHENSION OF THE COSMIC ALL OF GALACTUS. REED RICHARDS SHALL THUS BE THE FIRST TO SPEAK NOW...

HOW DO YOU PLEAD TO THE CHARGE HERE BROUGHT AGAINST YOU?
HOW ELSE CAN I PLEAD BUT...
...GUILTY!

GUILTY!"
A SINGLE WORD, SPOKEN SOFTLY, YET WITH GREAT RESOLVE. IT LANCES THROUGH THE ALIEN ASSEMBLY LIKE AN ELECTRIC CHARGE.

AND TO THE SMALL BAND OF WATCHING HUMANS THE EFFECT IS NO LESS GALVANIC...
NO! NO! DON'T SAY IT, REED! DON'T GIVE UP!
T-TAKE IT EASY, SUZIE... YER HUBBINS NEVER QUITS THAT EASY.
HE'S GOT SOME ACE UP HIS SLEEVE... HE'S GOTTA HAVE!

GUILTY? THEN YOU ACCEPT YOUR PART IN THIS MOST HEINOUS OF ALL CRIMES, REED RICHARDS?
YOU STAND PREPARED AND READY TO FACE THE FULL AND IRREVOCABLE WEIGHT OF SHI'AR LAW?

NOT AT ALL, MAJESTRIX.
I REMIND THE COURT THAT THE CHARGE AGAINST ME IS THAT OF WILLINGLY SAVING THE LIFE OF GALACTUS.
THAT ACTION IS A DOCUMENTED, HISTORICAL FACT. IT WOULD BE POINTLESS FOR ME TO ATTEMPT TO DISCLAIM IT, AND THEREFORE I MUST PLEAD GUILTY AS CHARGED.
BUT I FURTHER REMIND YOU THAT THE ISSUE BEFORE THIS BODY TODAY IS NOT WHETHER OR NOT I SAVED GALACTUS, BUT RATHER IF SO DOING IN FACT CONSTITUTES A CRIME.

OF THAT I CAN SAY ONLY THIS...
WHEN GALACTUS FIRST CAME TO EARTH ALL THOSE LONG YEARS AGO WE WERE TOLD BY THE WATCHER THAT HE WAS NOT EVIL--THAT GALACTUS IS IN FACT BEYOND GOOD AND EVIL.
THAT IS A STATEMENT WHICH HAS LONG TROUBLED ME, FOR IF A BEING IS TRULY NEITHER GOOD NOR EVIL HE IS BY DEFINITION NEUTRAL.
YET CLEARLY GALACTUS IS NOT A NEUTRAL BEING. WITH INCREASING FREQUENCY HE FEEDS UPON THE LIFE-ESSENCE OF WHOLE PLANETS, AND SHOULD THOSE PLANETS PROVE TO BE INHABITED HIS EFFECT IS CATASTROPHIC TO SAY THE LEAST.
HOW CAN ANY RATIONAL MAN JUDGE THAT TO BE NEUTRAL?
11.

ALBERT EINSTEIN ONCE SAID THAT "GOD DOES NOT PLAY AT DICE." HE MEANT THAT THERE IS AN ORDER OF THINGS IN OUR UNIVERSE.

AND IT DOES NOT REQUIRE ANY BELIEF IN A SUPREME BEING TO REALIZE THAT *GALACTUS* MUST SOMEHOW BE PART OF THAT ORDER--AND, I SUSPECT, AN *IMPORTANT* PART.

FOR IF HE IS TRULY TO BE CONSIDERED *NEUTRAL* THEN THE APPARENT *EVIL* OF HIS ACTIONS, MUST, IN THE END RESULT, NOT BE EVIL.

AND SO, THEY MUST BE PART OF SOME GREATER *GOOD.*

I CANNOT BELIEVE HE WOULD BE *ALLOWED* TO EXIST, IF THIS WERE NOT THE CASE.

IS THAT YOUR DEFENSE, REED RICHARDS? A CHILD'S GAME OF *ARITHMETIC*?

WHERE THEN IS YOUR *PROOF?* PROOF THAT THE DEATHS OF UNCOUNTED BILLIONS WORK TOWARD A GREATER GOOD?

ULTIMATELY I HAVE NO PROOF, MAJESTRIX. I HAVE ONLY LOGIC...

...LOGIC AND FAITH.

MEASURE NOW THE POWER OF THE *INTELLECT* OF THIS LONE EARTHMAN, FOR HE HAS REASONED *ORDER* OUT OF *CHAOS.*
AND HE HAS REASONED *CORRECTLY,* AS WILL BE SHOWN WITH THE TESTIMONY OF MY SECOND WITNESS...

"LOOK NOW TO THE CENTER OF THE COURT..."
WATCHER, HE CAME! HE *CAME!*
AND WOULD HAVE DONE SO E'EN *WITHOUT* THY PLEA LAD. THERE ARE MATTERS HERE THAT BE OF GREAT CONCERN TO *ODIN!*

ODIN?! HOLY FRIJOLES! THE WATCHER MUST HAVE SENT THE TORCH TO ASGARD!!!
HE... HE'S SO... IMPOSING! WE'VE ALL MET THOR HALF A DOZEN TIMES...
...BUT SOMEHOW I NEVER MADE THE CONNECTION-- ASGARD! THE ANCIENT NORSE GODS! AND ODIN-- THEIR RULER!
AN' HE SAID HE WUZ GONNA COME AN' TESTI-FY FER REED EVEN IF TH' WATCHER HADN'T ASKED!
REMIND ME TA BE IMPRESSED--WHEN I GET OVER BEIN' FLABBERGASTED!
THIS WITNESS IS, I BELIEVE, KNOWN TO THE MEMBERS OF THE COURT.
HE IS CALLED AS AN EXPERT WITNESS ON THE SUBJECT OF GALACTUS. ARE HIS... CRE-DENTIALS ACCEPTABLE TO THE PROSECUTION?
Y-YES...
THEN HEAR THE WORDS OF ODIN, FOR THE NATURE AND ORIGIN OF GALACTUS IS KNOWN TO US.
HEAR THESE WORDS, AS GALACTUS HIM-SELF DID SAY THEM UNTO THOR, MY NOBLE SON, AND KNOW ALL THAT THEY BE TRUE!
"ONCE THERE WAS A WORLD. A WORLD OF SUCH MAGNIFICENCE THAT EVEN FABLED ASGARD MIGHT SUFFER IN THE COMPARISON --THE PLANET TAA!
"BUT FOR ALL ITS GLORIES IT WAS A PLANET DOOMED, A PLANET DYING.
"AND IN ALL THAT WORLD ONE MAN ALONE HAD THE WISDOM TO KNOW WHAT IT WAS THAT SO DOOMED THEM, AND THE WORDS TO SPEAK ITS NAME...
THE PLAGUE THAT THREATENS US ALL HAS NO CURE, FOR IT IS THE FINAL PLAGUE OF ENTROPY!
OUR WORLD, OUR VERY UNIVERSE IS GRINDING TO ITS END!
"HIS NAME WAS GALEN, AND THO' HE KNEW IT NOT, HE WOULD BECOME GALACTUS!
13.

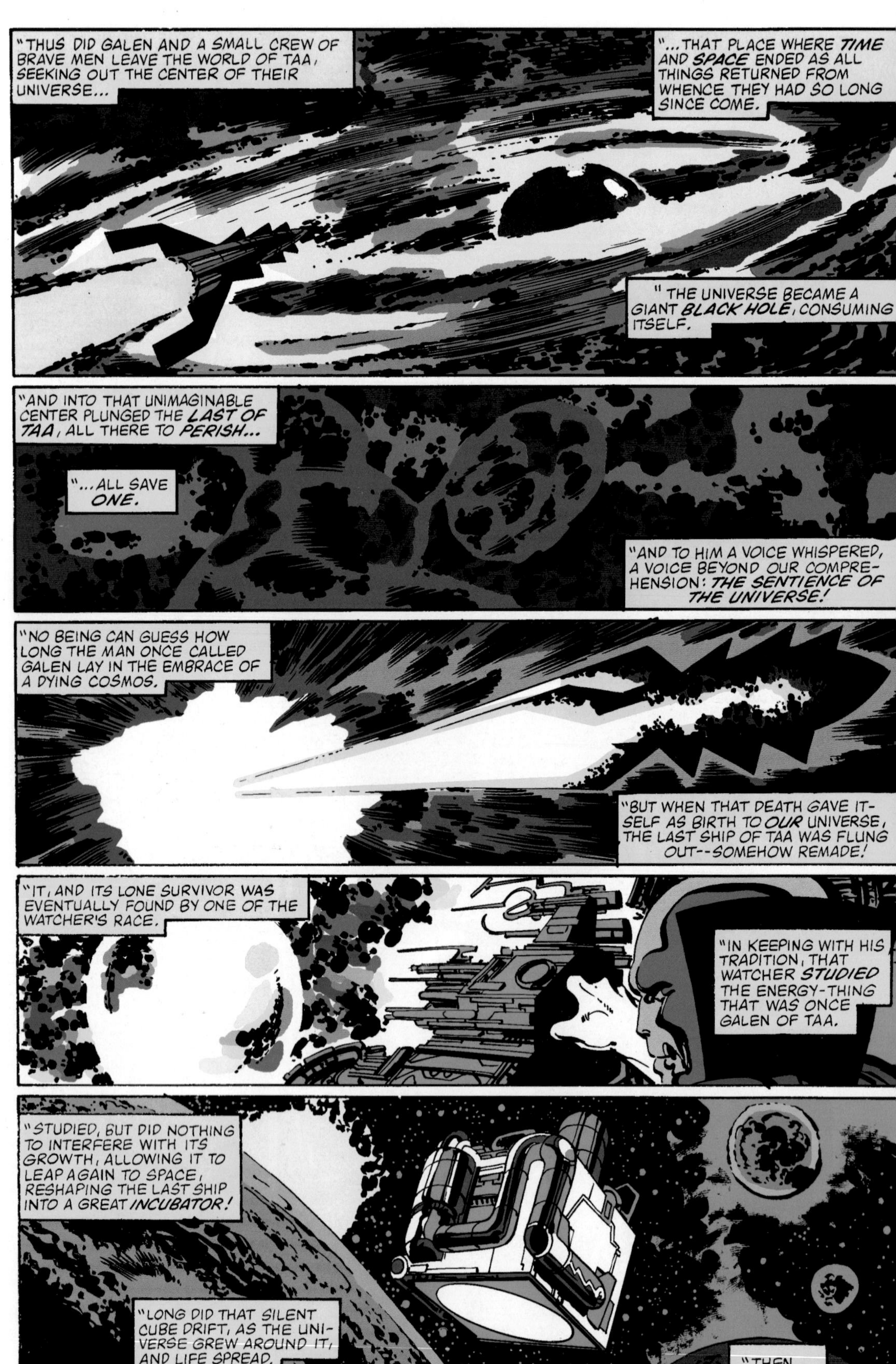
"THUS DID GALEN AND A SMALL CREW OF BRAVE MEN LEAVE THE WORLD OF TAA, SEEKING OUT THE CENTER OF THEIR UNIVERSE...
"...THAT PLACE WHERE TIME AND SPACE ENDED AS ALL THINGS RETURNED FROM WHENCE THEY HAD SO LONG SINCE COME.
"THE UNIVERSE BECAME A GIANT BLACK HOLE, CONSUMING ITSELF.
"AND INTO THAT UNIMAGINABLE CENTER PLUNGED THE LAST OF TAA, ALL THERE TO PERISH...
"...ALL SAVE ONE.
"AND TO HIM A VOICE WHISPERED, A VOICE BEYOND OUR COMPREHENSION: THE SENTIENCE OF THE UNIVERSE!
"NO BEING CAN GUESS HOW LONG THE MAN ONCE CALLED GALEN LAY IN THE EMBRACE OF A DYING COSMOS.
"BUT WHEN THAT DEATH GAVE ITSELF AS BIRTH TO OUR UNIVERSE, THE LAST SHIP OF TAA WAS FLUNG OUT--SOMEHOW REMADE!
"IT, AND ITS LONE SURVIVOR WAS EVENTUALLY FOUND BY ONE OF THE WATCHER'S RACE.
"IN KEEPING WITH HIS TRADITION, THAT WATCHER STUDIED THE ENERGY-THING THAT WAS ONCE GALEN OF TAA.
"STUDIED, BUT DID NOTHING TO INTERFERE WITH ITS GROWTH, ALLOWING IT TO LEAP AGAIN TO SPACE, RESHAPING THE LAST SHIP INTO A GREAT INCUBATOR!
"LONG DID THAT SILENT CUBE DRIFT, AS THE UNIVERSE GREW AROUND IT, AND LIFE SPREAD.
"THEN...

"...THEN CAME THAT FATEFUL DAY WHEN THE CUBE WAS OPENED...
"...AND GALACTUS LIVED!"
THUS WAS BORN INTO THE NEW UNIVERSE A NEW NATURAL FORCE. LIKE THE SOLAR WIND, LIKE THE SUPER-NOVA...
...LIKE THE ROILING SEAS THAT TESTED OUR VIKING WORSHIPPERS. TESTED THEM, AND MADE THEM STRONG.
SUCH IS THE FUNCTION OF GALACTUS. TO EACH WORLD IN TIME HE COMES AND HIS VERY COMING IS A TEST.
THOSE THAT PASS THE TEST ARE STRENGTHENED BY IT, AND MADE MORE WORTHY OF THAT GREAT FATE WHICH IS THE PROMISED END OF OUR UNIVERSE.
THOSE THAT FAIL, FAIL TOTALLY, AND ARE FOREVER EX-PUNGED, WIPED FROM THE SLATE OF TIME AND SPACE.
THE ACTIONS OF REED RICHARDS WERE IN NO WAY CRIMINAL. LET THIS TRIAL BE AT AN END! SO SPEAKS ODIN!!
AND, AS THE MYSTIC WINDS RISE, TO BEAR AWAY THE LORD OF ASGARD...
WA-HOOO! WE DID IT! WE WON!
I KNEW TH' BIG BRAIN WOULD GET CLEARED! I KNEW IT!
IT'S SO WONDERFUL! IT'S ALMOST TOO GOOD TO BE TRUE!
UMM... JUST A MINUTE GANG...
15

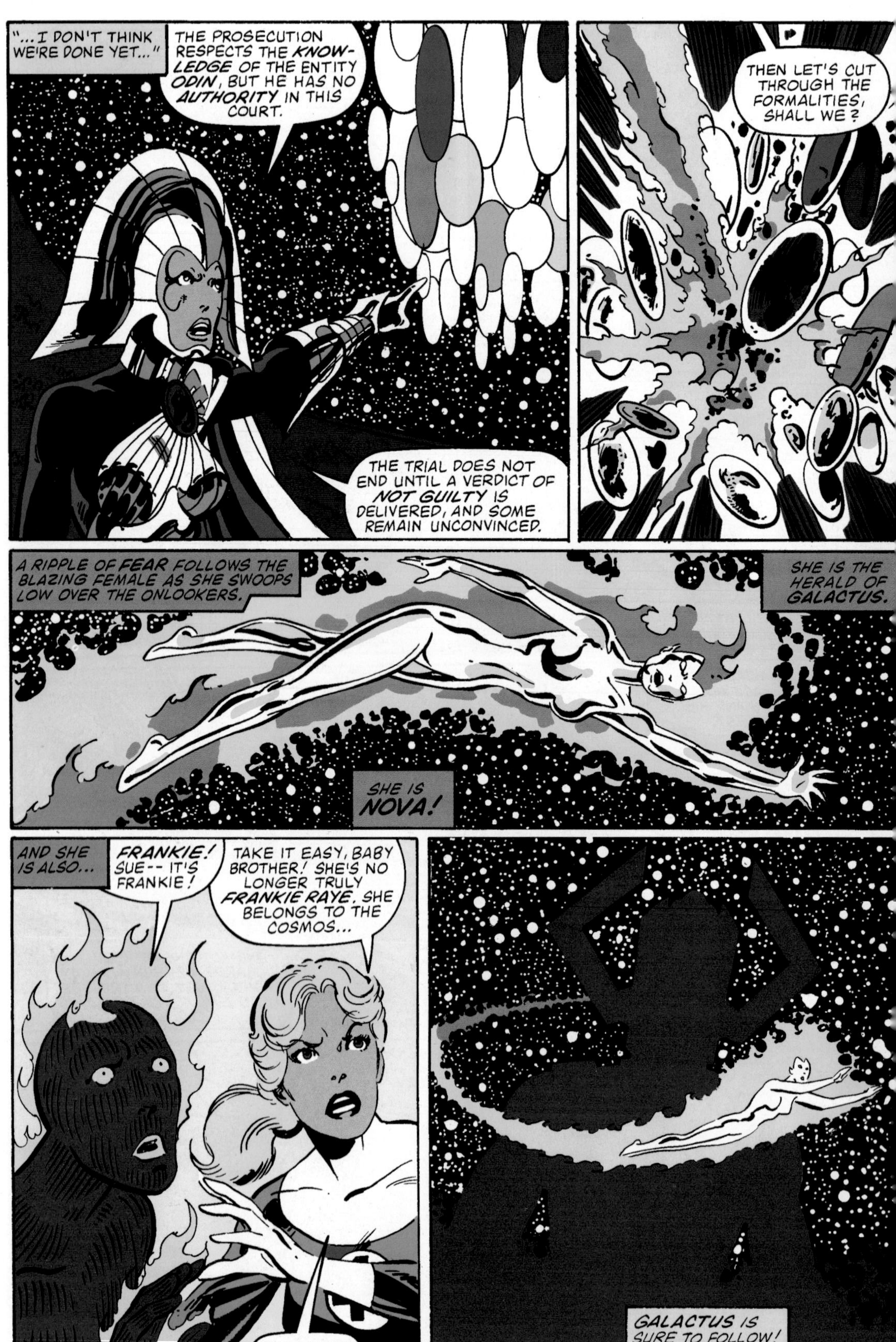
"...I DON'T THINK WE'RE DONE YET..."
THE PROSECUTION RESPECTS THE KNOWLEDGE OF THE ENTITY ODIN, BUT HE HAS NO AUTHORITY IN THIS COURT.
THE TRIAL DOES NOT END UNTIL A VERDICT OF NOT GUILTY IS DELIVERED, AND SOME REMAIN UNCONVINCED.
THEN LET'S CUT THROUGH THE FORMALITIES, SHALL WE?
A RIPPLE OF FEAR FOLLOWS THE BLAZING FEMALE AS SHE SWOOPS LOW OVER THE ONLOOKERS.
SHE IS THE HERALD OF GALACTUS.
SHE IS NOVA!
AND SHE IS ALSO...
FRANKIE! SUE-- IT'S FRANKIE!
TAKE IT EASY, BABY BROTHER! SHE'S NO LONGER TRULY FRANKIE RAYE. SHE BELONGS TO THE COSMOS...
AND WHERE SHE GOES...
GALACTUS IS SURE TO FOLLOW!

AND IF HIS HERALD BROUGHT FEAR, IMAGINE IF YOU CAN THE TERROR, THE BLIND, UNREASONING PANIC THAT NOW RIPS THROUGH THE ASSEMBLAGE.
A MILLION AND MORE ALIEN EYES LOOK UPON HIM WHO IS GALACTUS, AND FOR EACH RACE THE VISION DIFFERS.
FOR GALACTUS IS TRULY NO LONGER A BEING IN THE ABSOLUTE, PHYSICAL SENSE. HE IS AS ODIN NAMED HIM, A FORCE OF NATURE.
AND EACH MIND THAT VIEWS HIM STRUGGLES AS BEST IT CAN TO PERCEIVE THAT UNGUESSABLE FORCE AS AN IMAGE IT CAN COMPREHEND.
17.

BUT, AS PANIC TRANSFORMS CALM AUDIENCE INTO THUNDERING MOB...
GALACTUS! AT LAST!

THERE IS ONE FOR WHOM THE PRESENCE OF THE PLANET-KILLER BRINGS NOT FEAR, BUT GRIM RESOLVE.
A HUNDRED SPANS I HAVE WAITED FOR THIS MOMENT--WAITED FOR MY VENGEANCE!

STRANGE, ALIEN COMPONENTS SNAP AND CLICK TOGETHER, AND A WEAPON GROWS IN THE TREMBLING HANDS OF XXAN XXAR.
BUT GALACTUS DOES NOT NOTICE.

HE IGNORES ME! HE DOES NOT KNOW HIS DEATH IS IN THIS SMALL WEAPON. FOR IT FIRES A SINGLE TINY PELLET THAT WILL BEGIN A CHAIN REACTION!

A CHAIN REACTION THAT WILL CONSUME HIS ARMOR, UNLEASHING THE ENERGIES WITHIN, SCATTERING HIS BEING ACROSS A MILLION CUBIC PARSECS.

I THINK...
THERE WAS NO WAY TO TEST IT ...AND HE SEEMS SO... SO...
IF IT SHOULD FAIL...

IF IT SHOULD NOT DESTROY HIM... IF IT SHOULD INSTEAD ONLY ANNOY HIM...?
RESOLVE WEAKENS...

BEFORE THE IMPLACABLE POWER OF GALACTUS, XXAN XXAR FEELS SUDDENLY SMALL AND INSIGNIFICANT.

HE HOPES HIS LOST RACE WILL FORGIVE HIM, AS HIS OATH OF VENGEANCE MUST WAIT FOR ANOTHER DAY...

AND, NO MORE AWARE OF THIS BRIEF DRAMA THAN IS A MAN OF THE BACTERIA THAT THRIVE ON HIS LIVING FLESH, GALACTUS SPEAKS...
HEAR THE WORDS OF GALACTUS. I BRING NO DOOM TO THOSE GATHERED HERE THIS DAY. I BRING INSTEAD JUSTICE FOR THAT MORTAL I NAME FRIEND.
REED RICHARDS IS A NOBLE SPIRIT, UNTAINTED BY THE PETTINESS OF FEAR AND HATE. HIS DEED WAS HONORABLE AND GOOD.
SO SPEAKS GALACTUS. SO SPEAKS THE COSMIC TRUTH!
MAJESTRIX--HAVE A CARE! I AM SWORN EVER TO PROTECT YOU, BUT AGAINST GALACTUS I HAVE NOT THE POWER!
YET, SUMMONING HER COURAGE, LILANDRA FACES HER GREATEST FEAR.
Y-YOUR WORDS HAVE NO VALUE IN THIS COURT, RAVAGER.
BY NAMING HIM YOUR FRIEND YOU SERVE NOT TO SAVE REED RICHARDS, BUT TO CONDEMN HIM!
YOU ARE KNOWN TO ME, LILANDRA.
BUT I HAVE CONSUMED NO SHI'AR WORLD. WHY TROUBLE YOURSELF IN MATTERS OF NO CONCERN TO YOU?
THE MATTERS HERE CONCERN THE FATE OF ALL LIFE-KIND, GALACTUS.
I AM SWORN PROTECTOR OF ALL THAT LIVES, AGAINST THE LIKES OF YOU.
AND I REJECT YOUR TESTIMONY, UNLESS TO NAME IT A FINAL NAIL IN THE COFFIN OF THE ACCUSED.
I FEAR YOU HAVE DONE MORE ILL THAN GOOD BY YOUR APPEARANCE HERE, GALACTUS.
YET, STILL THERE IS A CHANCE--A CHANCE THAT WE MIGHT PLUCK SALVATION OUT OF HOPELESSNESS.
I KNOW WHEREOF YOU SPEAK, WATCHER. OUR POWER COMBINED MIGHT PEEL AWAY THE VEIL AND BRING HIM TO US!
THEN SO LET IT BE DONE!
THEIR HANDS DRAW NEAR, AND ANCIENT ENERGIES STIR...
19.

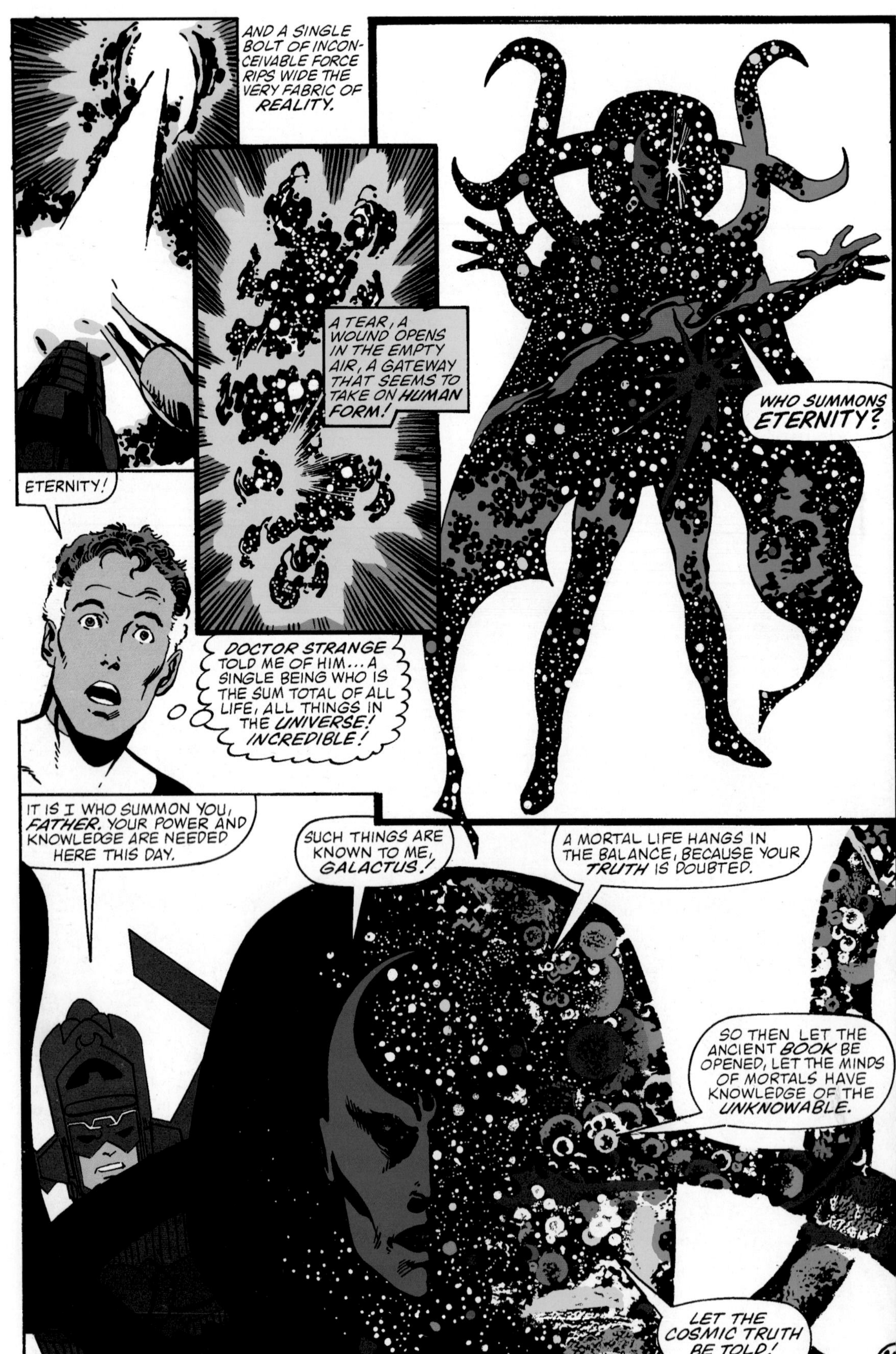
AND A SINGLE BOLT OF INCONCEIVABLE FORCE RIPS WIDE THE VERY FABRIC OF REALITY.
A TEAR, A WOUND OPENS IN THE EMPTY AIR, A GATEWAY THAT SEEMS TO TAKE ON HUMAN FORM!
WHO SUMMONS ETERNITY?
ETERNITY!
DOCTOR STRANGE TOLD ME OF HIM... A SINGLE BEING WHO IS THE SUM TOTAL OF ALL LIFE, ALL THINGS IN THE UNIVERSE! INCREDIBLE!
IT IS I WHO SUMMON YOU, FATHER. YOUR POWER AND KNOWLEDGE ARE NEEDED HERE THIS DAY.
SUCH THINGS ARE KNOWN TO ME, GALACTUS!
A MORTAL LIFE HANGS IN THE BALANCE, BECAUSE YOUR TRUTH IS DOUBTED.
SO THEN LET THE ANCIENT BOOK BE OPENED, LET THE MINDS OF MORTALS HAVE KNOWLEDGE OF THE UNKNOWABLE.
LET THE COSMIC TRUTH BE TOLD!
20

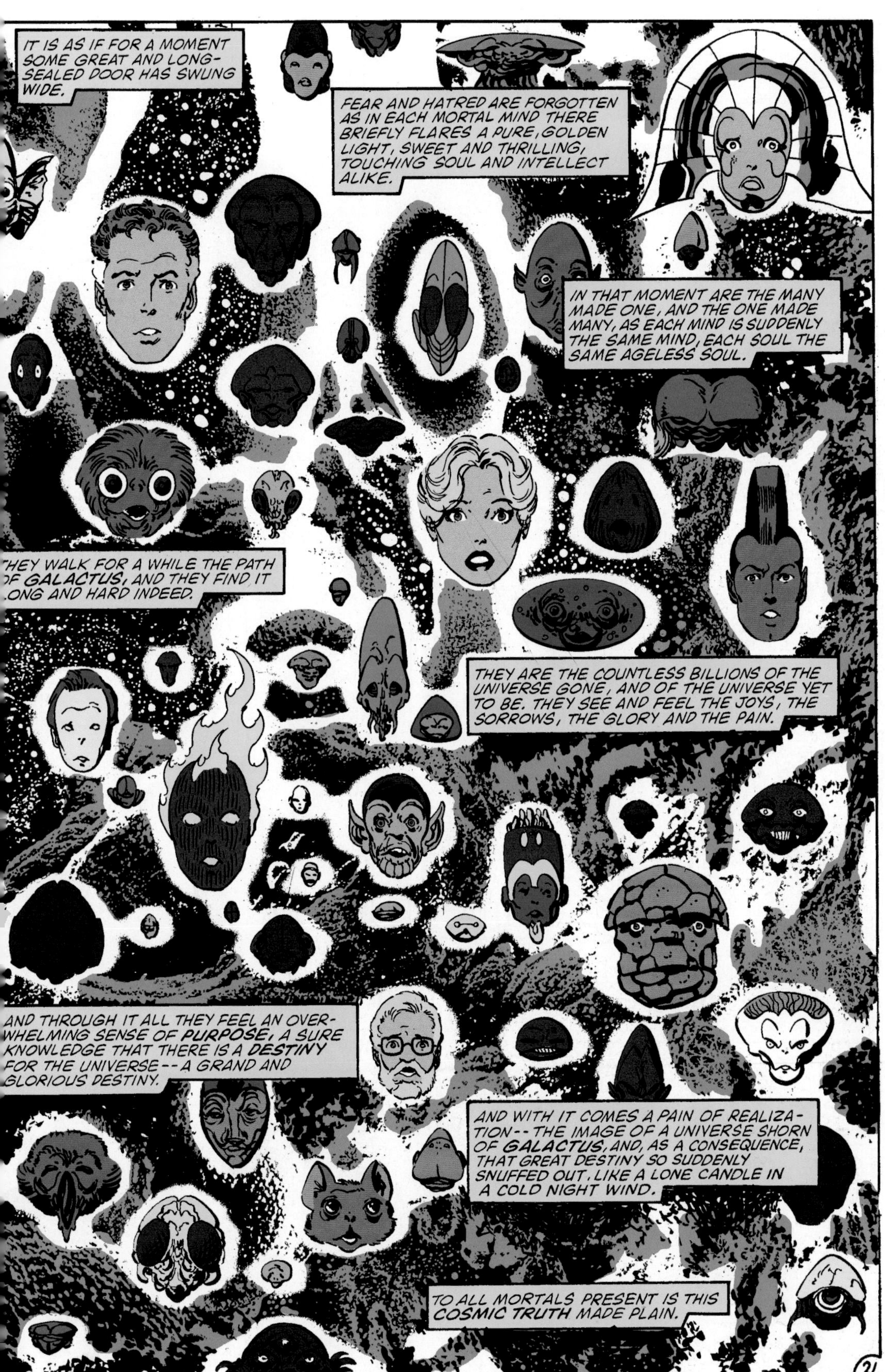
IT IS AS IF FOR A MOMENT SOME GREAT AND LONG-SEALED DOOR HAS SWUNG WIDE.
FEAR AND HATRED ARE FORGOTTEN AS IN EACH MORTAL MIND THERE BRIEFLY FLARES A PURE, GOLDEN LIGHT, SWEET AND THRILLING, TOUCHING SOUL AND INTELLECT ALIKE.
IN THAT MOMENT ARE THE MANY MADE ONE, AND THE ONE MADE MANY, AS EACH MIND IS SUDDENLY THE SAME MIND, EACH SOUL THE SAME AGELESS SOUL.
THEY WALK FOR A WHILE THE PATH OF GALACTUS, AND THEY FIND IT LONG AND HARD INDEED.
THEY ARE THE COUNTLESS BILLIONS OF THE UNIVERSE GONE, AND OF THE UNIVERSE YET TO BE. THEY SEE AND FEEL THE JOYS, THE SORROWS, THE GLORY AND THE PAIN.
AND THROUGH IT ALL THEY FEEL AN OVERWHELMING SENSE OF PURPOSE, A SURE KNOWLEDGE THAT THERE IS A DESTINY FOR THE UNIVERSE-- A GRAND AND GLORIOUS DESTINY.
AND WITH IT COMES A PAIN OF REALIZATION-- THE IMAGE OF A UNIVERSE SHORN OF GALACTUS, AND, AS A CONSEQUENCE, THAT GREAT DESTINY SO SUDDENLY SNUFFED OUT, LIKE A LONE CANDLE IN A COLD NIGHT WIND.
TO ALL MORTALS PRESENT IS THIS COSMIC TRUTH MADE PLAIN.
21.

THREE HOURS LATER...
...AND THAT'S WHAT HAPPENED, MIKE. ETERNITY MADE EVERYONE... ONE WITH THE UNIVERSE, AND WE ALL JUST KNEW GALACTUS HAD A PLACE IN IT.
LILANDRA--EVERYONE THERE--ACCEPTED THAT REED HAD DONE WHAT HAD TO BE DONE, AND EVERYONE JUST SORT OF... DRIFTED AWAY. THE FF AND I WERE SENT BACK TO EARTH.
GOSH, JOHN, UH... MAYBE YOU'VE BEEN INHALING TOO MUCH OF YOUR PENCIL SHAVINGS OR SOMETHING--THAT'S A WILD STORY!
WELL, JUST GET IT ALL ON PAPER, AND GET IT OFF TO ME ASAP.
THE FF'S FANS ARE GONNA PLOTZ WHEN THEY READ THIS ONE.

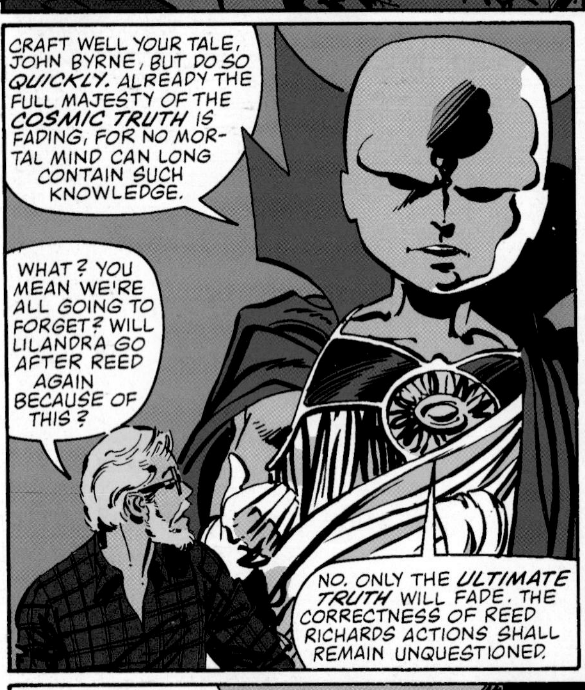
CRAFT WELL YOUR TALE, JOHN BYRNE, BUT DO SO QUICKLY. ALREADY THE FULL MAJESTY OF THE COSMIC TRUTH IS FADING, FOR NO MORTAL MIND CAN LONG CONTAIN SUCH KNOWLEDGE.
WHAT? YOU MEAN WE'RE ALL GOING TO FORGET? WILL LILANDRA GO AFTER REED AGAIN BECAUSE OF THIS?
NO. ONLY THE ULTIMATE TRUTH WILL FADE. THE CORRECTNESS OF REED RICHARDS ACTIONS SHALL REMAIN UNQUESTIONED.

BUT... WHAT ABOUT GALACTUS, WATCHER? IS HIS TASK ENDED NOW? OR WILL EVERYONE JUST HAVE TO CONTENT THEMSELVES WITH WATCHING HAPPILY THE NEXT TIME HE CONSUMES A WORLD?
TO RENDER THINGS THUS WOULD BE TO ROB LIFE-KIND OF FREE WILL, AND IN ALL THE COSMOS BUT ONE BEING IS DEPRIVED OF THAT FREEDOM: GALACTUS.
THEN, WHAT WILL HAPPEN, WATCHER?

GALACTUS WILL GO ON. THE TESTING WILL CONTINUE, UNTIL THAT DISTANT DAY HE FINDS A WORLD WITH POWER ENOUGH TO STOP HIM, TO END FOR ALL TIME HIS COSMIC HUNGER.
ON THAT DAY SHALL GALACTUS PERISH.
ON THAT DAY LET THE UNIVERSE MOURN.
NEXT ISSUE: THE MESSIAH!

fantastic four # 263

THE WORLD'S GREATEST COMIC MAGAZINE!

Fantastic Four

60¢
263
FEB
02462

APPROVED BY THE COMICS CODE AUTHORITY

JOHNNY--!

FEBRUARY 1984

R. AND R.
WELL, HONEY, I'M OFF TO "WORK"...
SUSAN!
THE RECENTLY PURCHASED HOME OF REED AND SUSAN RICHARDS, BETTER KNOWN AS REED AND SUSAN BENJAMIN TO ALL THEIR NEW NEIGHBORS IN BELLE PORTE, CONNECTICUT.
TODAY SUSAN IS PREPARING A NURSERY FOR THE CHILD THE COUPLE SOON EXPECT.
EDITOR'S NOTE: IT'S BEEN ONLY ONE ISSUE SINCE "THE TRIAL OF REED RICHARDS", BUT SEVERAL MONTHS HAVE ELAPSED FOR THE MEMBERS OF THE FANTASTIC FOUR-- MONTHS OF PEACE AND TRANQUILITY, OF PHYSICAL AND EMOTIONAL RECUPERATION.
IT CAN'T POSSIBLY LAST...
STAN LEE PRESENTS:
JOHN BYRNE / WORDS AND PICTURES
JIM NOVAK LETTERS
GLYNIS WEIN COLORS
BOB BUDIANSKY / EDITING
JIM SHOOTER / EDITOR IN CHIEF

OH, DRAT!
GOT IT!

BRAVO DARLING! A PERFECT CATCH! SOMETIMES BEING THE *INVISIBLE GIRL* CAN HAVE ITS DOMESTIC ADVANTAGES.
WELL, BEING ABLE TO PROJECT AN INVISIBLE FORCE FIELD DOES HAVE USES OTHER THAN BATTLING BAD GUYS

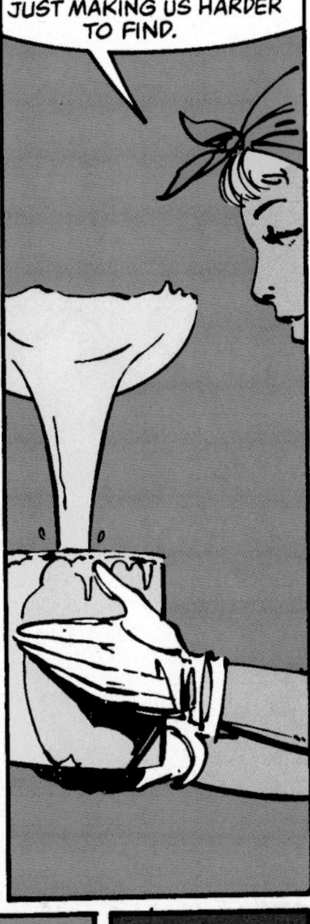
NOT THAT WE'VE BEEN DOING A WHOLE LOT OF *THAT* LATELY. IT'S BEEN MONTHS SINCE WE'VE SEEN HIDE OR HAIR OF ANY WORLD-THREATENING MENACES. MAYBE OUR NEW "SECRET IDENTITIES" ARE JUST MAKING US HARDER TO FIND.

WILL YOU NEED ANYTHING FROM THE CITY?
NO. I WAS PLANNING ON PICKING UP SOME GROCERIES LATER MYSELF.
YES. I'LL HAVE TO CALL THE *AVENGERS* AND ASK IF THEIR WORK LOAD HAS INCREASED ANY. HA HA.

YOU GONNA PUT ON YOUR *DISGUISE* NOW, DADDY? I LOVE IT WHEN YOU PUT ON YOUR DISGUISE.
INDEED I AM, *FRANKLIN*. AND WITH MY ELASTIC BODY IT'S AS EASY AS ONE...

...TWO...

...THREE.
2.

IMPRESSIVE AS EVER, DARLING. BUT I THINK I'D STILL HAVE PREFERRED-- OH-- ROBERT REDFORD, OR SEAN CONNERY.
PERHAPS. BUT IF I'D WANTED TO DRIVE THE NEIGHBORHOOD LADIES WILD... WELL, I COULD JUST KEEP MY OWN FACE!
TRUE. IT'S ALWAYS BEEN MORE THAN GOOD ENOUGH FOR ME. NOW, YOU'LL TAKE PROPER CARE IN THE CITY?
OF COURSE. IN FACT, I SHOULDN'T BE MORE THAN FOUR OR FIVE HOURS. I JUST WANT TO CHECK SOME OF THE AUTOMATED SCANNERS.
WELL, JUST DON'T GO CHARGING OFF TO SAVE THE WORLD ON YOUR OWN WHILE I'M... OUT OF ACTION, AND JOHNNY AND BEN ARE IN CALIFORNIA.
THUS, A FEW MINUTES' PLEASANT WALK THROUGH SUBURBAN BELLE PORTE, AND...
THIS RECENT ADOPTION OF SECRET IDENTITIES HAS CERTAINLY PROVED AN INTERESTING VENTURE.
WE'VE BEEN OUT OF OUR BAXTER BUILDING HOME AND HEADQUARTERS FOR FOUR AND A HALF MONTHS NOW...
YET IT'S STILL A STRANGE FEELING, TAKING THE BUS TO "WORK" EACH DAY.

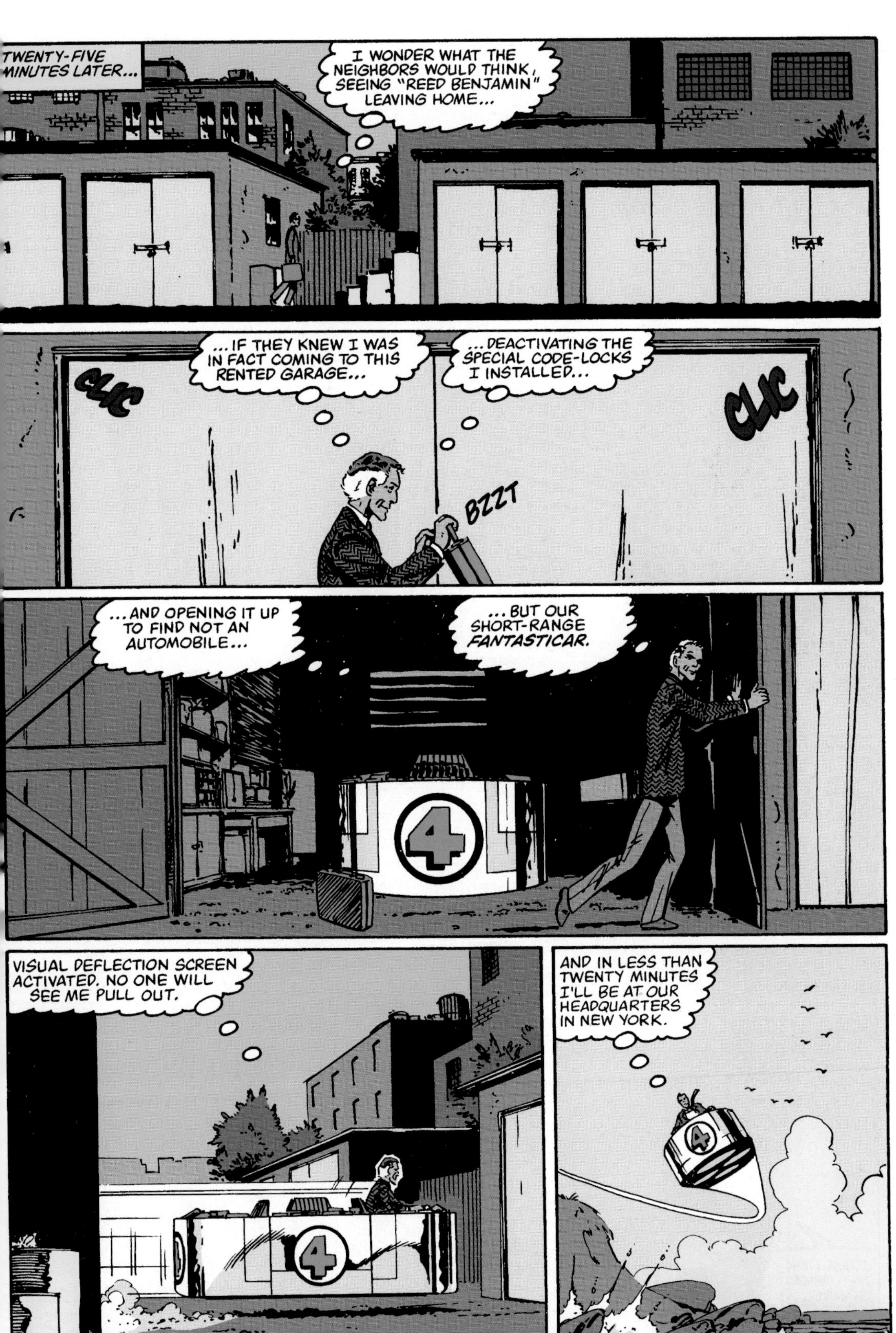
TWENTY-FIVE MINUTES LATER...
I WONDER WHAT THE NEIGHBORS WOULD THINK, SEEING "REED BENJAMIN" LEAVING HOME...
...IF THEY KNEW I WAS IN FACT COMING TO THIS RENTED GARAGE...
...DEACTIVATING THE SPECIAL CODE-LOCKS I INSTALLED...
CLIC
CLIC
BZZT
...AND OPENING IT UP TO FIND NOT AN AUTOMOBILE...
...BUT OUR SHORT-RANGE FANTASTICAR.
VISUAL DEFLECTION SCREEN ACTIVATED. NO ONE WILL SEE ME PULL OUT.
AND IN LESS THAN TWENTY MINUTES I'LL BE AT OUR HEADQUARTERS IN NEW YORK.
4.

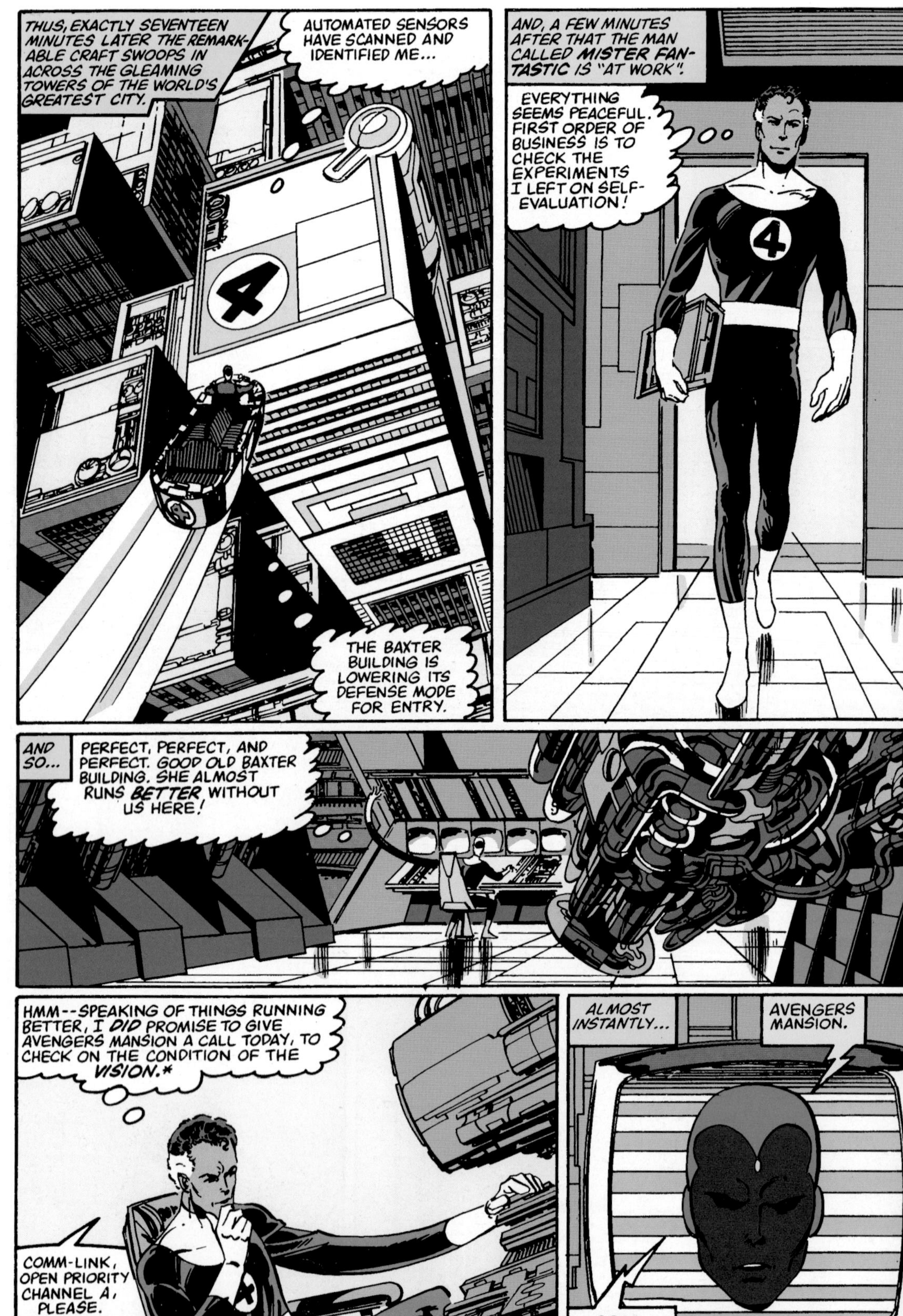
THUS, EXACTLY SEVENTEEN MINUTES LATER THE REMARKABLE CRAFT SWOOPS IN ACROSS THE GLEAMING TOWERS OF THE WORLD'S GREATEST CITY.
AUTOMATED SENSORS HAVE SCANNED AND IDENTIFIED ME...
THE BAXTER BUILDING IS LOWERING ITS DEFENSE MODE FOR ENTRY.
AND, A FEW MINUTES AFTER THAT THE MAN CALLED MISTER FANTASTIC IS "AT WORK".
EVERYTHING SEEMS PEACEFUL. FIRST ORDER OF BUSINESS IS TO CHECK THE EXPERIMENTS I LEFT ON SELF-EVALUATION!
AND SO...
PERFECT, PERFECT, AND PERFECT. GOOD OLD BAXTER BUILDING. SHE ALMOST RUNS BETTER WITHOUT US HERE!
HMM--SPEAKING OF THINGS RUNNING BETTER, I DID PROMISE TO GIVE AVENGERS MANSION A CALL TODAY, TO CHECK ON THE CONDITION OF THE VISION.*
COMM-LINK, OPEN PRIORITY CHANNEL A, PLEASE.
*FELLED BY A NULL-FIELD IN AVENGERS #233 --BOB.
ALMOST INSTANTLY...
AVENGERS MANSION.
REED RICHARDS. GOOD OF YOU TO CALL.

VISION! I DIDN'T EXPECT TO SEE YOU BACK ON YOUR FEET. HOW ARE YOU... FEELING?

I AM NEARLY RECOVERED, THANK YOU--ALTHOUGH I AM NOT, AS YOU PUT IT, "BACK ON MY FEET."

IN POINT OF FACT, I AM STILL IN MY RESTORATIVE CYLINDER, BUT MY CIRCUITS ARE TIED INTO THE AVENGERS' COMPUTER-LINKS.

AND FROM THERE YOU ARE ABLE TO ARTIFICIALLY GENERATE AN IMAGE OF YOURSELF ON THE MONITOR? I'M IMPRESSED. I DID NOT THINK EVEN *YOUR* SOPHISTICATED SYSTEMS CAPABLE OF SUCH A THING.

MY RECUPERATIVE PROCESSES HAVE ENABLED ME TO TAP... UNSUSPECTED ABILITIES, REED.

BUT, IF YOU WILL EXCUSE ME, THERE ARE CERTAIN MATTERS OF PRIORITY I MUST NOW ATTEND.

VISION, WAIT, I...
CONFOUND IT, HE'S CUT TRANSMISSION. I COULD PROBABLY ACTIVATE AN OVERRIDE, BUT...
REED'S UNMATCHED INTELLECT PONDERS THE SITUATION...

HE SOUNDED MOST... *ODD*, EVEN FOR THE VISION. I HOPE NOTHING IS AMISS. PERHAPS I SHOULD...
HMM?
THE AUTOMATIC SCANNERS... WHAT ON EARTH!?
6.

BUT WE MUST WAIT A WHILE TO LEARN WHAT REED RICHARDS HAS DISCOVERED.
FOR NOW WE TURN OUR EYES WESTWARD, AND OUR CLOCKS BACK THREE HOURS...
...AND LOOK IN ON THE INTERNATIONALLY RENOWNED WONDERWORLD AMUSEMENT PARK IN CALIFORNIA...
...SPECIFICALLY, THE NEWLY COMPLETED GRAND PRIX RACE COURSE, AND TWO VERY SPECIAL MEMBERS OF OUR CAST.
AW, BEN, DON'T BE SUCH AN OLD STICK-IN-THE-MUD.
I JUST SAID I DON'T LIKE IT...
OMNIROYAL
BUT THAT'S WHAT YOU ALWAYS SAY. YOU'RE ALWAYS THE ONE TO SEE THE DARK CLOUD INSIDE EVERY SILVER LINING. BEING ASKED TO THE FIRST WONDERWORLD INVITATIONAL RACE IS AN HONOR. AND I'VE BEEN DYING FOR AN EXCUSE TO GET BACK INTO MY RACING THREADS.
SURE, SURE. BUT WHAT'S THIS IDEA OF KEEPIN' WHO ALL THE CONTESTANTS ARE A SECRET? WOULDN'T THEY GET A BIGGER CROWD IF THEY ANNOUNCED WHO WAS RACIN'?
OURS IS NOT TO REASON WHY, BEN. IT'S PROBABLY SOME P.R. GUY'S STROKE OF GENIUS. I MEAN, IT'LL BE INTERESTING WHEN WE ALL "UNMASK" AT THE END OF THE RACE.
YEAH, YEAH. I'LL GO SOAK UP SOME SUN. THAT'S WHY I TAGGED ALONG ANYWAY. HAVE FUN, HOTSHOT.
NOW, MAYBE YOU SHOULD LEAVE BEFORE YOU BLOW MY COVER.
I STILL DON'T LIKE IT.
AND, AS A DISGRUNTLED BEN GRIMM MOVES THROUGH THE CROWD...
THE THING!
7.

A FEW MOMENTS LATER...
I SURE WISH BEN WOULD KICK THE "O-WOE-IS-ME" TRIP HE'S BEEN ON FOR THE PAST FEW MONTHS. SURE, BEING THE THING IS NO PICNIC, BUT...
JOHNNY! JOHNNY STORM!
HUH?
JULIE ANGEL...?!
IN THE... AH... FLESH! HEY, GREAT TO SEE YOU AGAIN, CUTIE. WELCOME TO SUNNY CALIFORN-EYE-AY.
ER, YEAH, THANKS. HOW'S EVERYTHING BEEN WITH YOU? SHARON* TOLD ME YOU'D MOVED OUT HERE WITH GREY LANDERS.
WELL, NOT EXACTLY. GREY GOT OFFERED THE LEAD IN "SON OF THE RETURN OF THE EMPIRE STRIKES OUT," OR SOMESUCH. HE THOUGHT THERE MIGHT BE A PART FOR ME, SO I TAGGED ALONG, STRICTLY FOR PROFESSIONAL REASONS.
*SHARON SELLECK IS JULIE'S N.Y. ROOMIE --BOB.
AND THEY'RE FILMING HERE?
OH, NO. THE JOB FELL THROUGH, SO I GOT AN AGENT AND HUNG AROUND A WHILE. HE TRIED TO GET ME A MAGAZINE LAYOUT, BUT I COULDN'T GET INTO THAT "SUCK IN YOUR TUMMY AND POINT YOUR TOE" ROUTINE.
SO YOU THOUGHT YOU'D HANG AROUND A RACETRACK IN YOUR BIKINI?
NOT QUITE. I'M DOING A MOTOR-OIL SPOT. YOU KNOW, GIRLS IN SWIMSUITS, AND GREASY MECHANICS.
8.

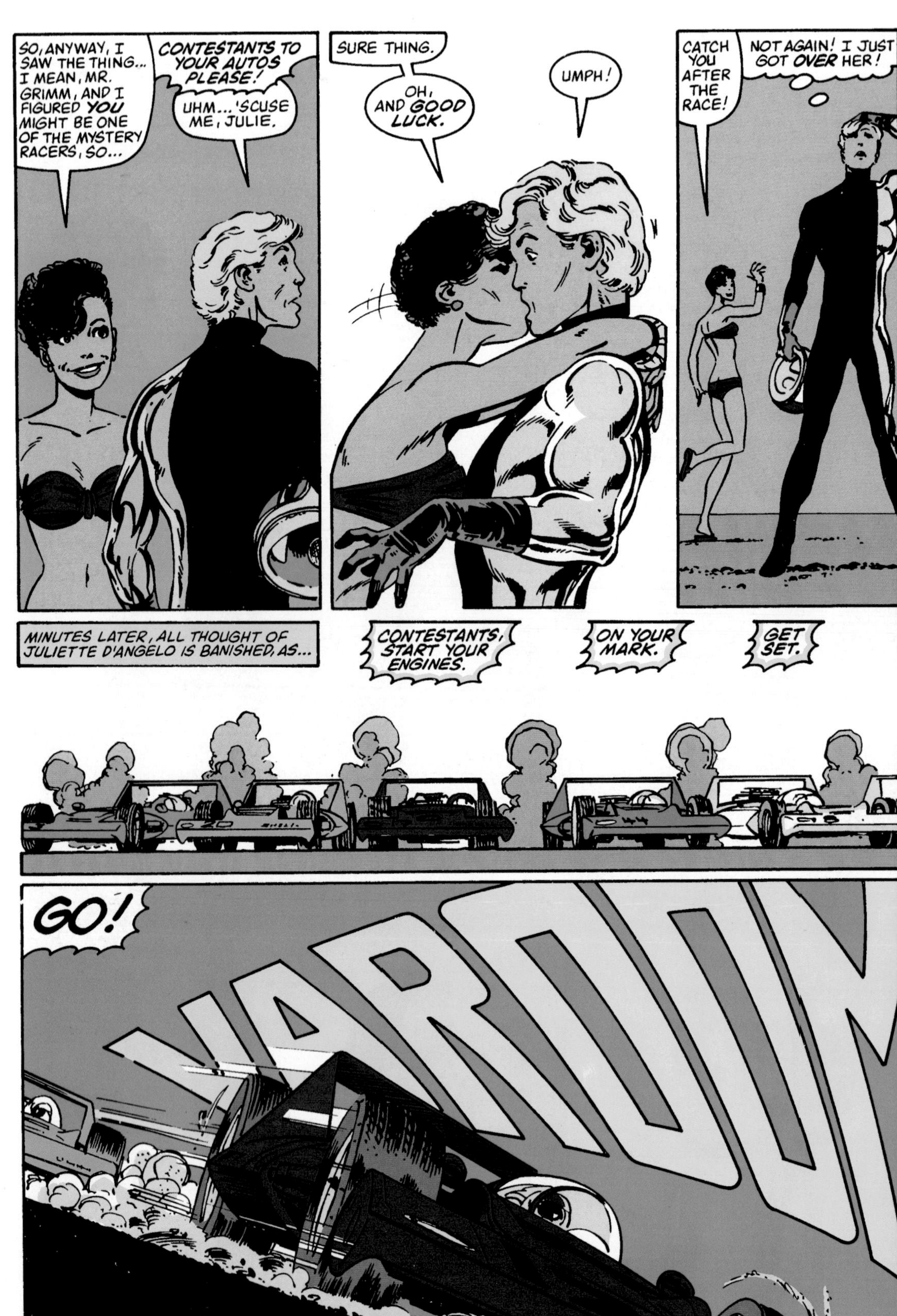
SO, ANYWAY, I SAW THE THING... I MEAN, MR. GRIMM, AND I FIGURED YOU MIGHT BE ONE OF THE MYSTERY RACERS, SO...
CONTESTANTS TO YOUR AUTOS PLEASE!
UHM... 'SCUSE ME, JULIE.
SURE THING.
OH, AND GOOD LUCK.
UMPH!
CATCH YOU AFTER THE RACE!
NOT AGAIN! I JUST GOT OVER HER!
MINUTES LATER, ALL THOUGHT OF JULIETTE D'ANGELO IS BANISHED, AS...
CONTESTANTS, START YOUR ENGINES.
ON YOUR MARK.
GET SET.
GO!
VAROOM

LMOST FROM THE STARTING GUN
T SEEMS THERE WILL BE LITTLE
OUBT ABOUT THE OUTCOME OF
HIS RACE.
JOHNNY'S CAR SEIZES AN IMMEDIATE LEAD AND HOLDS ON.
I'M LEAVING THE OTHERS WAY BEHIND.
NOT BAD EITHER, CONSIDERING HOW LONG IT'S BEEN SINCE I'VE DONE ANY SERIOUS RACING.
TWENTY MINUTES INTO THE CONTEST AND NOTHING HAS CHANGED.
THE OTHERS DRIVE HARD AND FAST, BUT COMPARED TO JOHNNY, THEY ARE MIRED IN MOLASSES.
THE THIRD TIME INTO THE TUNNEL AND JOHNNY'S NUMBER 17 HANGS ON TO A STRONG LEAD.
AND IT IS 17 FIRST OUT OF THE DARKNESS, TO THE JOYOUS WHOOPS OF THE CROWDS.
THEY DO NOT KNOW WHO IS DRIVING, ONLY THAT HE IS DRIVING VERY WELL!
10.

UNTIL...

JOHNNY!!

HE AIN'T FLYIN' AWAY FROM TH' WRECK.
WHAT COULD HAVE HAPPENED? HE'S GOTTA BE OKAY...
HE'S GOTTA!

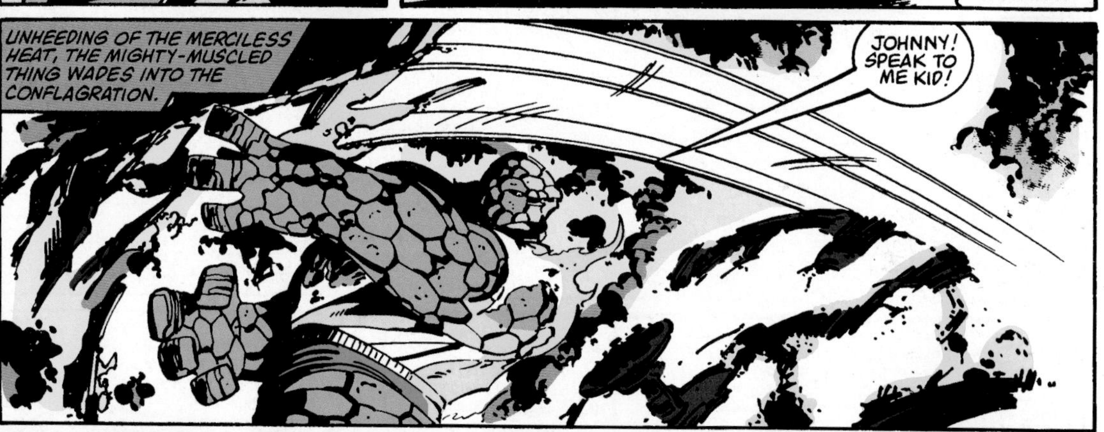
UNHEEDING OF THE MERCILESS HEAT, THE MIGHTY-MUSCLED THING WADES INTO THE CONFLAGRATION.
JOHNNY! SPEAK TO ME KID!

AWFUL IMAGES FLASH ACROSS BEN GRIMM'S MIND. IMAGES FROM HIS DAYS AS A TEST-PILOT.
HE HAS SEEN FIRES LIKE THIS BEFORE.
SEEN FRIENDS CONSUMED IN THE AWFUL, IMPARTIAL FLAMES.

AND TODAY, ANOTHER FRIEND SEEMS TO HAVE MET THE SAME FATE...
...FOR WHATEVER REMAINS OF THE DRIVER IS NOW...
... BURNED BEYOND RECOGNITION.
12

SOON...

EASY, MR. GRIMM. I DON'T KNOW IF THIS MEDICATION WILL DO ANY GOOD ON YOUR HIDE, BUT WE HAVE TO DO SOME-THING WITH THESE BURNS.

JUST DO TH' BEST YA CAN, KID. I'VE HAD A LOT WORSE HAPPEN TA ME SINCE I GOT ZAPPED INTA THIS BOD BY THEM ***COSMIC RAYS.***

THE AFTERMATH OF TRAGEDY. TWO HOURS AFTER THE CRASH THE WRECK HAS COOLED SUFFICIENTLY THAT CLEAN-UP CREWS MAY BEGIN THEIR GRIZZLY WORK.

THE BLACKENED HUSK THAT WAS ONCE A MAN IS TRANSFERRED FROM THE RUINED CAR TO A BODY-BAG, AND THENCE TO AN AMBULANCE, AND AWAY.

WELL, WHAT'S TH' WORD? YOUR GUYS FIGGERED OUT WHAT HAPPENED?

I'D SAY THAT'S PRETTY WELL OBVIOUS, MR. GRIMM. YOU GOT TO THE SCENE BEFORE ANY-ONE ELSE. YOU ***SAW*** WHAT WAS LEFT OF MR. STORM.

ANYWAY, YOU KNOW NO ONE COULD SUR-VIVE A CRASH LIKE THAT.

"WE AIN'T TALKIN' ABOUT JUST ANYONE, POPS. WE'RE TALKIN' ABOUT TH' HUMAN TORCH.
"I'VE SEEN HIM BLOW JET FIGHTERS OUTTA THE AIR. AN' JET FUEL BURNS A LOT HOTTER AN' FASTER THAN GASOLINE.
"THERE JUST AIN'T NO WAY IN TH' WORLD THAT... THING THEY TOOK OUTTA TH' WRECK COULDA BIN JOHNNY. THERE MUSTA BIN A SWITCH."

OKAY, YOU TELL ME WHEN, GRIMM. BEFORE THE CRASH? OUT ON THE TRACK AT TWO HUNDRED-PLUS MILES PER HOUR?
LOOK, I REALIZE HOW HARD THIS MUST BE, AFTER ALL YOU'D BEEN THROUGH TOGE-THER, BUT FACE THE FACTS, MAN.
THE HUMAN TORCH IS DEAD!

THEN, AS AN ANGRY AND CONFUSED THING MOVES INTO THE SURROUNDING AMUSEMENT PARK...
M-MISTER GRIMM? I'M JULIE D'ANGELO. I DON'T KNOW IF YOU REMEMBER ME...
D'ANGELO? SURE, YOU'RE THAT ACTRESS FRIEND OF... OF...
I... I DON'T KNOW WHAT TO SAY, MR. GRIMM. IT'S JUST... HORRIBLE!
YEAH. WELL, SO FAR I AIN'T ALTOGETHER CONVINCED WHAT WE SAW HAPPEN REALLY HAPPENED.
WHAT DO YOU MEAN? I REALIZE IT'S KIND OF IRONIC THAT JOHNNY SHOULD... DIE IN SOMETHING AS ORDINARY AS A CAR-CRASH AFTER ALL HE'S BEEN THROUGH...
THERE'S MORE TO IT THAN THAT. I KNOW THERE IS.
MEBBE IT'S JUST MY SUSPICIOUS NATURE, BUT I'M GONNA FIND THE TOP BOSS A' THIS JOINT AN' ASK ME SOME POINTED QUESTIONS.
THE TOP BOSS? YOU MEAN ALDEN MAAS? BUT HE'S A COMPLETE RECLUSE. NO ONE'S EVEN SEEN HIM IN-- MUST BE FIFTEEN YEARS NOW!
HE BUILT THAT BIG STAR-SHAPED, ARTIFICIAL ISLAND ABOUT TEN MILES OFF THE COAST AND JUST DROPPED OUT OF THE PUBLIC EYE.
AN ISLAND, HUH? WELL, THAT SHOULD BE EASY ENOUGH TO FIND. SEE YA AROUND, KID.
THUS, AFTER A FORTY MINUTE TAXI-RIDE TO THE SMALL AIRPORT WHERE THE THING AND TORCH LANDED THE DAY BEFORE...
...IT IS THE LONG-RANGE FANTASTICAR THAT FLASHES OUT OVER THE SPRAWL OF CALIFORNIA'S BEAUTIFUL BEACHES.
14.

AND, WITHIN MINUTES...
THAT'S GOTTA BE THE ISLAND SHE MEANT. IT'S THE ONLY ONE EVEN SLIGHTLY STAR-SHAPED.
FUNNY. I WUZ EXPECTIN' SOMETHIN' MORE CLEARLY DEFINED, NOT JUST THE TREES AN' STUFF CUT T' TH' SHAPE.
WONDER IF THEY'VE GOT ANY GIZMOS TA LET 'EM KNOW COMPANY'S COMIN'?
I'LL LAND ON THE BEACH, NICE AN' OPEN AN' FRIENDLY.
IF I HAFTA GET NASTY-- WELL, THERE'LL BE TIME FOR THAT LATER.
THEN, AFTER SEVERAL LONG MINUTES HAVE TICKED BY...
HM.
GUESS THEY DON'T HAVE ANY RADAR OR STUFF LIKE THAT, OR I'D SURELY HAVE BEEN MET BY...
GOOD MORNING, SIR!
AM I CORRECT TO ASSUME THAT I HAVE THE PLEASURE OF ADDRESSING BENJAMIN GRIMM, ALSO KNOWN AS THE THING?
HUH? WHAT IS THIS? HAVE I DIED AN' GONE TA JUNIOR EXECUTIVE HEAVEN?
YEAH, I'M BEN GRIMM. I WANNA SEE TH' BIG BOSS, AN' NO GUFF!
OF COURSE. MR. MAAS DOES NOT NORMALLY RECEIVE VISITORS...
... BUT IN THE CASE OF SO ILLUSTRIOUS A GUEST I'M SURE AN EXCEPTION CAN BE MADE.

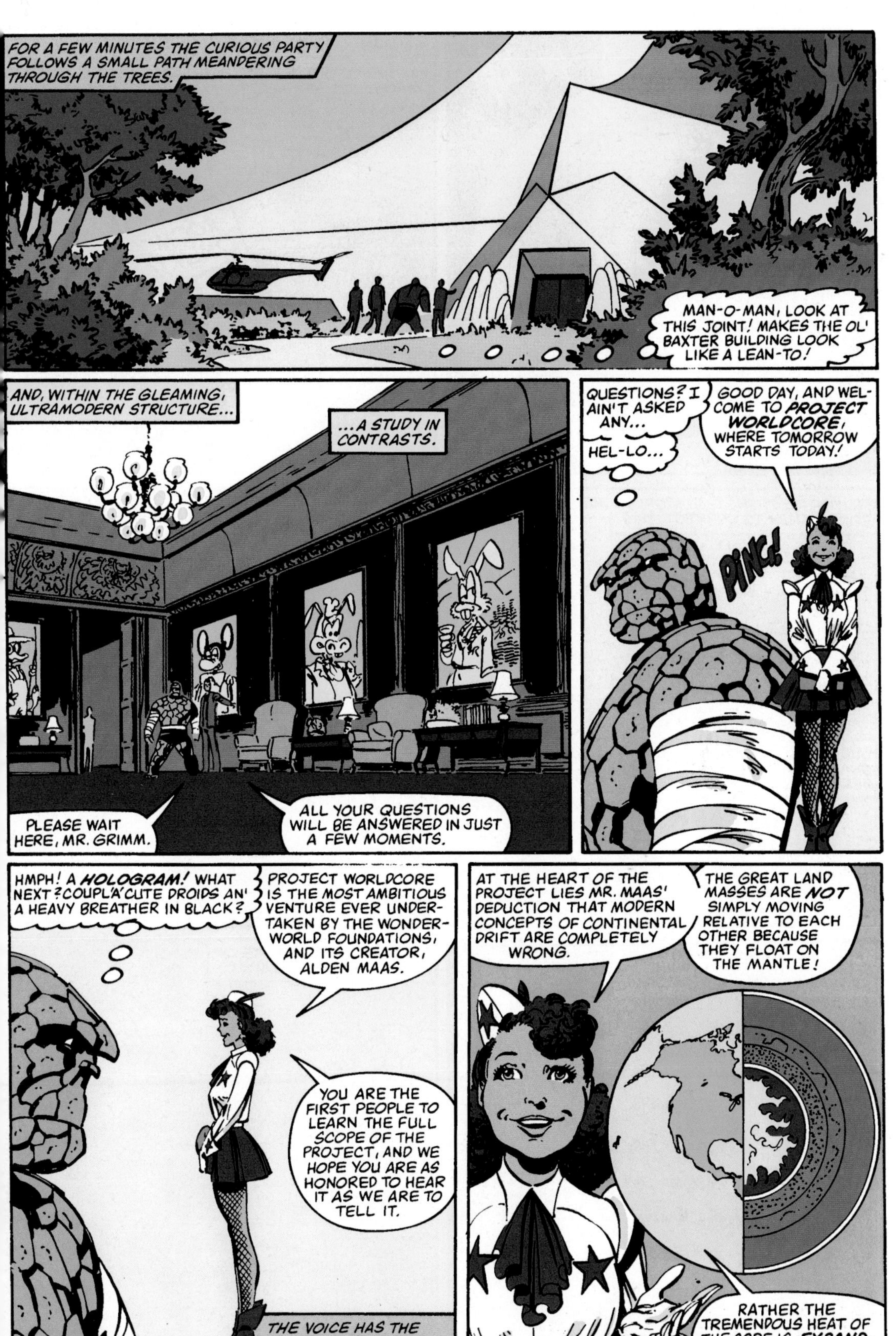
FOR A FEW MINUTES THE CURIOUS PARTY FOLLOWS A SMALL PATH MEANDERING THROUGH THE TREES.
MAN-O-MAN, LOOK AT THIS JOINT! MAKES THE OL' BAXTER BUILDING LOOK LIKE A LEAN-TO!
AND, WITHIN THE GLEAMING, ULTRAMODERN STRUCTURE...
...A STUDY IN CONTRASTS.
PLEASE WAIT HERE, MR. GRIMM.
ALL YOUR QUESTIONS WILL BE ANSWERED IN JUST A FEW MOMENTS.
QUESTIONS? I AIN'T ASKED ANY...
HEL-LO...
GOOD DAY, AND WELCOME TO PROJECT WORLDCORE, WHERE TOMORROW STARTS TODAY!
PING!
HMPH! A HOLOGRAM! WHAT NEXT? COUPL'A'CUTE DROIDS AN' A HEAVY BREATHER IN BLACK?
PROJECT WORLDCORE IS THE MOST AMBITIOUS VENTURE EVER UNDERTAKEN BY THE WONDERWORLD FOUNDATIONS, AND ITS CREATOR, ALDEN MAAS.
YOU ARE THE FIRST PEOPLE TO LEARN THE FULL SCOPE OF THE PROJECT, AND WE HOPE YOU ARE AS HONORED TO HEAR IT AS WE ARE TO TELL IT.
THE VOICE HAS THE CONDESCENDING SING-SONG RHYTHM OF A KIDDIE-SHOW HOSTESS.
AT THE HEART OF THE PROJECT LIES MR. MAAS' DEDUCTION THAT MODERN CONCEPTS OF CONTINENTAL DRIFT ARE COMPLETELY WRONG.
THE GREAT LAND MASSES ARE NOT SIMPLY MOVING RELATIVE TO EACH OTHER BECAUSE THEY FLOAT ON THE MANTLE!
RATHER THE TREMENDOUS HEAT OF THE CORE IS EXPANDING THEIR GLOBE LIKE A BALLOON.
16.

"BUT THE EARTH'S CORE HAS **COOLED** OVER THE MILLIONS AND BILLIONS OF YEARS OF ITS LIFE.

"BECAUSE OF THAT, THE EXPANSION HAS SLOWED ALMOST TO A STOP -- AND, SINCE PEOPLE CONTINUE TO HAVE LOTS AND LOTS OF BABIES...

STANDING ROOM ONLY!!

"...SOON ALL THE AVAILABLE SPACE ON EARTH WILL BE ***FILLED UP!***

"BUT HERE AT PROJECT WORLDCORE STEPS ARE BEING TAKEN TO CORRECT THIS.

"A SPECIAL SHAFT HAS BEEN DRILLED...

"...ALL THE WAY TO THE POOR OLD CORE.

"AND DOWN THAT SHAFT WILL BE PUMPED LOTS AND LOTS OF LOVELY ***HEAT.***
"THE CORE WILL BE REKINDLED, EVEN ***HOTTER*** THAN BEFORE.
"...UNTIL THERE'S LOTS OF ROOM FOR EVERYBODY!"

"AND, ONCE AGAIN, LIKE A GIANT BALLOON, THE EARTH WILL GROW AND GROW AND ***GROW...***

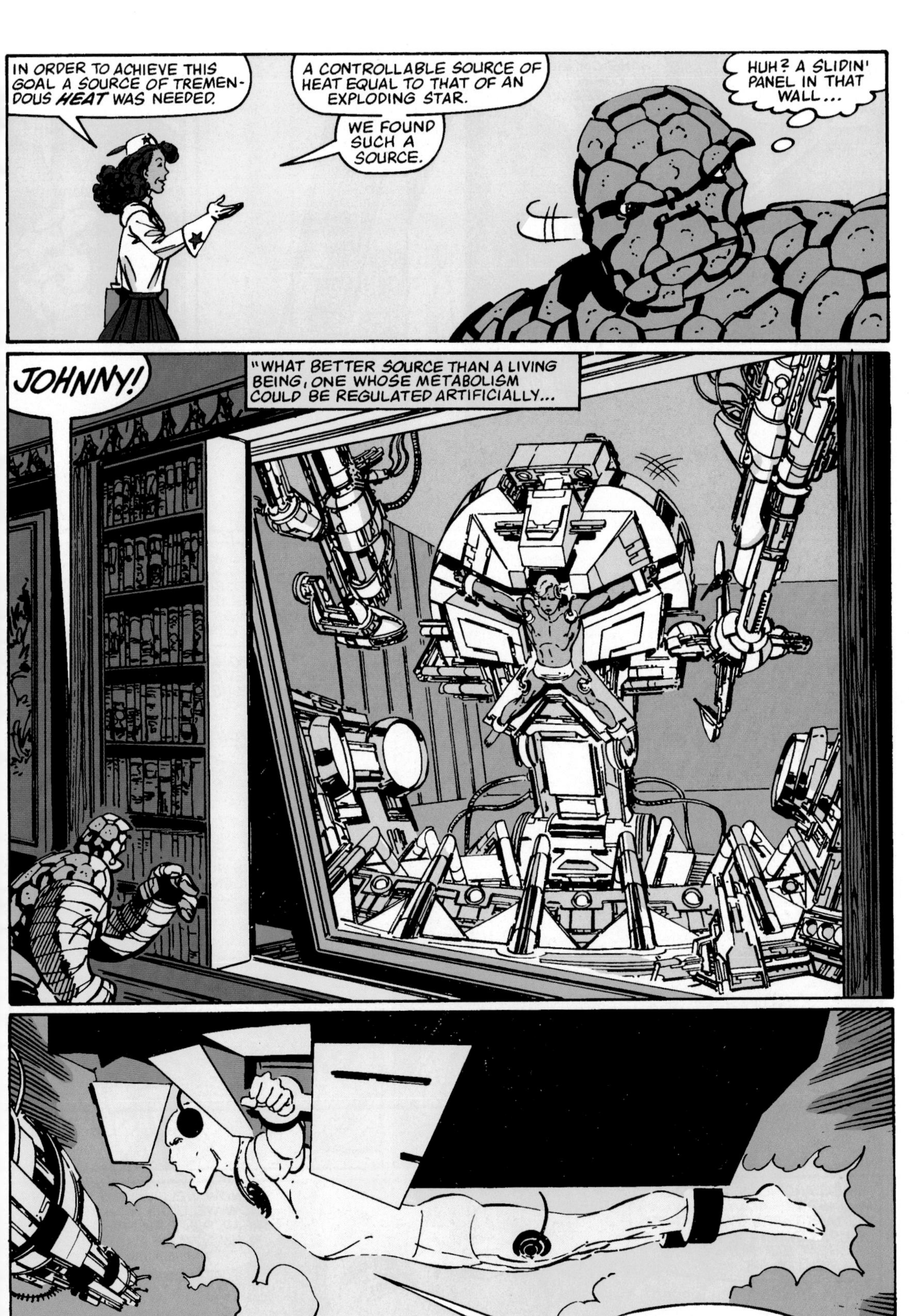
IN ORDER TO ACHIEVE THIS GOAL A SOURCE OF TREMENDOUS HEAT WAS NEEDED.
A CONTROLLABLE SOURCE OF HEAT EQUAL TO THAT OF AN EXPLODING STAR.
WE FOUND SUCH A SOURCE.
HUH? A SLIDIN' PANEL IN THAT WALL...
JOHNNY!
"WHAT BETTER SOURCE THAN A LIVING BEING, ONE WHOSE METABOLISM COULD BE REGULATED ARTIFICIALLY...
"SO AS TO GENERATE THE EXACT QUANTITIES AND QUALITIES OF HEAT REQUIRED."
ARRGH!!

HOLY CATS! THEY'RE KILLIN' HIM! AN' DYIN' ONCE IN ONE DAY IS ENOUGH!
HANG ON, KID! I'M COMIN'! IT'S CLOBBERIN' TIME!
NO!
HUH?
PLEASE RESTRAIN YOURSELF, MR. GRIMM. AN ASSAULT ON THAT PANEL WILL AVAIL YOU NOUGHT.
ALDEN MAAS! THE BIG KAHUNA HIMSELF. IF YOU DON'T WANT ME PULVERIZIN' THIS JOINT, YA BETTER GET JOHNNY OFF THAT CONTRAPTION.
ALL IN DUE COURSE, MR. GRIMM. THE POWER OF THE HUMAN TORCH MUST FIRST BE PUT TO GOOD AND PROPER USE, REKINDLING THE LOST HEAT OF OUR PLANET'S CORE.
BUT THAT'S HIS NOVA FLAME YA TURNED ON, YA BLASTED IDJIT! HE CAN ONLY BURN LIKE THAT FER A FEW SECONDS WITHOUT KILLIN' HIMSELF!
OR DON'T ONE HUMAN LIFE COUNT IN THIS NUTSO PLAN?
THE BALANCING OF THE ONE AGAINST THE MANY IS EVER THE TASK THAT BEFALLS THOSE OF US ELEVATED TO POSITIONS OF GREAT EARTHLY RESPONSIBILITY, SIR.
IF THE HUMAN TORCH INDEED PERISHES, A MONUMENT SHALL BE ERECTED TO COMMEMORATE HIS NOBLE SACRIFICE. BUT, I BEG YOU, DO NOT INTERFERE.
I KNOW WELL WHAT I AM DOING, KNOW WELL THE PATH I MUST TREAD, FOR I AM THE APPOINTED SAVIOUR OF ALL MANKIND, MR. GRIMM.
I AM THE MESSIAH!

THE MESSIAH?! OKAY, THAT DOES IT! FIRST I'M GONNA BUST JOHNNY OUTTA THAT HORROR-BOX...
...THEN I'M GONNA TEACH YOU A LITTLE HUMILITY.
GRIMM! NO! DON'T!
SAVE IT, PAL! I AIN'T...

...LISTENIN'...
SKRASKT
AW, NUTS!

JOHNNY WUZ ANOTHER BLASTED HOLOGRAM!

AN' NOW I'M FALLIN' RIGHT DOWN TH' MIDDLE A' THAT SHAFT THEY WUZ TALKIN' ABOUT.
NO WAY I BELIEVE IT GOES ALL THE WAY T' THE EARTH'S CORE...

...BUT IT LOOKS LIKE IT GOES DOWN FAR ENOUGH TA FINISH ME OFF.
SORRY, TORCHIE. LOOKS LIKE I LET YA DOWN IN A BIG WAY THIS TIME.
20.

THEN, AFTER WHAT SEEMS AN ETERNITY...
OOF!
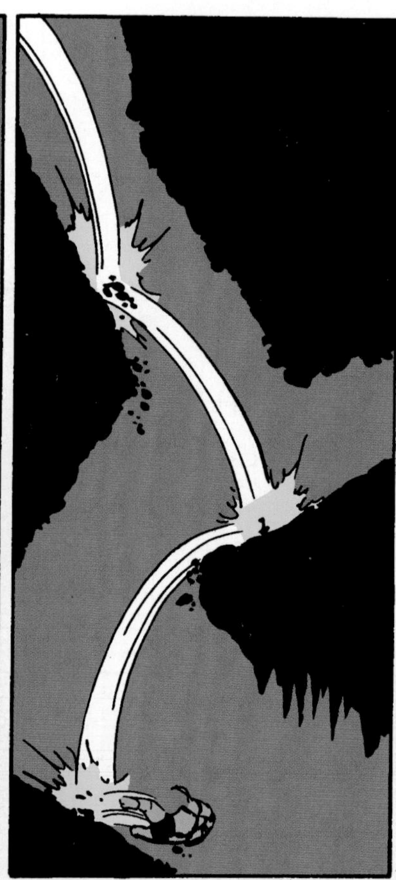

UNGH!
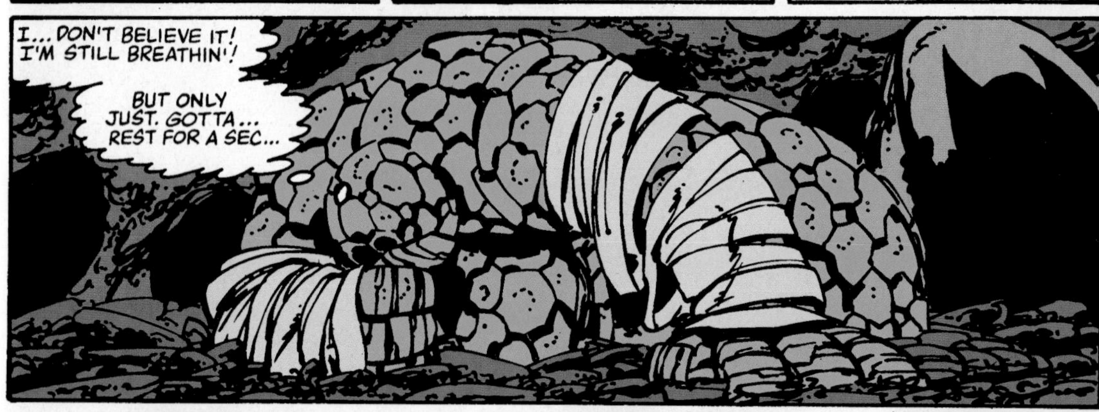
I... DON'T BELIEVE IT! I'M STILL BREATHIN'!
BUT ONLY JUST. GOTTA... REST FOR A SEC...

GOTTA...
ARGHH!
SKTZT!
21.

NEXT ISSUE: THERE ARE STILL A LOT OF QUESTIONS TO BE ANSWERED, AND MORE ON THE WAY! BE HERE IN THIRTY DAYS FOR... INFERNO!

Fantastic Four Fan Page

% MARVEL COMICS GROUP
387 Park Avenue South
New York, New York 10016

BOB BUDIANSKY
EDITOR
MICHAEL HIGGINS
ASSISTANT EDITOR

We were hoping Sue's Coiffure Contest might generate a little interest among our readers, but we had no idea just *how* much! At the point of this writing the official close of the contest is still a couple of months away, yet we have already received a grand total of 538 individual entries! 538 potential new styles for Sue.

Well, not quite that many different *styles*, actually. A lot of you suggested the same styles, and a lot automatically disqualified yourselves by suggesting either (a) the hairstyle she's presently wearing or (b) the style she had before issue #232. The whole idea of this contest was to pick a NEW style, remember, not to comment on what she's worn in the past.

In any case, a winner is yet to be picked (obviously, since the contest hasn't closed yet) but we thought we'd take a moment here to list the names of those of you who sent in such wonderful drawings that, even though the styles themselves haven't won, we felt we couldn't let your work pass without an HONORABLE MENTION:

In no particular order:

Scott McClung of Grand Junction, Colorado
Vincent Stone of Evansville, Indiana
Tom Mehs of Jamestown, New York
Frank Patrick Squillace of Phoenix, Arizona
Janet Taglianetti of Baldwin, New York
Tim Alvis of Exeter, Nevada
Kevin Crumble of London, England
Grant Sandground (No Address Given)
and last, but by no means least . . .
Larry A. Johnson of South Beloit, Illinois.

All of you turned in such beautifully rendered pieces that John was just about ready to hang up his pencils and look for honest work. Sorry none of your entries have actually won, but we hope this will soothe the pain of losing at least a little.

(In case you're wondering how we can have decided on anyone who *hasn't* won when we haven't yet decided on who *has*, we are considering entries on the basis of practicality, attractiveness, suitability for Sue and, *ahem*, how difficult they are to draw. Remember, you might send in a single sketch of a beautiful, elaborate hairstyle, but if that's the one Sue picked, poor John would have to draw it twenty-five or thirty times per issue.)

A second thing we thought you might find of interest is the numerical balance of the entries — that is, if this were strictly a quantity contest, as opposed to a quality contest, which style would be in the "lead". Below are the two "front-running styles" as rendered by John. We point out, again, that neither of these have won. We've just received more letters suggesting these two styles than any other.

By the way, this issue officially ENDS the contest, so send NO MORE ENTRIES as of the moment you read this!

AN EXPLANATION

As an editor for Marvel Comics, I find that sometimes my job demands my presence in places other than the Bullpen. This was the case this past August when I went to visit the San Diego Comic Convention. Upon my return, I quickly discovered what my assistant, Michael Higgins, had been up to in my absence: not only had he chosen to put himself in the most recent adventure of the Fantastic Four (recounted last issue), but he actually allowed John Byrne to go along with our heroes on their trip across the universe! True, John wanted to go — he always wants to tag along — but he's too valuable a talent to risk like that. Why, Marvel's insurance policy doesn't even cover intergalactic accidents! That's one of my responsibilities as editor — to keep John safely grounded and working. As for Higgins — the only way he'll ever get in the FF again is if he's bombarded by cosmic rays first!

— Bob Budiansky

OMPH
AND READY FOR NEXT YEAR, SUE... ER, SUSAN? WHERE ARE YOU?
ASTOUND ME! HOW COULD YOU DO SOME-THING... SO... SO PRACTICAL?
BUT SURELY THIS IS BETTER THAN CELEBRATING THE SEASON OF LIFE BY KILLING A TREE?
THIS DISCUSSION CAN SS FURTHER, HOWEVER...
VOOOSH
WHAT IN...?
EED HONED BY YEARS OF CE MISTER FANTASTIC HIS PLIABLE BODY TO INTER- E SMALL MISSILE.
WHILE THE INVISIBLE GIRL TENDS TO THEIR SON...
THAT WAS VERY NAUGHTY, FRANKLIN. YOU KNOW YOU'RE NOT SUPPOSED TO PLAY WITH SUCH TOYS IN THE HOUSE!
I'M AFRAID THERE'S MORE TO IT THAN THAT, SUE.
LOOK AT THIS!
THIS IS NOT A FLYING TOY
OH, MY!

fantastic four # 264

MARCH 1984

Stan Lee PRESENTS: THE FANTASTIC FOUR!®

JOHN BYRNE STORY & ART / MICHAEL HIGGINS LETTERING / JULIANNA FERRITER COLORING / BOB BUDIANSKY EDITING / JIM SHOOTER EDITOR IN CHIEF

CARRY HIM CAREFULLY, MY MINDLESS SLAVES. DO NOT HARM HIM AS YOU TRANSPORT HIM INTO THE DEEP, DARK BOSOM OF THE EARTH.

I DO NOT WISH HIM HURT IN ANY WAY... UNTIL THE MOMENT WHEN HE *DIES!*

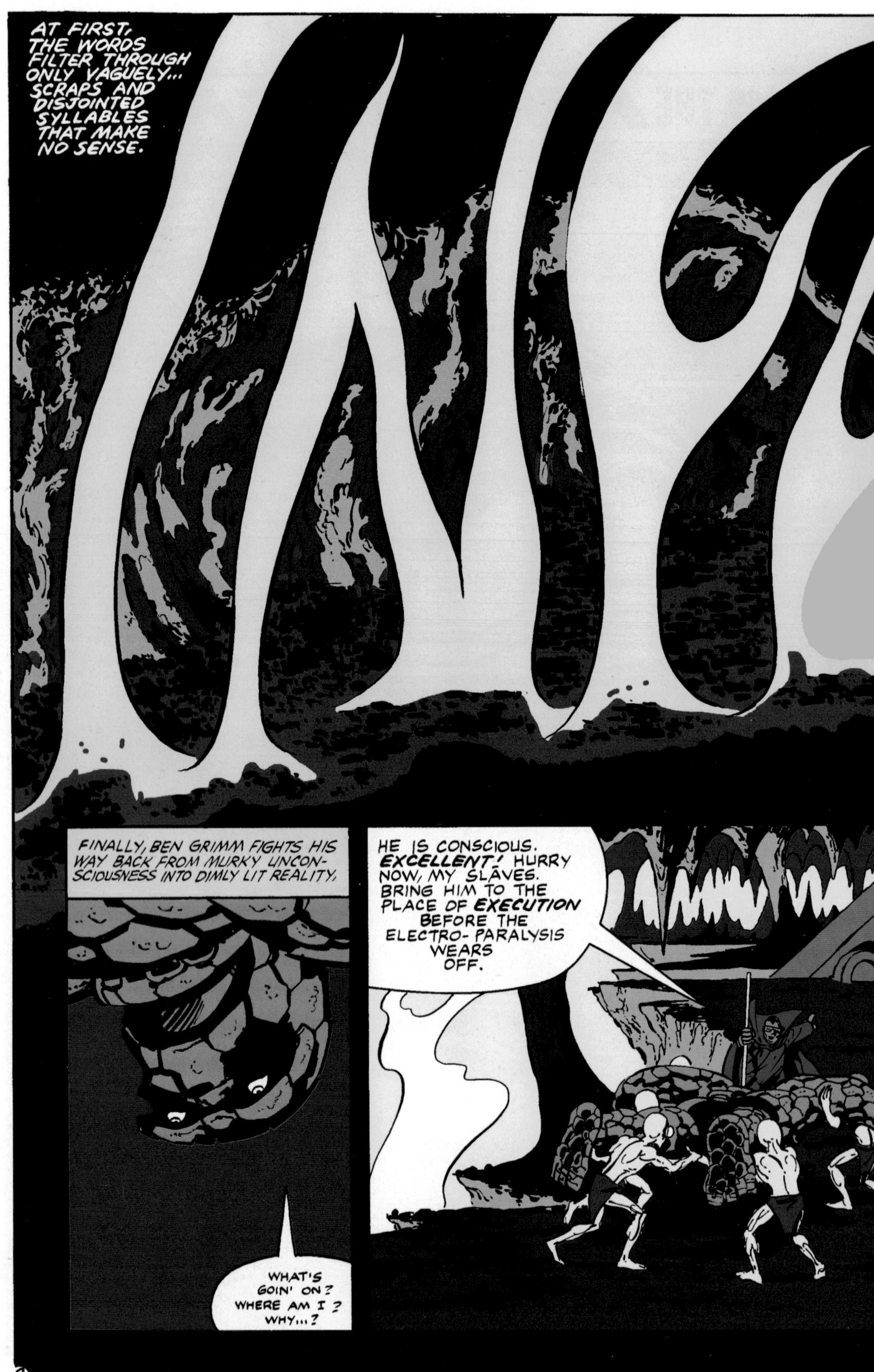
AT FIRST, THE WORDS FILTER THROUGH ONLY VAGUELY... SCRAPS AND DISJOINTED SYLLABLES THAT MAKE NO SENSE.
FINALLY, BEN GRIMM FIGHTS HIS WAY BACK FROM MURKY UNCONSCIOUSNESS INTO DIMLY LIT REALITY.
WHAT'S GOIN' ON? WHERE AM I? WHY...?
HE IS CONSCIOUS. EXCELLENT! HURRY NOW, MY SLAVES. BRING HIM TO THE PLACE OF EXECUTION BEFORE THE ELECTRO-PARALYSIS WEARS OFF.
2.

THIS WAY! THIS WAY! DO NOT LET HIM FALL INTO THE BLAZING LAVA. THAT IS NOT TO BE HIS FATE.
NOT YET!
THE VOICE IS A NASAL WHINE, PICKING AT THE EDGES OF HIS CONSCIOUSNESS LIKE AN ITCH ONE IS UNABLE TO SCRATCH.
NY HANDS, ROUGH AND NEWY-STRONG LIFT HIM NTO THE HOT, STONE SLAB.
ENEATH HIS OUR HUNDRED UNDS AN CIENT ROCKY NGE GROANS FEEBLE ROTEST.
M-MOLE MAN... HOW DID YOU GET... MIXED UP... IN THIS MESS? WHY'RE... YA... DOIN' THIS... TA ME?
YOU DARE? YOU DARE MOCK ME WITH SUCH A QUESTION?
3.

"I HAD MADE MY PEACE WITH YOU OF THE FANTASTIC FOUR, AS I HAD AT LAST MADE MY PEACE WITH ALL THE ACCURSED SURFACE WORLD.
"I HAD GATHERED TO MY UNDERGROUND KINGDOM ALL THE OUTCASTS, THE PHYSICALLY AND EMOTIONALLY DEFORMED, SPURNED BY THEIR FELLOW MEN, AS I HAD BEEN SPURNED.*
"I HAD CREATED FOR THEM A UTOPIA OF PEACE AND BEAUTY.
*AS SEEN IN FANTASTIC FOUR ANNUAL #13--Bob

"THEN ONE DAY, IN THE WESTERN REGIONS OF MY REALM...

"A GIANT DRILL-BIT RIPPED THROUGH TO THE SEETHING MAGMA HEART OF OUR PLANET, UNLEASHING THE BOILING, MOLTEN ROCK.

"IT FLOODED THROUGH MY TUNNELS, A GREAT, UNENDING RIVER OF LIQUID ROCK, SEARING ALL IN ITS PATH.
"THE UNUTTERABLE DEVASTATION SUFFERED BY MY OUTCASTS, MY SUBTERRANEANS... I CANNOT DESCRIBE.

"MY DREAMS OF PEACE AND TRANQUILITY WERE BURNT AWAY.
"AND AS I LOOKED UPON THE TERRIBLE SEA OF LAVA I SWORE I WOULD HAVE MY VENGEANCE UPON THOSE RESPONSIBLE!"

BUT, WHEN I CAME HERE TO INVESTIGATE, WHAT DID I FIND?
I FOUND YOU! THE THING! ONE OF THE FANTASTIC FOUR! I SHOULD HAVE KNOWN YOU WOULD FIND A WAY TO DESTROY MY DREAMS.
M-MOLE, LISTEN TA ME...

HE STRUGGLES AGAINST THE PARALYSIS THAT GRIPS HIS ROCK-LIKE FORM,

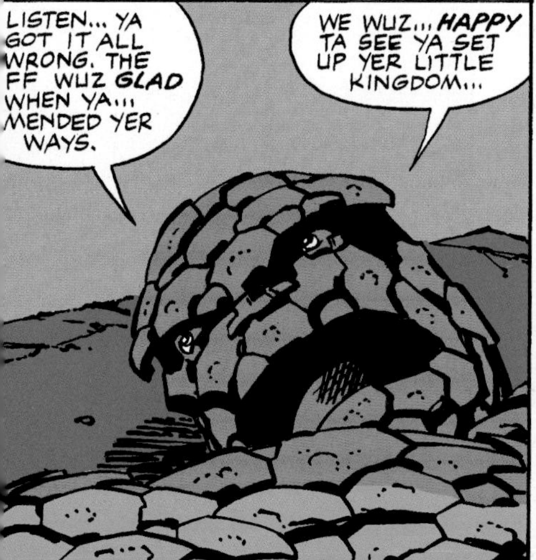
LISTEN... YA GOT IT ALL WRONG. THE FF WUZ GLAD WHEN YA... MENDED YER WAYS.
WE WUZ... HAPPY TA SEE YA SET UP YER LITTLE KINGDOM...

"WE AIN'T THE ONES WHO CAUSED ALL THAT DESTRUCTION AND DEATH.
"THE REAL VILLAIN IS ALDEN MAAS, THE CREATOR OF WONDERWORLD AMUSEMENT PARK. *
*AS SHOWN LAST ISSUE-- Bob.

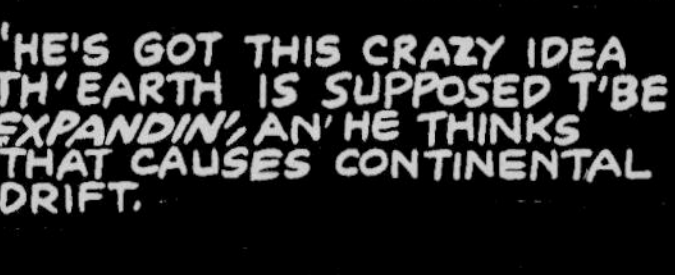
'HE'S GOT THIS CRAZY IDEA TH' EARTH IS SUPPOSED T'BE EXPANDIN', AN' HE THINKS THAT CAUSES CONTINENTAL DRIFT.

"AN' HE'S SNATCHED MY PARTNER, TH' HUMAN TORCH, TA USE HIS FLAME POWERS...

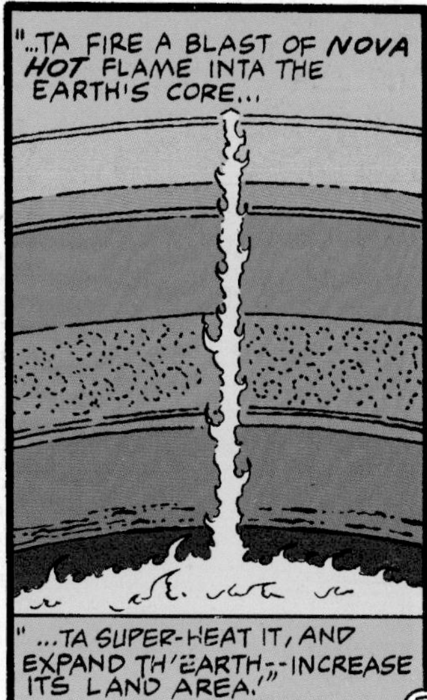
"...TA FIRE A BLAST OF NOVA HOT FLAME INTA THE EARTH'S CORE...
"...TA SUPER-HEAT IT, AND EXPAND TH' EARTH--INCREASE ITS LAND AREA."
5.

ALDEN MAAS? YES, I REMEMBER HIM. HE HAD BECOME A BILLIONAIRE RECLUSE EVEN BEFORE I CAME TO MY UNDER-GROUND WORLD.
BUT YOU CANNOT EXPECT ME TO BELIEVE THAT EVEN A PANDERING **FANTASY MERCHANT** SUCH AS HIM COULD HAVE CONCOCTED SO OUTLANDISH A PLAN.
THE EARTH WOULD NOT EXPAND. THE CRUST WOULD **RUPTURE.** ALL THE SURFACE WOULD BE INUNDATED.

THAT'S WHAT I THOUGHT. THAT'S WHY HE'S GOTTA BE **STOPPED!** BEFORE BILLIONS A' PEOPLE GET KILLED. THAT'S WHY... WHY YOU GOTTA **HELP ME!**
HELP YOU? ARE YOU **MAD?**
I MEAN TO **EXECUTE** YOU.

"EVEN NOW MY SUBTERRANEANS POSITION THE INSTRUMENT OF YOUR DEATH --
"--A GIANT BOULDER CAREFULLY BALANCED ON THE LEDGE ABOVE US."

IT WILL ROLL DOWN ITS CARVED CHANNEL TO STRIKE THE END OF THE SLAB ON WHICH YOU LIE HELP-LESSLY...
...AND YOU WILL BE HURLED INTO THE SEA OF LAVA BEYOND THIS PLATEAU.

'AN THAT'D COOK EVEN **ME.**
O...KAY, MOLE. ONE WAY... OR ANOTHER... I'M GONNA MAKE YA LISTEN!

MEANWHILE...
EVEN AS THE MIGHTY-MUSCLED THING TURNS EVERY IOTA OF HIS COSMIC RAY-SPAWNED STRENGTH TO THE TASK OF OVERCOMING THE PARALYSIS WHICH GRIPS HIM...
ACROSS THE CONTINENT A FAMILIAR VEHICLE RISES FROM THE HANGAR DECK ATOP THE FAR-FAMED BAXTER BUILDING.
AT THE CONTROLS IS REED RICHARDS, THE MAN CALLED MISTER FANTASTIC, LONG-TIME FRIEND OF BEN GRIMM AND LEADER OF THE FANTASTIC FOUR.
THE AUTOMATED SCANNERS HAVE BEEN PICKING UP AN UNIDENTIFIED ENERGY GLICH HERE IN MANHATTAN FOR SEVERAL DAYS NOW.
BUT THIS LATEST OCCURRENCE IS AT LEAST PARTIALLY DIRECTIONAL. IT CAME FROM SOMEWHERE IN CENTRAL PARK.
"SOMEWHERE IN CENTRAL PARK..."
ONLY A NEW YORKER CAN TRULY APPRECIATE THE ENORMITY OF THOSE WORDS. TWO AND A HALF MILES LONG, HALF A MILE WIDE, THE PARK COVERS 840 ACRES IN THE VERY HEART OF MANHATTAN.
AND AS REED RICHARDS CIRCLES AND RECIRCLES THE OCEAN OF GREENERY, HE REALIZES THE TASK HE HAS SET FOR HIMSELF HAS NIGH-PROVERBIAL PROPORTIONS.
HE IS SEEKING A FLEETING ENERGY NEEDLE IN A MOST FRUSTRATING HAYSTACK.
IT'S BEEN A LONG TIME SINCE THERE WERE ACTUAL SHEEP GRAZING ON THE ROLLING GRASSES OF THE SHEEP MEADOW...
...BUT THE GATHERED PICNICKERS ARE SURELY NO LESS ASTONISHED BY THE ARRIVAL OF THE FANTASTICAR THAN THOSE FOUR-LEGGED CREATURES WOULD HAVE BEEN.
7.

TYPICALLY HEEDLESS OF THE STIR HIS VERY PRESENCE CREATES, REED RICHARDS DIRECTS HIS PHENOMENAL INTELLECT TO MORE PRESSING CONCERNS THIS DAY.
THIS PORTABLE DIO-ETHERIC SCANNER SHOULD BE ABLE TO MONITOR THE PRECISE SOURCE OF THE ENERGY FLUCTUATIONS.
AT LEAST I HOPE IT WILL. I ONLY HAD A FEW MINUTES TO COBBLE IT TOGETHER BEFORE THE ALARM SOUNDED.*
*LAST ISSUE. --Bob.

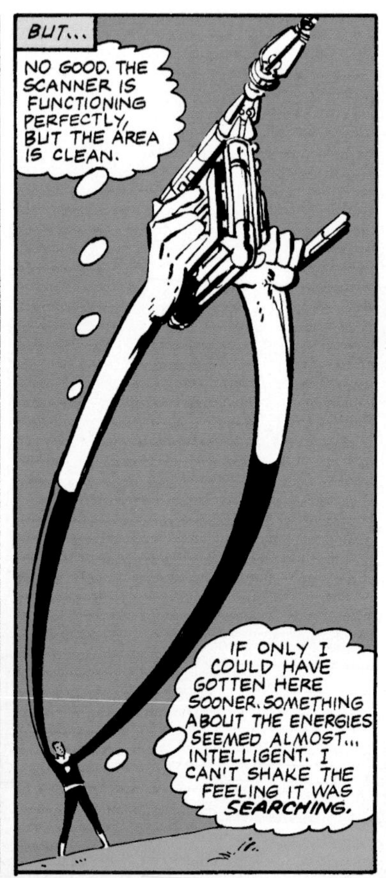
BUT...
NO GOOD. THE SCANNER IS FUNCTIONING PERFECTLY, BUT THE AREA IS CLEAN.
IF ONLY I COULD HAVE GOTTEN HERE SOONER. SOMETHING ABOUT THE ENERGIES SEEMED ALMOST... INTELLIGENT. I CAN'T SHAKE THE FEELING IT WAS SEARCHING.

AND, I SUSPECT, SEARCHING FOR SOMETHING THAT WILL HAVE TERRIBLE CONSE-QUENCES FOR THE PEOPLE OF EARTH.
*AND YOU CAN SEE THE MYSTERY BEGIN TO UNRAVEL IN THE THING #10, ON SALE IN ONE WEEK. --Bob.

MEANWHILE, ON A QUIET STREET IN SUBURBAN BELLE PORTE, CONNECTICUT...
MRS. BENJAMIN? ARE YOU HOME, MRS. BENJAMIN?

IS THAT YOU, KATE?
YES, I'VE BROUGHT FRANKLIN HOME FROM THE PLAY-GROUND.

GOOD... GOOD GIRL. THERE ARE SOME MILK AND COOKIES IN THE KITCHEN. HELP YOUR-SELVES.
I'LL BE DOWN IN JUST A MINUTE...
...I HOPE...
8

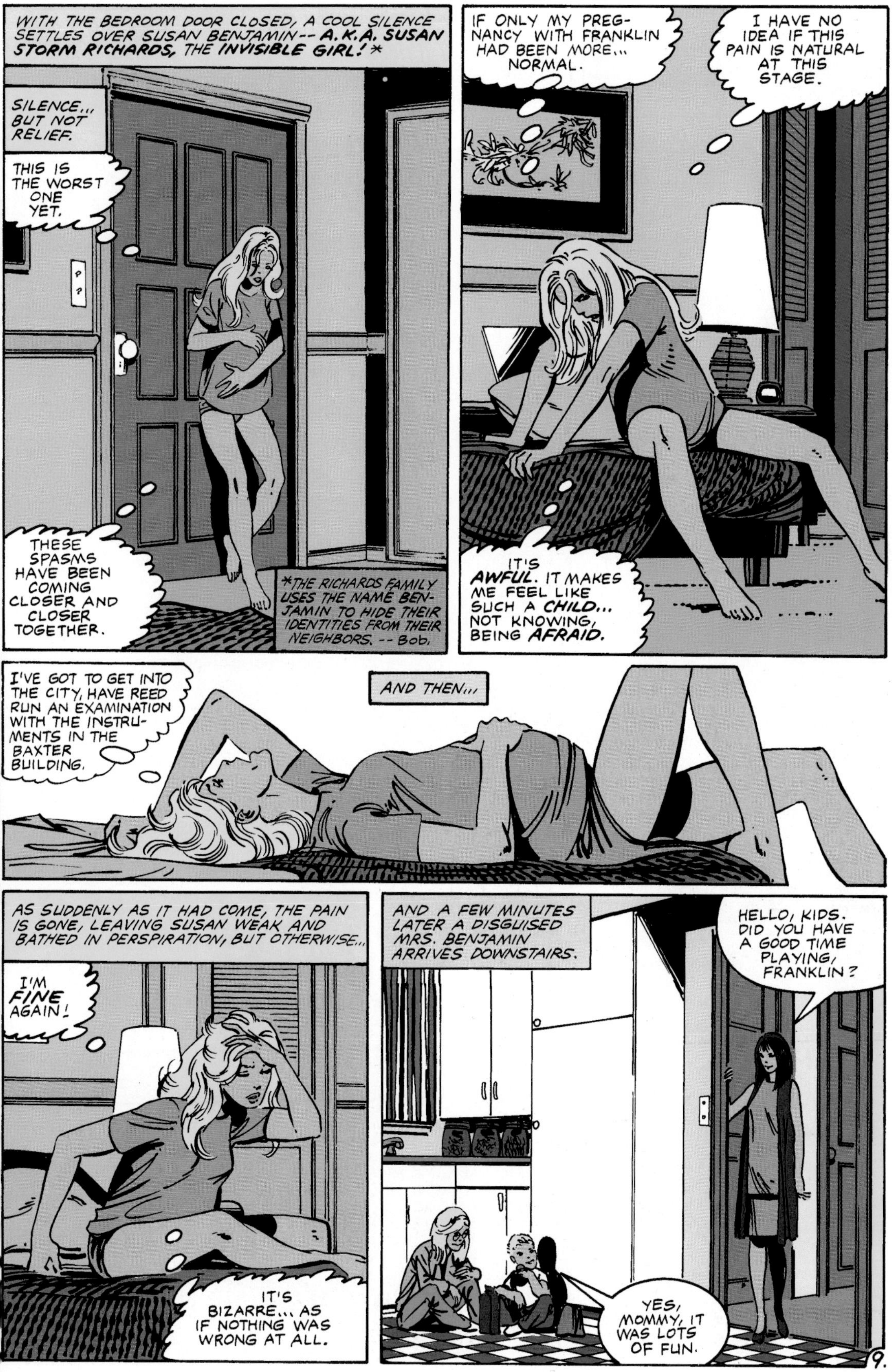

WITH THE BEDROOM DOOR CLOSED, A COOL SILENCE SETTLES OVER SUSAN BENJAMIN -- A.K.A. SUSAN STORM RICHARDS, THE INVISIBLE GIRL! *

SILENCE... BUT NOT RELIEF.

THIS IS THE WORST ONE YET.

THESE SPASMS HAVE BEEN COMING CLOSER AND CLOSER TOGETHER.

*THE RICHARDS FAMILY USES THE NAME BENJAMIN TO HIDE THEIR IDENTITIES FROM THEIR NEIGHBORS. -- Bob.

IF ONLY MY PREGNANCY WITH FRANKLIN HAD BEEN MORE... NORMAL.
I HAVE NO IDEA IF THIS PAIN IS NATURAL AT THIS STAGE.
IT'S AWFUL. IT MAKES ME FEEL LIKE SUCH A CHILD... NOT KNOWING, BEING AFRAID.

I'VE GOT TO GET INTO THE CITY, HAVE REED RUN AN EXAMINATION WITH THE INSTRUMENTS IN THE BAXTER BUILDING.

AND THEN...

AS SUDDENLY AS IT HAD COME, THE PAIN IS GONE, LEAVING SUSAN WEAK AND BATHED IN PERSPIRATION, BUT OTHERWISE...
I'M FINE AGAIN!
IT'S BIZARRE... AS IF NOTHING WAS WRONG AT ALL.

AND A FEW MINUTES LATER A DISGUISED MRS. BENJAMIN ARRIVES DOWNSTAIRS.
HELLO, KIDS. DID YOU HAVE A GOOD TIME PLAYING, FRANKLIN?
YES, MOMMY, IT WAS LOTS OF FUN.
9.

ELSEWHERE...
IN A HIDDEN CHAMBER, ON AN ISLAND TEN MILES OFF THE COAST OF SOUTHERN CALIFORNIA...
SOME VACATION THIS HAS TURNED OUT TO BE...

VAINLY, THE HUMAN TORCH FIGHTS AGAINST THE NUMBING FATIGUE THAT MAKES IT A HERCULEAN EFFORT EVEN TO RAISE HIS HEAD...
BEN AND I CAME OUT HERE FOR SOME FUN AND SUN...
INSTEAD I END UP GETTING SNATCHED BY A BOZO WITH A MESSIAH COMPLEX.*
AN' STRAPPED INTO THIS GIZMO THAT ROBS ME OF CONTROL OF MY POWER.
*LAST ISSUE. --Bob.

UH-OH! HERE COMES ONE OF MAAS' FEMALE FLUNKIES.
LISTEN TO ME, PLEASE! YOU'RE TAXING MY POWER TOO MUCH. YOU'LL KILL ME!
OH, I ASSURE YOU, WE WON'T DO THAT, MR. STORM.

YOU ARE FAR TOO VITAL AN ELEMENT OF THE MESSIAH'S PLAN FOR US TO ALLOW ANY HARM TO BEFALL YOU.
MR. MAAS HAS CALCULATED THE PRECISE AMOUNT OF TIME YOU NEED TO RE-CUPERATE FROM EACH NOVA BLAST.

AND THAT TIME HAS NOW PASSED, SO, SINCE THE FIRST ATTEMPT TO FIRE UP THE CORE WAS UN-SUCCESSFUL...
...IT'S TIME TO TRY AGAIN!
10

HER VOICE HAS THE SAME SYRUPY SING-SONG SWEETNESS THAT THE THING HEARD WHEN HER HOLOGRAM IMAGE SPOKE TO HIM EARLIER.*
THEN, BEFORE THE FATEFUL SWITCH CAN BE THROWN...
*LAST ISSUE AGAIN--Bob.
WITH INCREDIBLE SPEED THE HARD YELLOW HANDS DRAG HER INTO THE SUDDEN OPENING.
SHE HAS NO CHANCE TO SOUND AN ALARM BEFORE SHE IS SILENCED AND SPIRITED AWAY.
AND THEN...
EXCELLENT, MY SLAVES. YOU HAVE LOCATED THE EXACT CHAMBER.
THE MOLE MAN!
DON'T TELL ME YOU'VE GOT YOUR BIG NOSE IN THIS, TOO?
CAN THE WISECRACKS, JUNIOR. IT'S TAKEN ME QUITE A WHILE TA CONVINCE HIM WE'RE ON HIS SIDE THIS TIME.
DON'T BLOW IT!
WISE WORDS, BEN GRIMM. I AM STILL NOT WHOLLY CONVINCED.
SLAVES, FREE THE HUMAN TORCH.
11.

AND, WITHIN SECONDS...
HEY--YOU SURE ABOUT THIS, BEN? IT'S ONE THING TO SAY MOLE'S ON OUR SIDE, BUT BEING TOUCHED BY THESE GUYS STILL GIVES ME THE CREEPS.
YEAH, WELL DON'T GO ALL DELICATE ON ME NOW, TORCHIE. HOW ARE YA FEELIN'? CAN YA FLAME ON YET?
JUST ABOUT. I'VE REALLY HAD MY POWER PUT THROUGH THE WRINGER... ALTHOUGH I GUESS I SHOULD FEEL LUCKY TO BE ALIVE.
"THE WHOLE WONDERWORLD GRAND PRIX WAS A PLOY TO CAPTURE ME.*
"THE RACE TRACK TUNNEL WAS RIGGED SO THAT ON THE THIRD TIME ROUND MY CAR GOT SHUNTED INTO AN UNDERGROUND VACUUM CHAMBER, AND A DUPLICATE CAR HAD THE CRASH."
*LAST ISSUE-- Guess Who.
YEAH, I FIGGERED IT MUSTA BIN SOMETHIN' LIKE THAT. I JUST COULDN'T ACCEPT YOU WUZ DEAD!
TOUCHING...
...BUT A WASTE OF TIME. BY NOW THE CONTROLLERS OF THIS COMPLEX WILL HAVE REALIZED SOMETHING HAS DELAYED THE TORCH'S BLAST.
EVEN WITHOUT AN ALARM BEING SOUNDED THEY ARE CERTAIN TO SEND SOMEONE TO INVESTIGATE.
WE MUST BE READY!
SUBTERRANEANS FORWARD!!

AND, TRUE TO THE MOLE MAN'S WORDS...
WE'RE BEIN' ATTACKED!

BUT NOTHING COULD HAVE PREPARED THEM FOR THE IDENTITY OF THE ATTACKERS.
C'MON MEN! STOP THEM! FOR MISTER MAAS! FOR THE MESSIAH!

THE FAMILIAR CARTOON VOICES ECHO STRANGELY IN THE VAULTED CORRIDOR.
TOO STRANGELY FOR AT LEAST ONE OF THE COMBATANTS.
I KNEW IT! I KNEW THEY COULDN'T BE GUYS IN COSTUMES!

THEY'RE ROBOTS!
NICE GOIN', THING! WE CAN HANDLE THEM EASY!
FLAME ON!
13

GOOD SHOOTING, MAXIE, BUT EVEN WITH MY FLAME AT THIS LOW EBB I CAN STILL MELT YOUR BULLETS BEFORE THEY HIT.
SQUAWK!
JUST LIKE I CAN MELT YOU!

THE TRADITIONAL BANTER OF THE FF IS NOT MIRRORED BY THE MOLE MAN.
HIS DARK THOUGHTS HE CONSIGNS TO SILENCE.

MEANWHILE HIS SUBTERRANEAN SLAVES FIND THEMSELVES OUTMASSED IF NOT OUTNUMBERED.
LITTLE WORMIES, YOU'RE NO MATCH FOR HOPALONG HIPPO!™

MAYBE NOT. BUT I AM.
THIS IS WEIRD. MAAS NEVER GOT TO QUITE THE LEVEL OF DISNEY, BUT HIS CARTOONS ARE REAL POPULAR.
I FEEL A LITTLE BIT LIKE I'M ATTACKIN' TH' FLAG OR MOM'S APPLE PIE!

NOT FAR AWAY...
I DON'T LIKE THIS, MR. SMITH. IT IS NOT AT ALL IN ACCORDANCE WITH THE **PLAN.**

QUITE SO, MR. JONES. BUT THEN WE HAD NOT CALCULATED THE PRESENCE OF THE **MOLE MAN** IN OUR CONTINGENCY PLANS.
THAT WAS A SERIOUS ERROR ON OUR PARTS. I FEAR IT MAY COST US VALUABLE TIME, IF NOT THE ENTIRE PROJECT.
THEN IT WOULD SEEM TIME FOR ME TO TAKE DIRECT CONTROL.

MR. MAAS! SIR, YOU SHOULD NOT BE OUT OF YOUR **E.A. CHAMBER.**
NEVER MIND THAT, JONES. GIVE ME THE FULL DETAILS ON THE PROBLEM.

IN A FLAT, UNEMOTIONAL MONOTONE, JONES COMPLIES.
...SO YOU SEE, SIR, THE PLAN IS, AT THE MOMENT, IN A POSITION OF EXTREME JEOPARDY.

WE CANNOT ALLOW THAT, MR. JONES. THE SALVATION OF MANKIND MUST NOT BE ALLOWED TO TOTTER AND FALL AT THIS STAGE, SO CLOSE TO THE ULTIMATE GOAL.
PREPARE THE **THERMO-NUCLEAR DEVICE.** IT IS DANGEROUS, AND NOT AS EFFICIENT AS THE TORCH'S NOVA FLAME...
...BUT IT IS THE **LAST HOPE** OF MANKIND.
15

AND...
WELL, LOOKS LIKE MAAS HAS RUN OUTTA ROBOT FUNNY ANIMALS.
'BOUT TIME, TOO. I WUZ STARTIN' TA FEEL LIKE THE CHAIRMAN OF ACTION FOR CHILDREN'S TELEVISION.
LOOKS LIKE WE'RE GETTING NEAR THE NITTY-GRITTY...
THAT DOOR LOOKS BIG ENOUGH TO GIVE EVEN YOU SOME PROBLEMS, BIG GUY.
YEAH, IT MAY SLOW US DOWN A BIT.
MORE THAN "A BIT". IT IS AT LEAST FIFTEEN FEET THICK.
BUT THERE IS NO NEED TO WASTE TIME...
THE SILVERY WHISTLE BARELY TICKLES THE EDGE OF PERCEPTION.
FOR SEVERAL MINUTES NOTHING SEEMS TO HAPPEN.
AWRIGHT, MOLE, WHAT'S YER GAME.
UNHAND ME!
THING! DON'T! YOU GOTTA TRUST HIM-- LIKE YOU TOLD ME TO!
THEN...
WHAT TH'...?
16.

WITH A SOUND LIKE A HUNDRED EARTHQUAKES THE GIANT CREATURE TEARS THROUGH THE REINFORCED FLOORING...
ITS PALE EYES SQUINT AND BLINK, AND FOR A MOMENT THERE IS SOMETHING LIKE A FLICKER OF RECOGNITION DEEP WITHIN THEM...
...FOR THE FANTASTIC FOUR HAVE ENCOUNTERED THIS BEAST BEFORE, YEARS AGO WHEN THEY FIRST MET AND BATTLED THE MOLE MAN'S HORDES.
BUT THE CREATURE HASN'T THE TIME TO TRY TO DRAW FROM ITS BRUTISH BRAIN THE DIM MEMORIES OF THOSE IT NOW SEES.
ALMOST AT ONCE THE MOLE MAN'S WHINY VOICE IS RAISED IN HARSH COMMANDS.
AND, LIKE SOME OUTLANDISH LAP-DOG, THE MONSTER OBEYS.
17.

WHAT FOLLOWS CAN IN NO WAY BE DESCRIBED AS DELIBERATE.

THERE IS NO THOUGHT, NO LOGIC, NO TACTICAL PLANNING BEHIND THE MONSTER'S MOVEMENTS.

THERE IS ONLY DIRECTION...
...FORWARD, AND EVER FURTHER FORWARD, NO MATTER WHAT MIGHT BAR THE WAY.
HOLY...! HE'S TEARIN' RIGHT THROUGH STEEL LIKE IT WAS CARDBOARD!
EVEN THE MIGHTY-MUSCLED THING CAN ONLY STAND AND GAPE BEFORE SUCH POWER UN-LEASHED.

IN THE END THE TINY HUMANS MUST RESIGN THEMSELVES TO THE ROLE OF FOLLOWERS, PICKING THEIR WAY ALONG A HIGHWAY OF RUBBLE.
IT IS A POSITION NOT AT ALL FAMILIAR OR COMFORTABLE TO THE TWO MOST FLAMBOYANT MEMBERS OF THE EARTH'S MOST AMAZING QUARTET.

AND...
THIS IS QUITE DISTRESSING, MR. JONES. I FEAR THE INTRUDERS MAY REACH US.
THAT IS PRESENTLY THE LEAST OF OUR CONCERNS, MR. SMITH. MR. MAAS IS DETERIORATING RAPIDLY. WE MUST RETURN HIM TO THE E.A. CHAMBER.
NO... NO. LISTEN TO ME.
MY LIFE IS NOT IMPORTANT. DO YOU UNDERSTAND? MY LIFE IS NOT IMPORTANT. ONLY THE PROJECT IS IMPORTANT. ONLY THE DREAM.
AS YOU WISH, SIR. BUT IF YOU COULD PLEASE TAKE MORE CARE OF...
THERE IS NO LONGER TIME FOR SUCH CONSIDERATIONS. IS THE NUCLEAR DEVICE PREPARED, MR. BROWN?
THE MASTER CONTROL CIRCUIT HAS BEEN PRIMED, SIR. IT REMAINS ONLY FOR THE SWITCH TO BE THROWN.
LET ME HELP YOU, SIR...
QUICKLY, MR. JONES. I HAVE ONLY SECONDS LEFT. I MUST REACH THE SWITCH. I MUST SEE THE CULMINATION OF THE DREAM SET IN MOTION BY MY OWN HAND.
I AM THE MESSIAH, THE SAVIOR. I MUST PREVAIL!
19.

AND, AS THE TREMBLING, PALSIED HAND GROPES FOR THE SWITCH...

THE MOLE MAN'S MONSTROUS SLAVE BURSTS BLINKING INTO THE BRIGHT CALIFORNIA SUN.

BUT THE THREE HUMANS ARE NO LONGER FOLLOWING.
THIS WAY! THE MAIN CONTROL CENTER'S GOTTA BE ALONG HERE.
HOW CAN YOU BE SO SURE?

'CAUSE OF THIS DOOR, HOT-SHOT.
WHAT ELSE'D NEED SUCH HEAVY PROTECTION?

BUT...
HOLY!
WHAT IN...?
MAAS?!?

YES, SIR, THIS IS ALDEN MAAS...
THE *LATE* ALDEN MAAS.

YOU MUST BE JOKING! YOU EXPECT US TO BELIEVE THIS DESSICATED CORPSE IS MAAS? THIS THING HAS BEEN DEAD FOR *TWENTY YEARS!*

SIXTEEN-POINT-OH-NINE-FIVE YEARS, SIR. MR. MAAS SUCCUMBED TO A DEGENERATIVE NERVOUS DISORDER, CHARACTERIZED BY FAILING METABOLIC FUNCTIONS AND DELUSIONS OF GRANDEUR.

IN THE LAST YEAR OF HIS *TRUE LIFE* HE CAME TO THINK OF HIMSELF AS THE SAVIOR OF HUMANKIND, THE LIVING MESSIAH, ALTHOUGH HE DID NOT BELIEVE HIMSELF A REINCARNATION OF THE *LAST* TO BEAR THAT TITLE.

AND SO HE BEGAN BUILDING ON THIS ISLAND THE MECHANISMS NECESSARY FOR *PROJECT WORLDCORE...*

...AND THE DEVELOPMENT OF THE *EXTENDED ANIMATION CHAMBER,* WHICH PROLONGED HIS EXISTENCE...

...UNTIL NOW.

WAIT A MINUTE... YOU MEAN YOU GUYS DID THIS KNOWING THE DANGER, THE POTENTIAL FOR DESTRUCTION?
THERE WAS NEVER ANY DANGER, SIR. EVEN HAD HE SUCCEEDED IN THE ACTIVATION OF IT...
THE THERMONUCLEAR DEVICE WOULD HAVE BEEN INSUFFICIENT TO FIRE THE CORE.

THEN... *WHY,* FER CRIPES SAKE, DIDJA GO ALONG WITH HIM?

TO KEEP HIM HAPPY AND CONTENTED, SIR...
...AS WE WERE PROGRAMMED TO DO.
21.

EPILOG
SO THAT'S HOW IT ENDS, HUH? THEY JUST WALK OUT INTO THE OCEAN UNTIL THE PRESSURE CRUSHES THEM... AND WHAT'S LEFT OF MAAS.
KINDA ANTICLIMACTIC, AIN'T IT? WE WON... BUT NOTHIN' WOULDA BIN MUCH DIFFERENT IF WE LOST.
WE DID NOT WIN. I WAS DENIED MY VENGEANCE!

AW, DON'T BE SUCH A GRUMP, MOLE. IF WE'RE ALL GONNA BE PALS NOW...
TAKE YOUR PAW OFF ME, YOU RIDICULOUS OAF!

HUH? BUT I THOUGHT...
I RETURN NOW TO SUBTERRANEA, AS MY MONSTER HAS ALREADY DONE BUT MY DREAMS OF AN UNDER-GROUND UTOPIA HAVE STILL BEEN CRUSHED. WHEN NEXT WE MEET...
... IT WILL NOT BE AS FRIENDS.

AND SO...
HEY, I JUST REALIZED WHY MAAS' ISLAND ISN'T STAR-SHAPED ANYMORE.
'CAUSE THEY DUMPED ALL THE EARTH FROM THE BORE-HOLE OFF-SHORE. I GUESSED THAT AS SOON AS I FOUND OUT WHAT THEY WUZ UP TA.
C'MON KID. TIME TA HEAD HOME. I FEEL LIKE BEIN' DEPRESSED FOR A WHILE.

OUR STORY GOES FROM HERE TO THING #10 FOR THE BEGINNING OF A DRAMATIC CHANGE FOR THE FANTASTIC FOUR.

THEN BACK HERE FOR A DOUBLE-STORY ISSUE IN #265: THE HOUSE THAT REED BUILT AND HOME ARE THE HEROES

DON'T MISS EITHER.

thing # 10

APRIL 1984

STAN LEE PRESENTS A TURNING POINT IN THE LIFE OF THE THING...
MARKING TIME
FORGET EVERYTHING YOU'VE HEARD ABOUT CENTRAL PARK.
CERTAINLY IT IS NOT A PLACE TO WANDER ALONE, IN THE SMALL HOURS OF MORNING. BUT ISN'T THAT TRUE OF ALMOST ANY-WHERE? ISN'T THERE A NEIGH-BORHOOD LIKE THAT IN YOUR HOME TOWN?
BUT CENTRAL PARK HAS CHANGED MUCH IN THE PAST FEW YEARS. THE TIME OF FEAR AND CRIME IS LARGELY PASSED. THE PEOPLE ARE TAKING BACK THE PARK. THE OLD FOLKS, THE KIDS, THE MOTHERS WITH THEIR BABIES, THE LIVING, BREATHING THRONGS OF THE CITY.
AND IN PARTICULAR, THESE TWO...
JOHN BYRNE SCRIPTER
RON WILSON PENCILER
HILARY BARTA, INKER
JIM NOVAK LETTERER
JULIANNA FERRITER COLORIST
BOB BUDIANSKY-EDITOR
JIM SHOOTER-TIMEKEEPER

HIS NAME IS **BEN GRIMM**, HERS **ALICIA MASTERS**, AND THEY ARE PERHAPS THE STRANGEST OF THE MANY COUPLES YOU MIGHT MEET IN THE PARK THIS AUTUMN AFTERNOON.

OH, BEN, IT'S SO BEAUTIFUL. THE SMELL OF THE LEAVES, THE CRISPNESS OF THE AIR. I LOVE THESE MOMENTS JUST BEFORE THE SEASONS CHANGE.

NEVER PAID ALL THAT MUCH ATTENTION, BABE. IT'S FUNNY HOW YOU, EVEN THOUGH YER *BLIND*... YOU SEEM TA APPRECIATE THINGS SO MUCH MORE'N I DO.

ONLY BECAUSE YOU WON'T ALLOW YOURSELF TO APPRECIATE THEM, DARLING. YOU DENY YOURSELF SO MUCH, LOCKING OUT THE WORLD THAT LOVES YOU, THAT RESPECTS AND HONORS YOU. LOCKING OUT SO MUCH BEAUTY AND LOVE.

I GOT ME ALL THE LOVE I NEED TUCKED UNDER MY ARM RIGHT NOW, BABY. AN' AS FER RESPECT... WELL, PEOPLE DON'T RESPECT LUMPY, ROCKY, *UGLY*, ORANGE MONSTERS. FEAR 'EM, MAYBE. CHEER 'EM WHEN THEY LAY THEIR LIVES ON THE LINE ONE MORE TIME TA SAVE THE WORLD.

BUT RESPECT? NAH. RESPECT IS FER BASEBALL PLAYERS AN' CONGRESSMEN.

US SUPER-FOLK JUST GET TH' LUMPS.

YOU STILL SOUND SO TROUBLED, BELOVED. PLEASE, CAN'T YOU LET ME INTO YOUR HEART? LET ME KNOW WHAT IT IS THAT TORMENTS YOU SO?
I WISH I COULD, ALICIA. YOU DON'T KNOW HOW MUCH I WISH I COULD.
BUT IT AIN'T THAT EASY. I BIN USIN' YOU FER A CRYIN' TOWEL FER A BIG PILE OF YEARS, AN' LATELY... WELL, LATELY IT JUST DON'T SEEM LIKE THAT'S ALTOGETHER FAIR.

LATELY IT SEEMS LIKE... MAYBE YOU AN' ME...
WELL, MAYBE WE'D BOTH DO ...BETTER WITHOUT THE OTHER.

B-BEN... YOU CAN'T MEAN...
I DUNNO WHAT I MEAN, BABY. I LOVE YOU. LOVE YOU WITH ALL MY HEART. YOU KNOW THAT.

BUT WHAT KINDA LIFE CAN I OFFER YOU? WE CAN'T EVER GET *MARRIED*. AT LEAST, NOT IN THE WAY REAL PEOPLE DO. TH' MOST I CAN OFFER IS OUR NAMES ON A PIECE OF PAPER.
AN'... WELL, YOU DESERVE A WHOLE LOT MORE THAN BEIN' THE GIRL-FRIEND OF A *FREAK*!
HOLY COW.

IT'S HIM! IT'S REALLY HIM! THE *THING*!
WHAT'S HE DOIN' HERE? SHOULDN'T HE BE OFF BEATIN' ON *DOC DOOM* OR SOMETHIN'?
HEY, WHERE YOU BEEN, SMARTIE? DOC DOOM IS *DEAD*. MY DAD READ IT IN THE PAPERS.
YEAH, WELL THAT'S STILL THE THING, AND WHERE HE GOES BAD GUYS FOLLOW!

THEN LET'S *US* FOLLOW.
WE MAY SEE SOMETHIN' SUPER-NEAT!

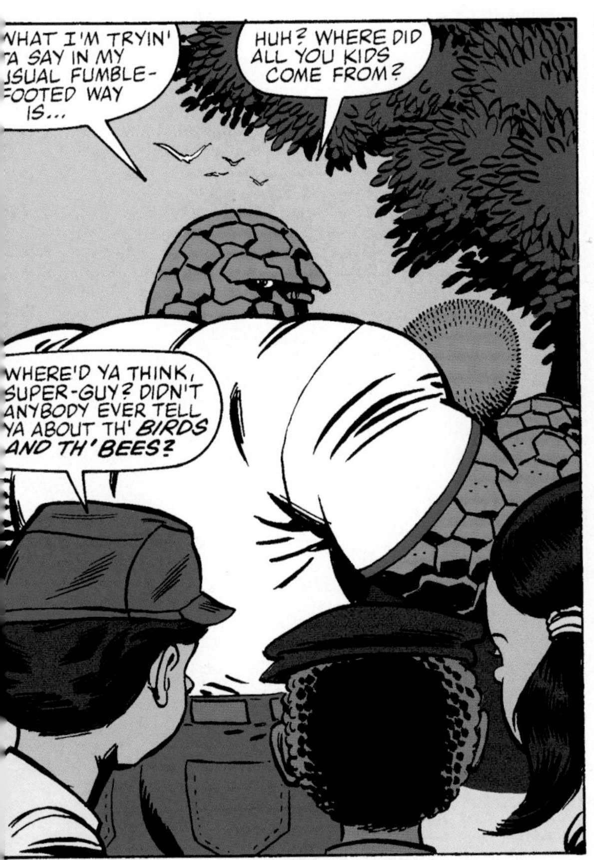
WHAT I'M TRYIN' TA SAY IN MY USUAL FUMBLE-FOOTED WAY IS...
HUH? WHERE DID ALL YOU KIDS COME FROM?
WHERE'D YA THINK, SUPER-GUY? DIDN'T ANYBODY EVER TELL YA ABOUT TH' BIRDS AND TH' BEES?

OH, CUTE. THAT'S JUST WHAT I NEED. A BUNCHA PINT-SIZED COMEDIANS.
TRASH IT
WHY DON'T YA GO PLAY IN HEAVY TRAFFIC OR SOMETHIN'?
BEN.

HEY, DON'T MIND CHUCK, MR. THING. WE JUST WANNA FOLLOW YOU AROUND AN' WATCH YA BEAT UP ON SOME BAD-GUYS!
YEAH? WELL, MAYBE I DON'T FEEL LIKE BEING FOLLOWED. DID YA THINK OF THAT?

OH, BEN, PLEASE TRY TO BE A LITTLE NICER. THEY'RE ONLY CHILDREN. FROM THE SOUNDS OF THEIR VOICES THEY'RE NOT MUCH OLDER THAN YOUR NEPHEW FRANKLIN*.
HMPH.
*SON OF REED AND SUE RICHARDS, TWO OF THE THING'S PARTNERS IN THE FANTASTIC FOUR -- BOB.

YEAH, DON'T BE SUCH A GROUCH, MR. THING. SHOW US HOW STRONG YOU ARE!
YEAH, DO SOMETHING STRONG!
LISTEN, I AIN'T IN THE MOOD, OKAY? ME AN' MY LADY GOT STUFF TA DISCUSS. IF YA HAFTA FOLLOW, JUST STAY OUT FROM UNDER...

...FOOT.
OH!

ALICIA!
BABY, ARE YOU OKAY? YOU AIN'T HURT?
I'M... FINE, BEN. JUST A LITTLE STARTLED, THAT'S ALL.

YEAH, WELL YOU STAND RIGHT HERE FER A MINUTE...

THESE LITTLE TWERPS WANTED TA SEE THE THING IN ACTION...
I'M GONNA SHOW 'EM!

OH, BEN!
NO! WHAT ARE YOU THINKING?

I'M THINKIN'...

...THAT I'M SICK AN' TIRED OF BEING PESTERED WHERE-EVER I GO!

I'M THINKIN' MAYBE IT'S TIME I LET EVERYONE KNOW I AIN'T YOUR BASIC CELEBRITY WHO LOVES HIS ADORIN' FANS!

I'M THINKIN' I'D LIKE TA BE *ALONE*!!
O-OMIGOSH!

BEN... ALL THAT TERRIBLE CRUNCHING NOISE...!
BEN, IN HEAVEN'S NAME, WHAT DID YOU DO?!
NOTHIN'.

CENTRAL PARK JUST GOT REDUCED BY ONE PIGEON PERCH, IS ALL.

BUT JUST IN CASE THERE'S STILL SOME RUBBER-NECKERS WHO DIDN'T GET THE POINT OF THAT LITTLE DEMONSTRATION...
NOT
TER

...YOU AN' ME ARE GOIN' SOMEWHERES WE CAN REALLY BE ON OUR OWN...
TAXI

...THE BAXTER BUILDING!

AFTERNOON, MR. GRIMM, MISS MASTERS.
HIYA, O'HOOLIHAN. SEE IF YA CAN KEEP THE GAWKERS AT BAY, WILL YA?

THE BUSTLING LOBBY GROWS STILL AND QUIET.
BUSINESS FOLK SLOW AND HALT IN THEIR DAILY ROUTINES AS THE THING PASSES AMONG THEM. EVEN AFTER ALL THE YEARS OF SHARING THIS MANHATTAN TOWER WITH THE FANTASTIC FOUR, THEIR REACTION TO THE SIGHT OF ONE OF EARTH'S GREATEST HEROES STILL IS A THRILL -- AND A SHUDDER.
HOLD ON A SEC, BABE.

LEMME ACTIVATE MY BELT-BUCKLE GIZMO AN' CALL DOWN THE FF'S PRIVATE ELEVATOR.
GHOST-LIKE, THE BEAM FLICKERS BRIEFLY TO THE CALL BUTTON.
SCARCELY VISIBLE IN THE SUNLIT LOBBY, THE SPECIAL RAY IS THE UNIQUE PRODUCT OF THE AMAZING INTELLECT OF REED RICHARDS, LEADER OF THE FANTASTIC FOUR, AND LONGTIME FRIEND OF BEN GRIMM.

OKAY, HERE'S TH' CAR. WATCH YER STEP KID.
SILENTLY, THE SPECIALLY DESIGNED ELEVATOR ZOOMS TO THE THIRTY-FIRST FLOOR RESIDENTIAL LEVEL, WHERE...

HEY, BEN YOU'RE LOOKING GLOOMY TO BEAT ALL...
OH, HI, ALICIA. DIDN'T SEE YOU FOR A MINUTE...
HELLO, JOHNNY, HOW ARE YOU TODAY?

I'M FINE. BUT YOUR BOYFRIEND LOOKS LIKE HE JUST GOT INVITED TO HIS OWN WAKE.
REAL FUNNY. THE WORLD'S FULLA COMEDIANS TODAY.

LEAVING THE YOUNGEST MEMBER OF THE FF TO DESCEND IN THE ELEVATOR, BEN AND ALICIA PASS THROUGH THE SECURITY DOORS TO FIND...
STRETCHO! SUE! I THOUGHT YOU TWO WERE OFF PLAYIN' MR. AND MRS. AVERAGE AMERICAN IN THE 'BURBS!
THAT'S A CURIOUS WAY TO REFER TO OUR HOME IN CONNECTICUT, BEN, BUT WE HAD IMPORTANT MATTERS TO ATTEND TO HERE IN TOWN.

YEAH? WHAT KINDA MATTERS?
WELL, FOR ONE THING SUE IS GETTING VERY NEAR HER TIME. THE BABY WILL BE BORN ANY DAY NOW, I SHOULD THINK, AND I WANTED TO RUN SOME TESTS.

FOR A MOMENT THE FACE OF THE MAN CALLED MISTER FANTASTIC DARKENS...
SINCE THIS CHILD WAS CONCEIVED WHILE WE WERE ALL IN THE NEGATIVE ZONE* THE PROGRESS OF THE PREGNANCY MUST BE CAREFULLY MONITORED. WE CANNOT RISK A RECURRENCE OF THE COMPLICATIONS ENCOUNTERED WHEN FRANKLIN WAS BORN.
ALSO, THERE HAVE BEEN SOME PECULIAR ENERGY READINGS OVER CENTRAL PARK IN THE LAST FEW DAYS. I WANTED TO DOUBLE-CHECK MY INSTRUMENTS.
*SEE FANTASTIC FOUR #'S 251-256 -- BOB.

CENTRAL PARK? YER BARKIN' UP TH' WRONG TREE, BIG BRAIN. ME AN' ALICIA JUST GOT BACK FROM THERE, AND IT'S PEACEFUL AS CAN BE.
AS IT WAS, WHEN I CHECKED IT MYSELF, NOT LONG AGO.* BUT IT ALWAYS PAYS TO BE CAREFUL AND SURE.
*SEE FANTASTIC FOUR #264 -- BOB.

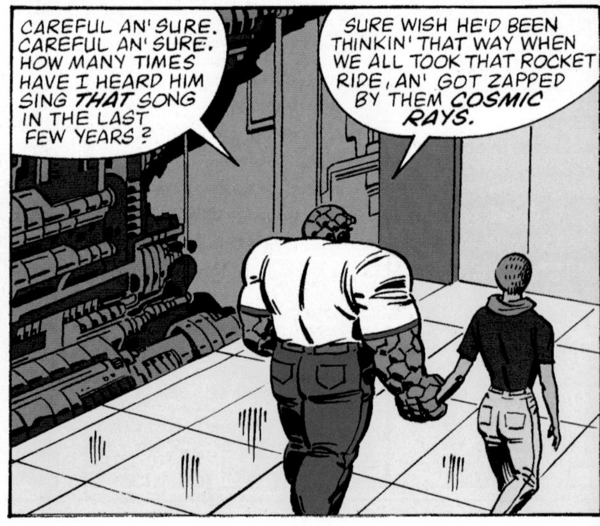
CAREFUL AN' SURE. CAREFUL AN' SURE. HOW MANY TIMES HAVE I HEARD HIM SING THAT SONG IN THE LAST FEW YEARS?
SURE WISH HE'D BEEN THINKIN' THAT WAY WHEN WE ALL TOOK THAT ROCKET RIDE, AN' GOT ZAPPED BY THEM COSMIC RAYS.

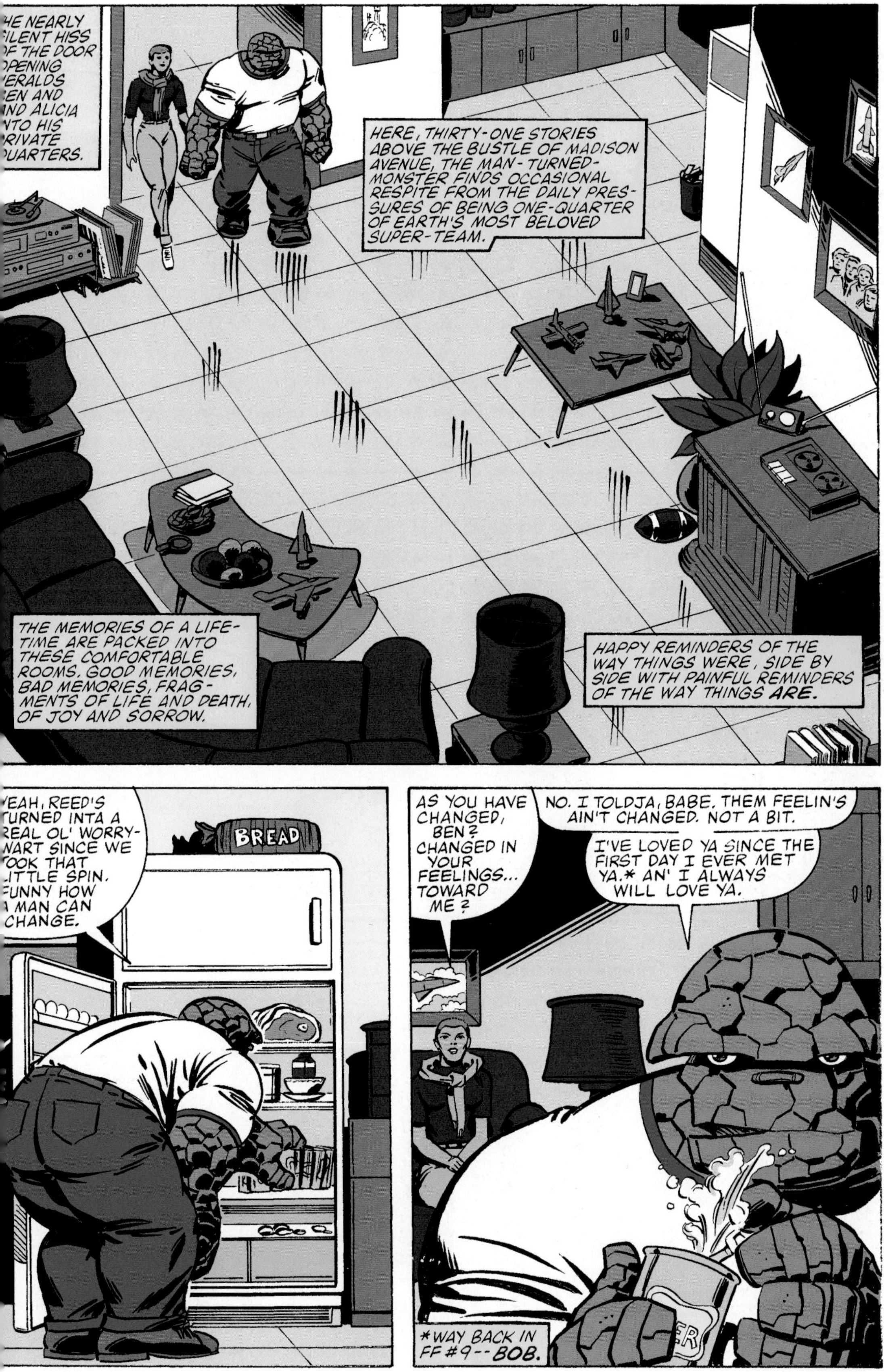

THE NEARLY SILENT HISS OF THE DOOR OPENING HERALDS BEN AND AND ALICIA INTO HIS PRIVATE QUARTERS.

HERE, THIRTY-ONE STORIES ABOVE THE BUSTLE OF MADISON AVENUE, THE MAN-TURNED-MONSTER FINDS OCCASIONAL RESPITE FROM THE DAILY PRESSURES OF BEING ONE-QUARTER OF EARTH'S MOST BELOVED SUPER-TEAM.

THE MEMORIES OF A LIFETIME ARE PACKED INTO THESE COMFORTABLE ROOMS. GOOD MEMORIES, BAD MEMORIES, FRAGMENTS OF LIFE AND DEATH, OF JOY AND SORROW.

HAPPY REMINDERS OF THE WAY THINGS WERE, SIDE BY SIDE WITH PAINFUL REMINDERS OF THE WAY THINGS *ARE*.

YEAH, REED'S TURNED INTA A REAL OL' WORRY-WART SINCE WE TOOK THAT LITTLE SPIN. FUNNY HOW A MAN CAN CHANGE.
BREAD

AS YOU HAVE CHANGED, BEN? CHANGED IN YOUR FEELINGS... TOWARD ME?
NO. I TOLDJA, BABE. THEM FEELIN'S AIN'T CHANGED. NOT A BIT.
I'VE LOVED YA SINCE THE FIRST DAY I EVER MET YA.* AN' I ALWAYS WILL LOVE YA.
*WAY BACK IN FF #9--BOB.

BUT IT AIN'T LOVE I'M TALKIN' ABOUT.
YOU'D BETTER GET COMFORTABLE, BABE. I FEEL A SPEECH COMIN' ON, AN' THAT DON'T HAPPEN OFTEN.

ALL RIGHT, MY DARLING. SAY WHATEVER IT IS YOU FEEL NEEDS TO BE SAID.
BEER
WELL, FIRST OFF, LET ME SAY IT ONE MORE TIME, JUST 'CAUSE I LIKE THE WAY IT SOUNDS.

I LOVE YOU, ALICIA. IF THERE WAS ANY WAY ON GOD'S GREEN EARTH TA DO IT, I'D MARRY YA AN' SETTLE DOWN TA RAISE A MESSA NORMAL KIDS.
BEER

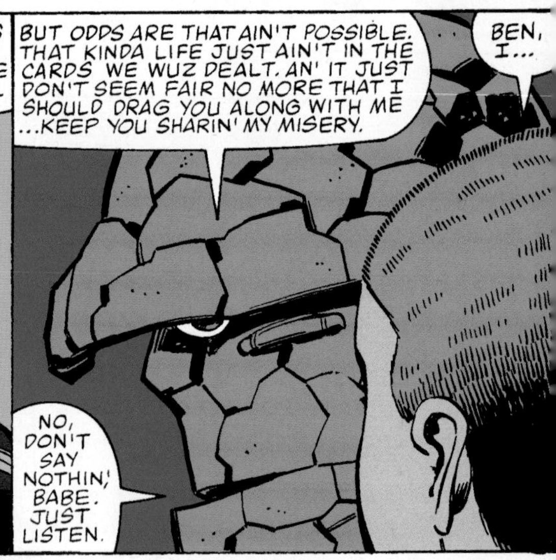
BUT ODDS ARE THAT AIN'T POSSIBLE. THAT KINDA LIFE JUST AIN'T IN THE CARDS WE WUZ DEALT. AN' IT JUST DON'T SEEM FAIR NO MORE THAT I SHOULD DRAG YOU ALONG WITH ME ...KEEP YOU SHARIN' MY MISERY.
BEN, I...
NO, DON'T SAY NOTHIN', BABE. JUST LISTEN.

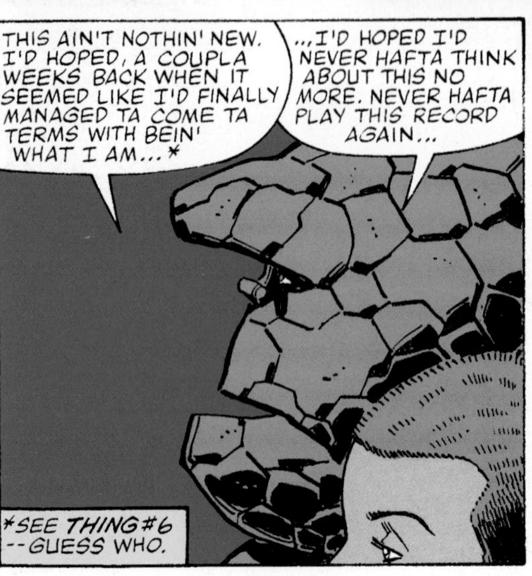
THIS AIN'T NOTHIN' NEW. I'D HOPED, A COUPLA WEEKS BACK WHEN IT SEEMED LIKE I'D FINALLY MANAGED TA COME TA TERMS WITH BEIN' WHAT I AM...*
...I'D HOPED I'D NEVER HAFTA THINK ABOUT THIS NO MORE. NEVER HAFTA PLAY THIS RECORD AGAIN...
*SEE THING #6 --GUESS WHO.

BUT IT SEEMS LIKE I'LL ALWAYS BE PLAYIN' IT...
SEEMS LIKE I ALWAYS HAVE BEEN PLAYIN' IT...
THE PICTURE IS A SIMPLE IMAGE...

FOUR FRIENDS, BROUGHT TOGETHER BY A COMMON GOAL, A COMMON NEED.
NEVER GUESSING WHAT LAY AHEAD OF THEM, NEVER GUESSING THAT THEIR CLANDESTINE FLIGHT TO THE STARS WOULD END IN NEAR TRAGEDY...
BOMBARDED BY A POTENTIALLY LETHAL DOSE OF COSMIC RAYS, THEY FOUND THEMSELVES RETURNED TO EARTH AND TRANSFORMED INTO...

...THE HUMAN TORCH...
...MISTER FANTASTIC...
...THE INVISIBLE GIRL...
...AND...

...A THING! A MONSTER! I'VE BECOME A MONSTER!
LISTEN TO ME, ALL OF YOU! THAT MEANS YOU TOO, BEN!

TOGETHER WE HAVE MORE POWER THAN ANY HUMANS HAVE EVER POSSESSED.

YA DON'T HAFTA MAKE A SPEECH, BIG SHOT. WE UNDERSTAND. WE GOTTA USE THAT POWER TA HELP MANKIND, RIGHT?
RIGHT, BEN. ABSOLUTELY RIGHT.

THUS, ON A LONELY, WOODED HILLSIDE NORTH OF ITHACA, N.Y., A MOMENTOUS PLEDGE IS MADE. A PROMISE TO A FUTURE YET UNBORN...
WE MUST SWEAR TO USE OUR POWERS ONLY FOR THE BETTERMENT OF THE HUMAN CONDITION...
BUT... WHERE IS BEN?

I AIN'T BEN ANYMORE. I'M THE THING.
AN'... I'M WITH YA. BUT DON'T ASK ME WHY!

SOMBER WORDS, AND BEFORE A REPLY CAN BE MADE ALL SPEECH IS DROWNED OUT BY THE FAMILIAR SOUND OF A HELI-COPTER...
BEN...
YA DON'T HAFTA SAY IT. I'LL MAKE MYSELF SCARCE FOR A BIT...

AND SO, ONLY THREE TRANSFORMED HUMANS ARE THERE TO GREET THE NEWCOMERS...
GET USED TA THIS, GRIMM. UNLESS THIS TRANSFORMATION WEARS OFF YER GONNA BE HIDIN' LIKE THIS FER A LONG TIME...

GENTLEMEN! GOOD TO SEE YOU. YOU MUST HAVE SEEN OUR... AH... LANDING.
LANDING? MISTER, I DON'T KNOW WHAT YOU WERE FLYIN', BUT THAT HAS TO HAVE BEEN THE BIGGEST BLAST SINCE... I DON'T KNOW WHAT.
WHO THE BLAZES ARE YOU PEOPLE?

AH... I WONDER IF YOU'D MIND TELLING US WHO YOU ARE FIRST? WE WERE ON A ...AH... SECURITY FLIGHT.
SECURITY? OKAY, WE'RE FROM THE SENECA ARMY DEPOT. WE'RE ALL CLEARED FOR SECURITY LEVEL 3B.

SENECA? THEN... THANK HEAVENS! THIS IS THE UNITED STATES!
I'M SORRY TO HAVE BEEN SO SECRETIVE, MEN! I'M REED RICHARDS, AND...
REED RICHARDS? THE BIG SHOT SCIENTIST FROM CALI-FORNIA? AIN'T YOU THE GUY WITH THE PRIVATE ROCKET BASE THAT MAKES CAPE CANAVERAL LOOK SICK?

THAT'S HIM, BRIGHT BOY. NOW LET'S STOW THE YAPPIN' AN GET OUTTA HERE.
HOLY.
IT'S SOME KINDA MONSTER! I READ ABOUT THINGS LIKE THAT...
BUT I AIN'T NEVER SEEN ONE...
WELL TAKE A GOOD LOOK, SOLDIER BOY! IT'LL BE SOMETHIN' TA TELL THE KIDDIES...
THE WORDS ARE ALMOST JOVIAL...
BUT SOMETHING BURNS IN THE SHADED BLUE EYES THAT MAKES ALL THOUGHT OF MIRTH EVAPORATE INTO THE COOL AUTUMN AIR...
SOMETHING THAT BREEDS PANIC.
LATER, OFFICIAL REPORTS OF THE INCIDENT WILL MAKE IT CLEAR THAT NO ONE ACTUALLY GAVE THE ORDER TO FIRE.
BUT THE FIRST SHOT TRIGGERS MANY MORE...
AND BEN GRIMM LEARNS HE HAS GAINED MORE THAN STRENGTH FROM HIS TRANSFORMATION...
WHADDAYA KNOW. I HARDLY EVEN FELT THEM SLUGS...
BRAAKKT!
BUT YOU BOYS ARE GONNA FEEL THIS!

BEN! NO!
BLAST IT, KEEP YER NOSE OUTTA THIS OR I'LL SNUFF YA LIKE A CRUMMY CANDLE!

BEN! GET A GRIP ON YOURSELF, MAN! THESE ARE AMERICAN SOLDIERS!
OUR SOLDIERS!

WHAT IN TH...
THAT CUTS IT! I'M SCRAMMIN' OUTTA HERE!

THIS IS TOO MUCH LIKE I WOKE UP IN THE MIDDLE OF A HORROR MOVIE!
WHAT'S THE RUSH, BOYS? YOU'RE NOT GOING TO LEAVE A GIRL STRANDED ARE YOU?
HUH? WHERE THE HECK DID YOU COME FROM?

WITH THE APPEARANCE OF THE BEAUTIFUL INVISIBLE GIRL, IT IS AS IF A SPELL IS BROKEN.
THE THING ALLOWS HIMSELF TO BE CALMED. THE SOLDIERS ACCEPT REED RICHARDS' PROMISE THAT HIS FRIEND WILL BEHAVE.

FEELING MUCH LIKE A CHILD WHO HAS RECEIVED A PARENTAL SCOLDING, BEN GRIMM CLIMBS INTO THE WAITING CHOPPER.
NO ONE FAILS TO NOTICE THE PONTOON'S CREAK OF PROTEST AS HIS WEIGHT BEARS BRIEFLY DOWN UPON IT.

TANGO ALPHA BRAVO TO CATBIRD SEAT. WE'VE PICKED UP FOUR, REPEAT, FOUR, SURVIVORS OF THE CRASH WE SIGHTED.
AND BOYS... YOU JUST AREN'T GONNA BELIEVE WHAT WE'RE BRINGING HOME.

THE LIGHT WORDS SEEM TO BRUSH AWAY FOR A MOMENT THE ENORMITY OF THE EVENTS OF WHICH THEY SPEAK.
BUT THEY CANNOT BRUSH AWAY THE FEELING THAT GROWS BIGGER AND BLACKER IN BEN GRIMM'S HEART AS HE SEES THE SOLDIERS, SEES EVEN HIS DEAR FRIENDS LEAN UNCONSCIOUSLY AWAY FROM HIM...
...AWAY FROM THE MONSTER HE HAS BECOME.

YEAH, THAT'S HOW IT ALL BEGAN. AN' FER A LONG TIME I THOUGHT MAYBE WE BURIED BEN GRIMM UP ON THAT HILLSIDE.
BURIED THE *MAN*. MAYBE FOREVER.

I MEAN, LOOK AT ALL THE TIMES REED'S COOKED UP SOME POTION, OR GADGET THAT WUZ SUPPOSED TA CURE ME, MAKE ME A MAN AGAIN. AN' EVERY TIME IT'S FAILED.
AN' LATELY...
WELL, LATELY IT SEEMS LIKE HE AIN'T EVEN TRYIN' NO MORE...*
*AN INSIGHT INTO *WHY* CAN BE FOUND IN FF #245--BOB.

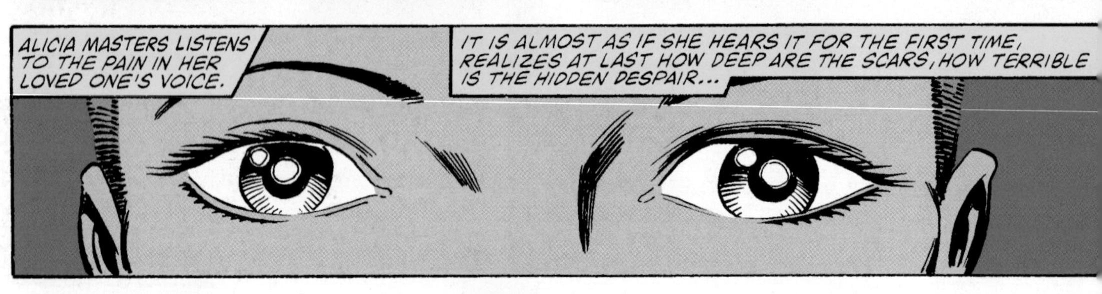
ALICIA MASTERS LISTENS TO THE PAIN IN HER LOVED ONE'S VOICE.
IT IS ALMOST AS IF SHE HEARS IT FOR THE FIRST TIME, REALIZES AT LAST HOW DEEP ARE THE SCARS, HOW TERRIBLE IS THE HIDDEN DESPAIR...

BUT BEFORE SHE CAN OFFER WORDS OF SOLACE OR COMFORT...
BEN! THANK GOODNESS YOU'RE STILL HERE!
HUH? WHAT...?

SOMETHING STRANGE IS HAPPENING, BEN! I DON'T KNOW WHAT, OR HOW, BUT ALL THE INSTRUMENTS JUST SHOT RIGHT OFF THE DIAL.
WHATEVER THAT ENERGY WAS THAT I WAS MONITORING OVER CENTRAL PARK HAS JUST SWITCHED *FULL ON*.
AND IT'S AS IF THE FABRIC OF THE UNIVERSE HAS RIPPED WIDE OPEN.

OKAY, LEADER-MAN. I HEAR YA. SOUNDS LIKE WE GOTTA GO SAVE THE WORLD AGAIN. WHO KNOWS, MAYBE THIS TIME WE'LL EVEN GET A STATUE FER OUR TROUBLES.
IF THAT'S SUPPOSED TO BE FUNNY, BEN, I'M AFRAID I MISS THE JOKE.
THE FANTASTICAR IS ALL WARMED UP. SUE IS TOO FAR ALONG TO GO ON THIS MISSION, SO SHE'LL STAY WITH ALICIA.

YEAH, SURE. TAKE CARE, BABY. I'LL... SEE YA...
THE BLIND SCULPTRESS DOES NOT HAVE TO SEE BEN GRIMM'S PAINED EXPRESSION TO HEAR THE HOLLOWNESS IN HIS WORDS.

BOTH MEN FEEL FOR A MOMENT AS IF THEY ARE HOVERING ON THE EDGE OF SOMETHING, SOMETHING WONDERFUL AND TERRIBLE...
SOMETHING THAT THEY SHOULD REACH OUT AND RESTRAIN, STOP IT FROM BLUNDERING ON TO ITS INEVITABLE CONCLUSION...

AND THEN THE MOMENT, LIKE THE MEN, IS GONE...
ALICIA...
ARE YOU ALL RIGHT, DEAR? BEN SOUNDED SO... SO...
I'M ALL RIGHT, SUSAN. THANK YOU FOR YOUR CONCERN...

BEN AND I HAVE BEEN... TALKING THINGS OVER.
WE HAVE... AGREED THAT A TIME HAS COME FOR A CHANGE IN OUR RELATIONSHIP. IT ONLY REMAINS TO BE DECIDED THE EXACT NATURE OF THE CHANGE.
A... CHANGE...?

IT'S SO HARD TO READ HER FACE, HER EYES. HOW MUCH WE DEPEND UPON THE SUBTLE SIGNALS OF THE FACE, SIGNALS A BLIND PERSON DOES NOT HAVE.

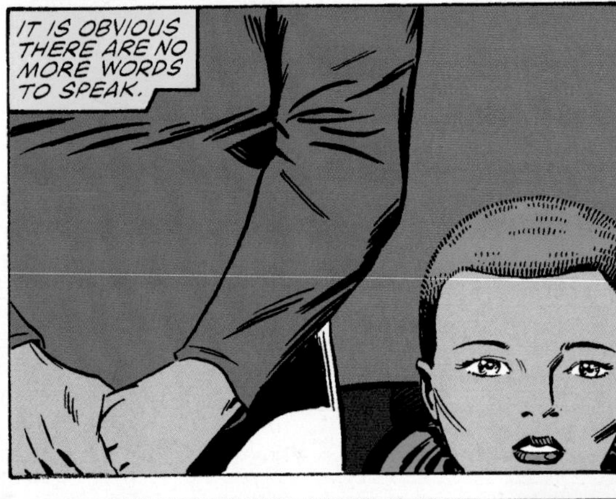
IT IS OBVIOUS THERE ARE NO MORE WORDS TO SPEAK.

SUSAN STORM RICHARDS FEELS A CHILL PASS THROUGH THE ROOM, REACHING OUT FROM SOME HIDDEN PLACE TO TOUCH HER, TO TOUCH THE UNBORN CHILD SHE CARRIES.

AS SHE WATCHES THE THREE MOST IMPORTANT MEN IN HER LIFE FLY OVER THE NEW YORK SKYLINE-- THE TORCH, HER BROTHER, ZOOMING UP TO JOIN THE HURTLING FANTASTICAR-- SHE KNOWS THAT A THRESHHOLD IS ABOUT TO BE CROSSED.
AND SHE KNOWS, TOO, THAT FROM THIS MOMENT FORWARD THINGS WILL NEVER BE QUITE THE SAME...

AND EVEN AS THAT THOUGHT CROSSES SUSAN'S MIND THE FANTASTICAR CROSSES THE SKYSCRAPING TOWERS OF MANHATTAN, DUE SOUTH OF CENTRAL PARK.
HOW ABOUT AN EXPLANATION, FEARLESS LEADER? I SAW THE EMERGENCY FLARE, BUT I DON'T SEE ANY SIGN OF ANYTHING I'D CALL AN EMERGENCY.
IF MY READINGS WERE CORRECT, JOHNNY, YOU SHOULD SEE SOMETHING ALL TOO SOON.
YEAH, HOTSHOT, TH' BIG BRAIN SAYS THE END OF THE WORLD'S ABOUT TA CRANK ITSELF UP, RIGHT IN TH' MIDDLE OF CENTRAL PARK.
HARDLY THE END OF THE WORLD, BEN. AT LEAST I HOPE NOTHING SO DRASTIC. BUT CLEARLY A FORCE, OR FORCES, UNLIKE ANY WE'VE EVER ENCOUNTERED.
BOY, REED, I'VE HEARD YOU DO YOUR DOOM AND GLOOM VOICE A WHOLE LOT OF TIMES, BUT THIS TIME YOU REALLY SOUND LIKE YOU MEAN IT.
I ALWAYS MEAN IT, LAD. IN A... "JOB" LIKE OURS WE CAN NEVER AFFORD TO OVERLOOK THE... WAIT A MINUTE.
THERE!
HOLY COW! IT LOOKS LIKE THE SETTING SUN... BUT THAT'S NORTH!
LOOKS A HECKUVA LOT BRIGHTER THAN THAT TA ME, KID. WHAT'RE WE GETTIN' INTO THIS TIME, REED?

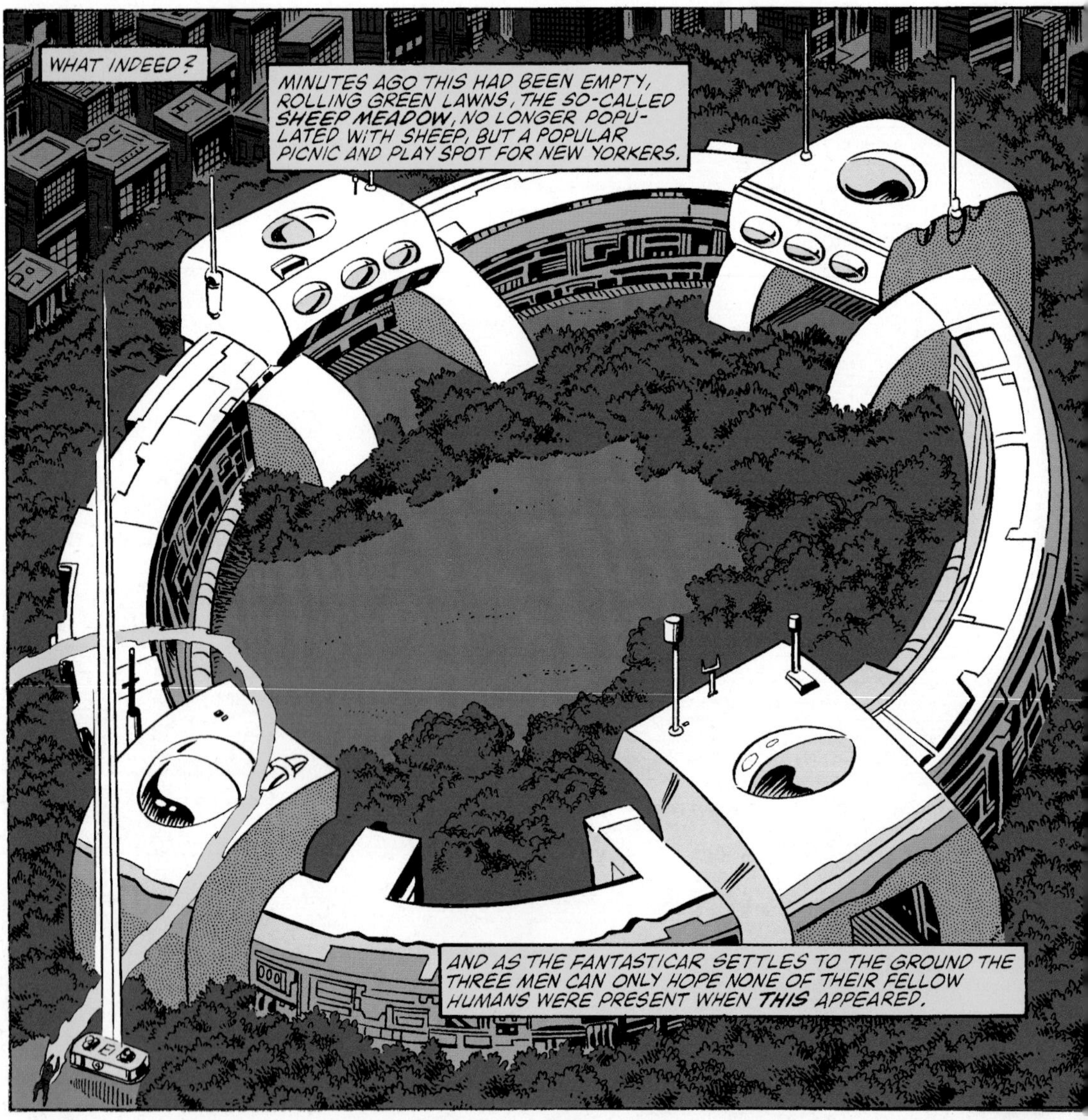

WHAT INDEED?

MINUTES AGO THIS HAD BEEN EMPTY, ROLLING GREEN LAWNS, THE SO-CALLED **SHEEP MEADOW**, NO LONGER POPULATED WITH SHEEP, BUT A POPULAR PICNIC AND PLAY SPOT FOR NEW YORKERS.

AND AS THE FANTASTICAR SETTLES TO THE GROUND THE THREE MEN CAN ONLY HOPE NONE OF THEIR FELLOW HUMANS WERE PRESENT WHEN **THIS** APPEARED.

REED... WHAT...?
SAVE YOUR QUESTIONS, JOHNNY. I HAVE NO ANSWER.

WELL, MARK THIS ONE ON YER CALENDER. THE BIG BRAIN STUCK FER WORDS.
THIS IS NOT TIME FOR YOUR PECULIAR BRAND OF MIRTH, BEN. MY INSTRUMENTS SHOW A PHENOMENAL AMOUNT OF RAW ENERGY RADIATING ABOUT THIS CONSTRUCT...
YET IT SEEMS UTTERLY BENIGN. IT IS HAVING NO EFFECT WHATSOEVER ON THE GRASS, THE TREES... OR US.
HEY... IS IT MY IMAGINATION OR DOES THIS THING SEEM BIGGER ON THE INSIDE THAN THE OUTSIDE?

YEAH... AND IT SEEMS... I DON'T KNOW QUITE HOW TO SAY IT...
NICER?
I GUESS THAT'S THE ONLY WORD. IT'S... *NICER* IN HERE.
THE AIR IS DEFINITELY CLEANER. AND THERE SEEMS TO BE SOME KIND OF... SOOTHING EFFECT. ALMOST LIKE A PSIONIC TRANQUILIZER.
YEAH, IT'S REAL NICE AND PEACEFUL AND SWEET AND CLEAN...

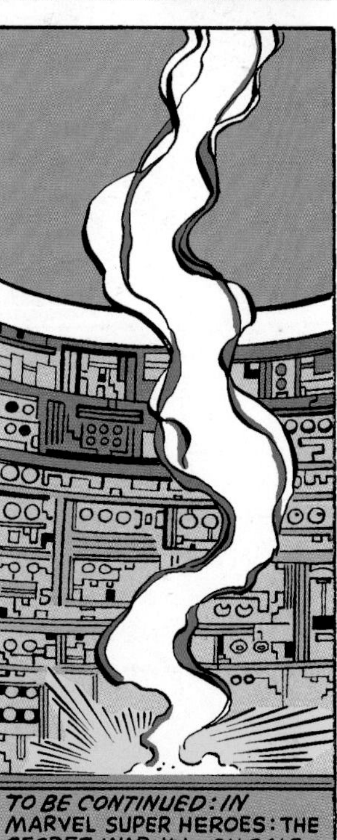

TO BE CONTINUED: IN MARVEL SUPER HEROES: THE SECRET WAR #1, *ON SALE NEXT MONTH. DON'T MISS* THING #11 *FOR THE BEGINNINGS OF THE STRANGEST ADVENTURE OUR HERO HAS EVER HAD! WE MEAN IT, TRUE BELIEVERS!!*

fantastic four # 265

APRIL 1984

Stan Lee PRESENTS:
THE HOUSE THAT REED BUILT
LOOK AT IT! DON'T IT SEEM ALL COZY AN' UNSUSPECTIN'...?
IT'S GONNA BE SO EASY TA DESTROY THEM.
JOHN BYRNE, EVERYTHING EXCEPT... LETTERING BY MIKE HIGGINS • COLORING BY GLYNIS WEIN
EDITING: BOB BUDIANSKY BUILDING: JIM SHOOTER

SO FAR, SO GOOD. I DON'T HEAR NO ALARMS GOING OFF.
PROBABLY WOULDN'T FROM HERE. THEY GOT TH' PLACE REAL WELL SOUND-PROOFED.
WIND DIRECTION'S CHANGIN'. THIS IS GONNA BE THE TRICKY PART.
THEM TALL BUILDIN'S ALL 'ROUND MAKE FOR SOME MEAN UPDRAFTS.
GOTTA BRING MYSELF AROUND. GOTTA COME IN FROM THE WEST.
ACCORDIN' T'THE WIZARD THAT'S THEIR MOST VULNERABLE SIDE.
4
AT LEAST, THAT'S THE SIDE I CLIMBED THAT TIME I WUZ POSIN' AS SPIDER-MAN.
GOOD, ACCORDIN' T'THIS SCANNER I'VE BEEN DETECTED...
...BUT NOT IDENTIFIED AS AN ATTACKER.
YET...
OKAY, LET'S SEE WHAT HAPPENS WHEN I LAND...
THREE SECONDS TO CONTACT...
2

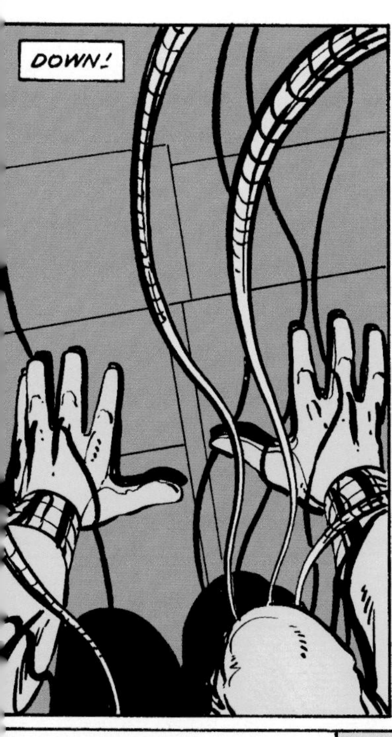
DOWN!

NOW, GOTTA EIGHTY-SIX THESE BALLOONS BEFORE SOME PASSIN' SUPER-DO-GOODER SEES 'EM AN' COMES TO INVESTIGATE.

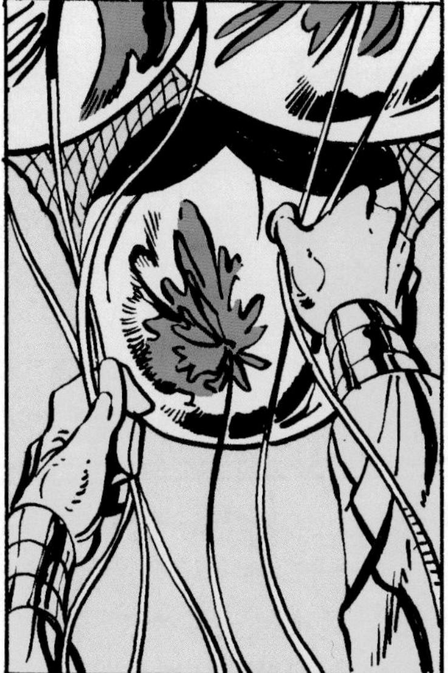

THERE, NOW...
WHASSAT?
BLAST, SOME KINDA SECURITY EYE-BALL, I BET. MUST BE NEW. WASN'T HERE LAST TIME.

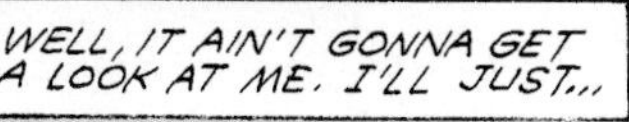
WELL, IT AIN'T GONNA GET A LOOK AT ME. I'LL JUST...

HEY, ANOTHER ONE!

AN' ANOTHER! BUT MY PASTE-GUN CAN IMMOBILIZE AN' CLOG 'EM ALL.

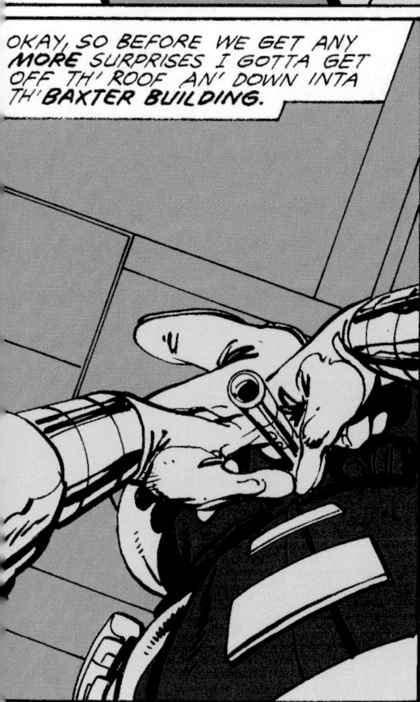
OKAY, SO BEFORE WE GET ANY MORE SURPRISES I GOTTA GET OFF TH' ROOF AN' DOWN INTA TH' BAXTER BUILDING.

LET'S JUST SEE IF THIS OL' MULTI-PHASE ELECTRONIC SKELETON KEY STILL WORKS.
FWEEEEP

BINGO!
SHUNK!
3.

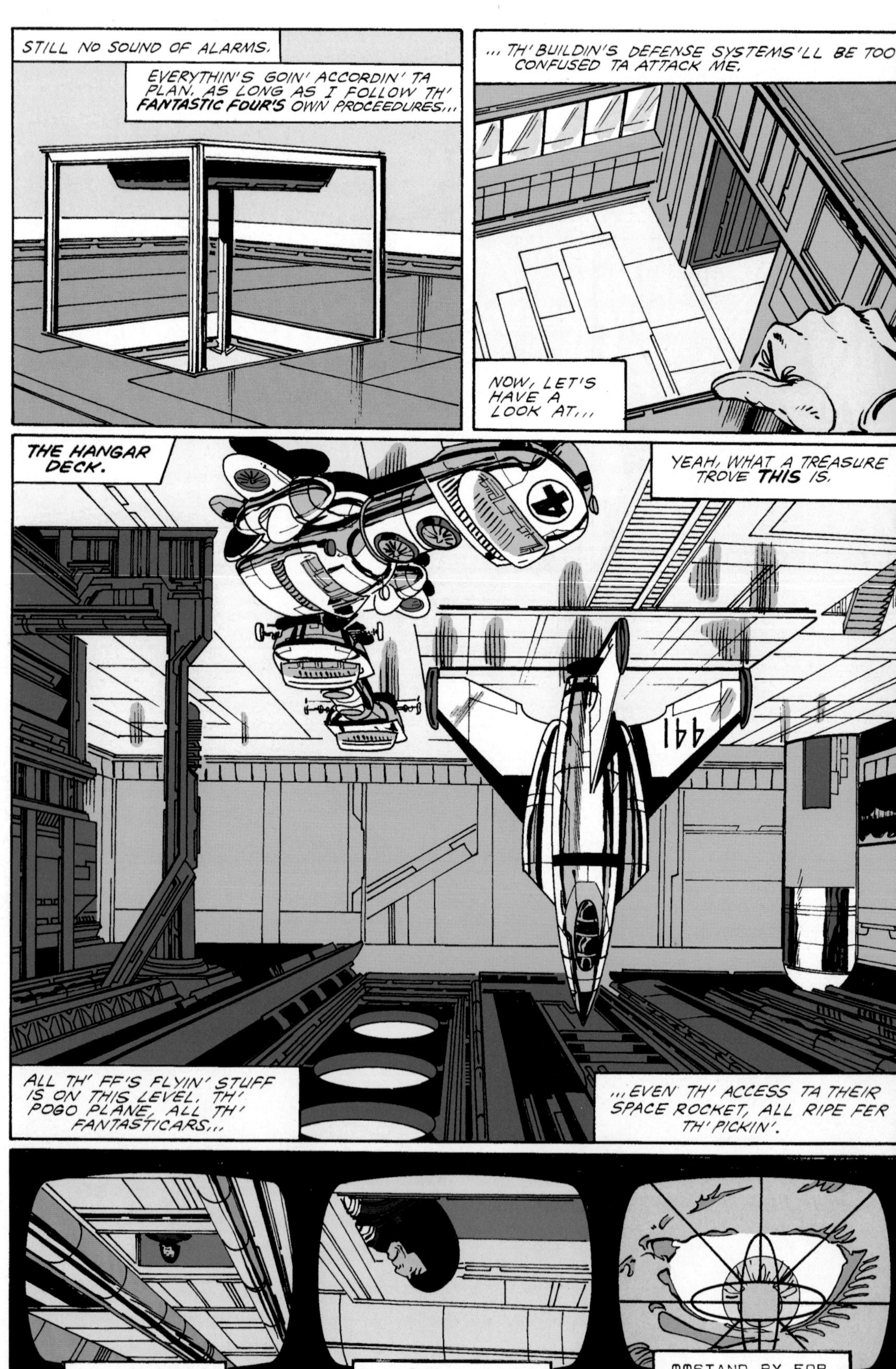
STILL NO SOUND OF ALARMS.
EVERYTHIN'S GOIN' ACCORDIN' TA PLAN, AS LONG AS I FOLLOW TH' **FANTASTIC FOUR'S** OWN PROCEEDURES...
...TH' BUILDIN'S DEFENSE SYSTEMS'LL BE TOO CONFUSED TA ATTACK ME.
NOW, LET'S HAVE A LOOK AT...
THE HANGAR DECK.
YEAH, WHAT A TREASURE TROVE **THIS** IS.
4
441
ALL TH' FF'S FLYIN' STUFF IS ON THIS LEVEL. TH' POGO PLANE, ALL TH' FANTASTICARS...
...EVEN TH' ACCESS TA THEIR SPACE ROCKET, ALL RIPE FER TH' PICKIN'.
ⅢINTRUDERⅢ
ⅢHANGAR DECKⅢ
ⅢSTAND BY FOR RETINA SCANⅢ

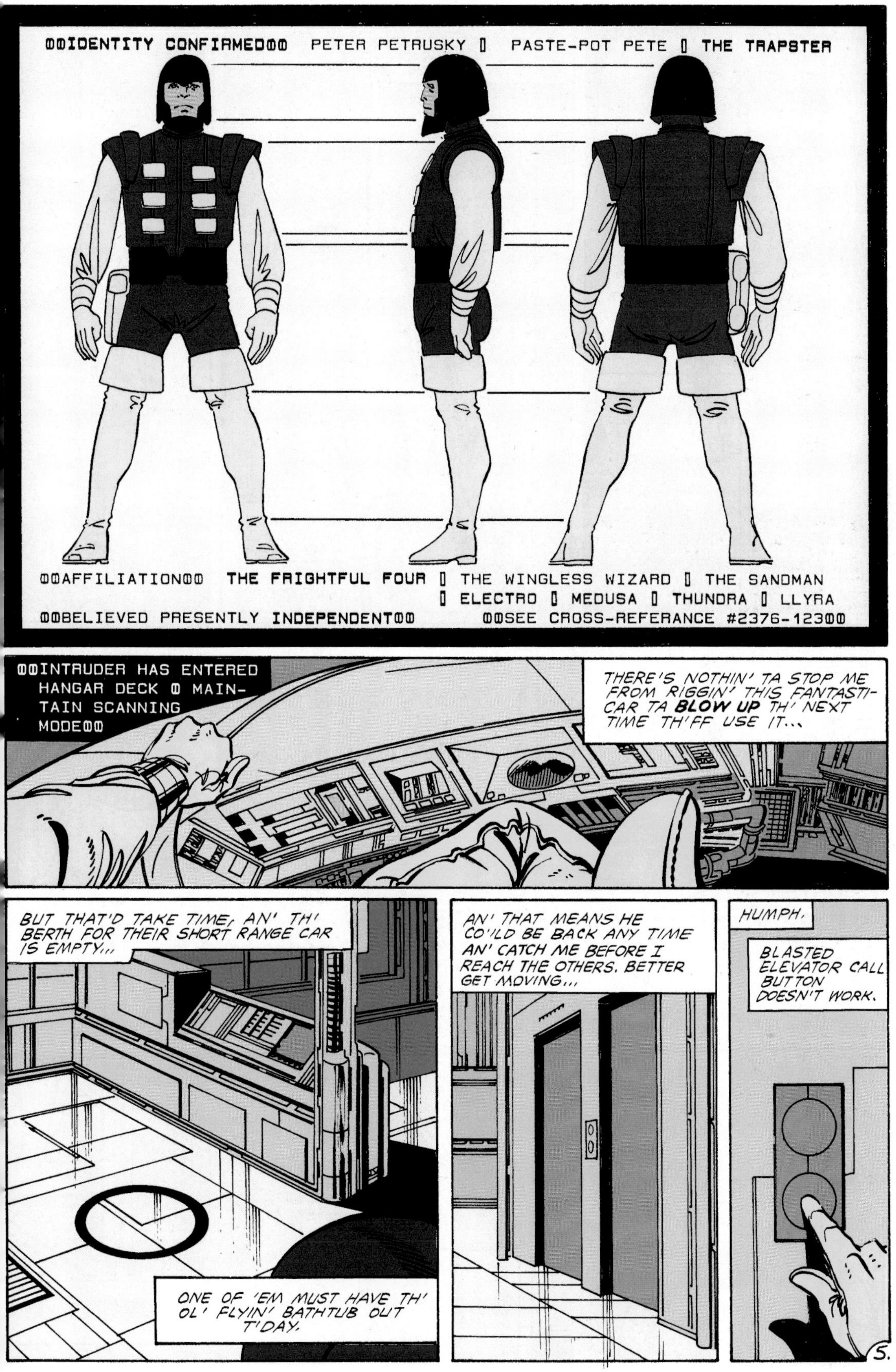

▯▯IDENTITY CONFIRMED▯▯ PETER PETRUSKY ▯ PASTE-POT PETE ▯ **THE TRAPSTER**

▯▯AFFILIATION▯▯ **THE FRIGHTFUL FOUR** ▯ THE WINGLESS WIZARD ▯ THE SANDMAN ▯ ELECTRO ▯ MEDUSA ▯ THUNDRA ▯ LLYRA

▯▯BELIEVED PRESENTLY **INDEPENDENT**▯▯ ▯▯SEE CROSS-REFERANCE #2376-123▯▯

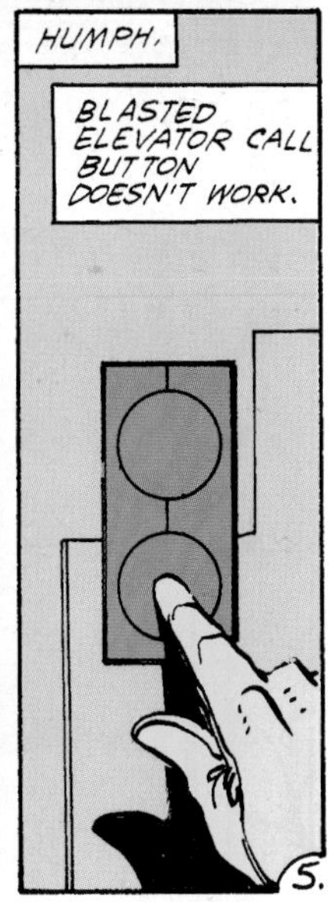

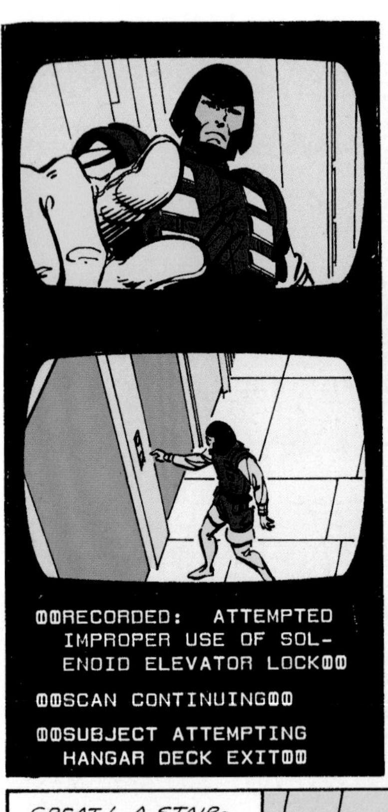
◘◘RECORDED: ATTEMPTED IMPROPER USE OF SOL-ENOID ELEVATOR LOCK◘◘
◘◘SCAN CONTINUING◘◘
◘◘SUBJECT ATTEMPTING HANGAR DECK EXIT◘◘

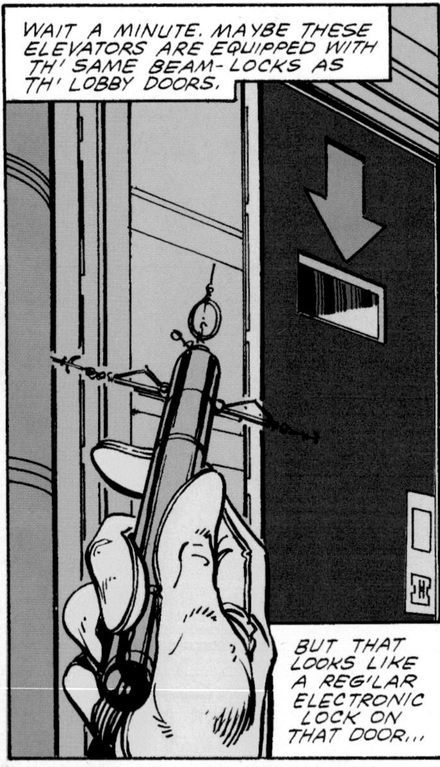
WAIT A MINUTE. MAYBE THESE ELEVATORS ARE EQUIPPED WITH TH' SAME BEAM-LOCKS AS TH' LOBBY DOORS.
BUT THAT LOOKS LIKE A REG'LAR ELECTRONIC LOCK ON THAT DOOR...

I WUZ RIGHT.

GREAT! A STAIR-WELL. I FIGGERED THERE'D BE SOME OTHER WAY BE-TWEEN FLOORS IN CASE TH' POWER FAILED.

NOW, IF I REMEMBER RIGHT, THE NEXT LEVEL DOWN SHOULD BE TH' ASTRO-SCIENCE...
WHO'S THAT?!?
AW...CRUD! THIS PLACE IS STARTIN' TA SPOOK ME.
I'LL BE JUMPIN' AT MY OWN SHADOW NEXT.

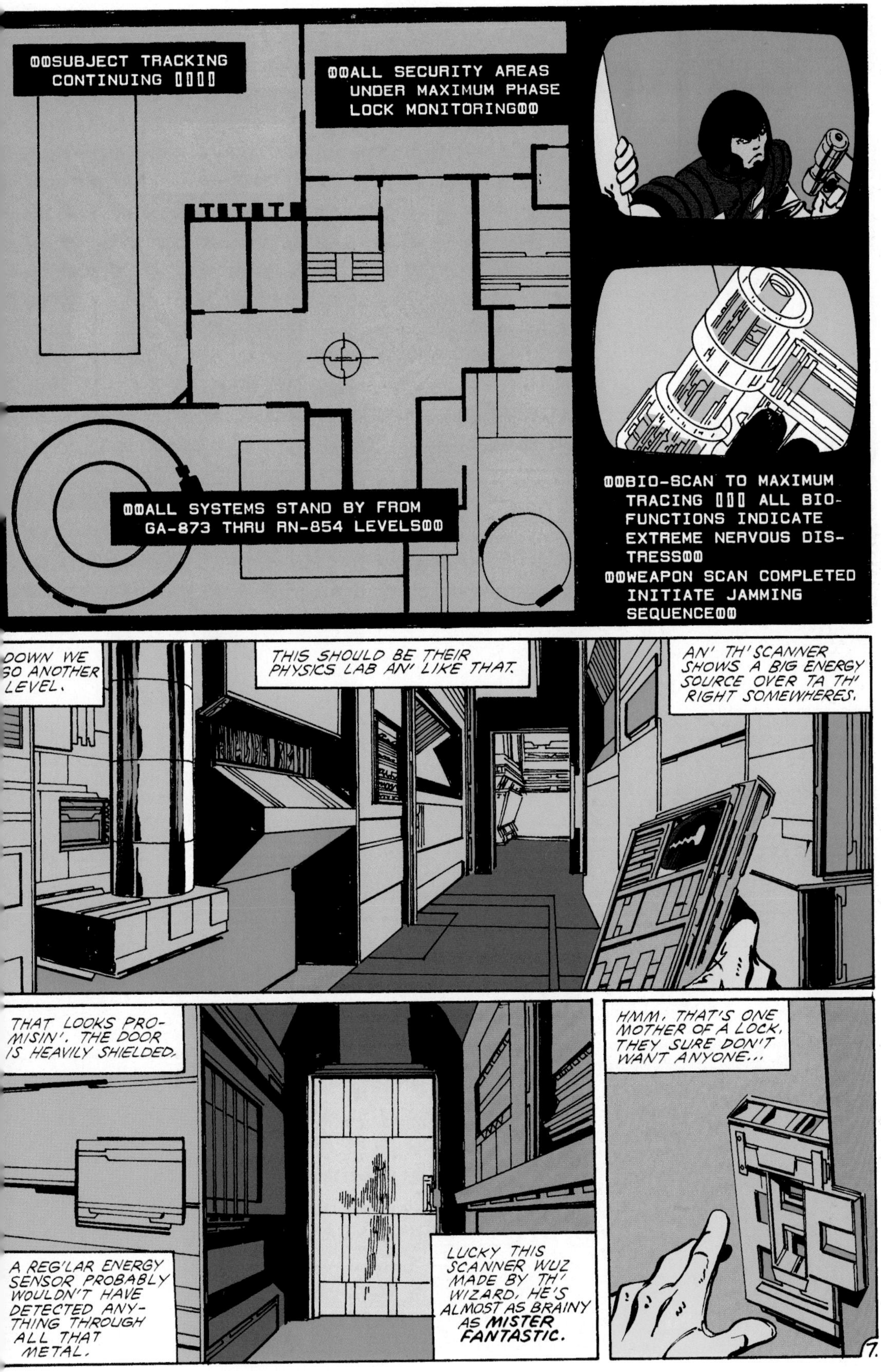

SUBJECT TRACKING CONTINUING

ALL SECURITY AREAS UNDER MAXIMUM PHASE LOCK MONITORING

ALL SYSTEMS STAND BY FROM GA-873 THRU RN-854 LEVELS

BIO-SCAN TO MAXIMUM TRACING ALL BIO-FUNCTIONS INDICATE EXTREME NERVOUS DISTRESS

WEAPON SCAN COMPLETED INITIATE JAMMING SEQUENCE

DOWN WE GO ANOTHER LEVEL.
THIS SHOULD BE THEIR PHYSICS LAB AN' LIKE THAT.
AN' TH' SCANNER SHOWS A BIG ENERGY SOURCE OVER TA TH' RIGHT SOMEWHERES.

THAT LOOKS PROMISIN'. THE DOOR IS HEAVILY SHIELDED.
A REG'LAR ENERGY SENSOR PROBABLY WOULDN'T HAVE DETECTED ANYTHING THROUGH ALL THAT METAL.
LUCKY THIS SCANNER WUZ MADE BY TH' WIZARD. HE'S ALMOST AS BRAINY AS MISTER FANTASTIC.

HMM. THAT'S ONE MOTHER OF A LOCK. THEY SURE DON'T WANT ANYONE...
7.

YEOW!

BLAST! SOME KINDA ELECTRO-SHOCK DEFENSE SYSTEM. TH' SCANNER DIDN'T PICK IT UP.
BUT I CAN FIX IT REAL QUICK WITH MY PASTE-GUN...

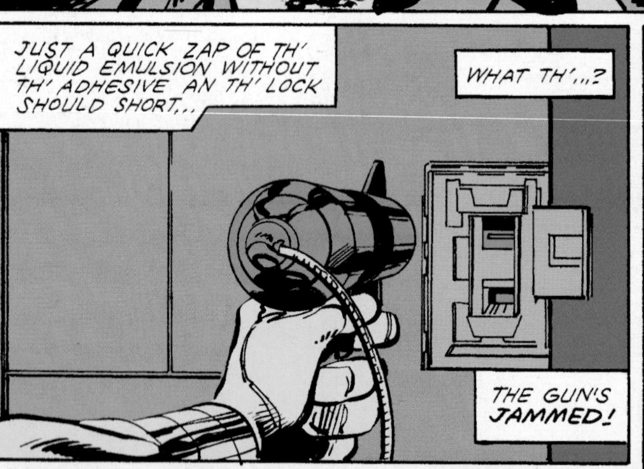
JUST A QUICK ZAP OF TH' LIQUID EMULSION WITHOUT TH' ADHESIVE AN TH' LOCK SHOULD SHORT...
WHAT TH'...?
THE GUN'S JAMMED!

CONFIRMATION OF WEAPON DEACT-IVATION SCAN CONTINUING
SUBJECT PROCEEDING TO STAIRS
SWITCHING TO LATERAL SCAN

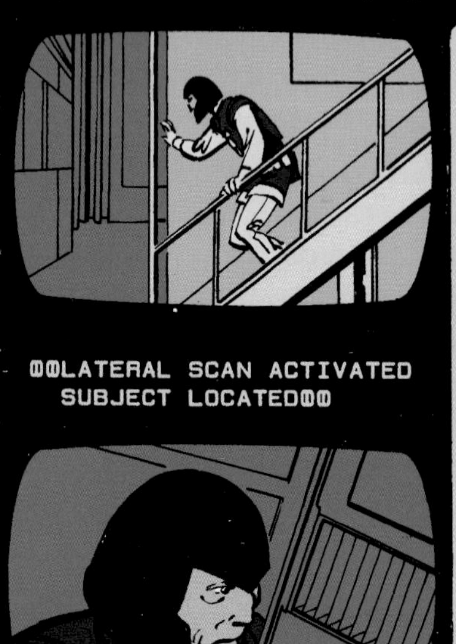
LATERAL SCAN ACTIVATED SUBJECT LOCATED

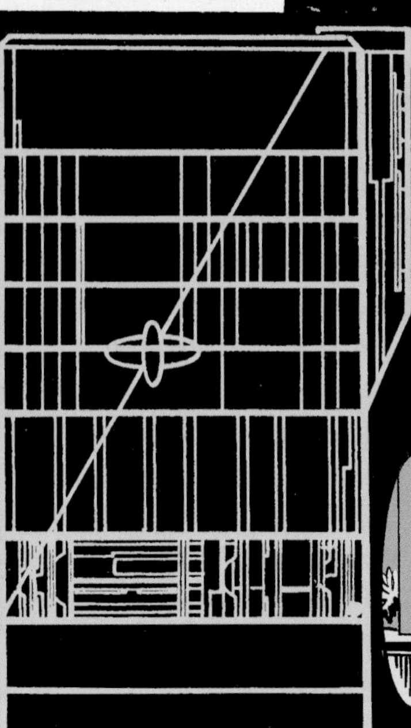
SUBJECT APPROACHING RESIDENTIAL LEVEL
DEFENSE ALERT TO ALL FIRST LEVEL SYSTEMS
DEFEN-MODE KL8-0037 SCAN FOR SUBJECT'S PRIME VULNERABILITIES AND COMMENCE CAPTURE SEQUENCE

WHERE TH' HECK IS EVERYBODY?
THE WHOLE BLASTED TOWER COMPLEX IS **DESERTED!**
IT AIN'T **FAIR!** I CAME TA PROVE I'M NOT TH' **LOSER** EVERY-ONE THINKS I AM...
...TA PROVE I COULD BEAT TH' **FF** WITHOUT TH' REST OF TH' **FRIGHTFUL FOUR.**
MEEP!

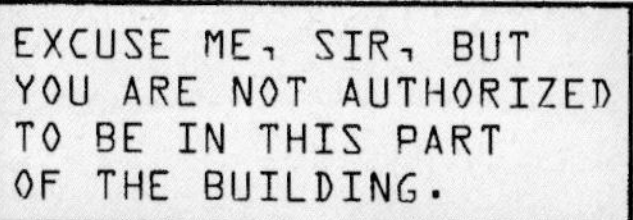
EXCUSE ME, SIR, BUT YOU ARE NOT AUTHORIZED TO BE IN THIS PART OF THE BUILDING.

HOLY!
A FLYIN' ROBOT!

I KNEW IT WAS TOO GOOD TO BE TRUE!
TH' SECURITY SYSTEM MUSTA BIN TRACKIN' ME ALL ALONG.

H.U.B.E.R.T. TO CENTRAL...
SUBJECT IS FLEEING. SHALL I DETAIN HIM?

NEGATIVE

SUBJECT IS ABOUT

TO DETAIN HIMSELF
9.

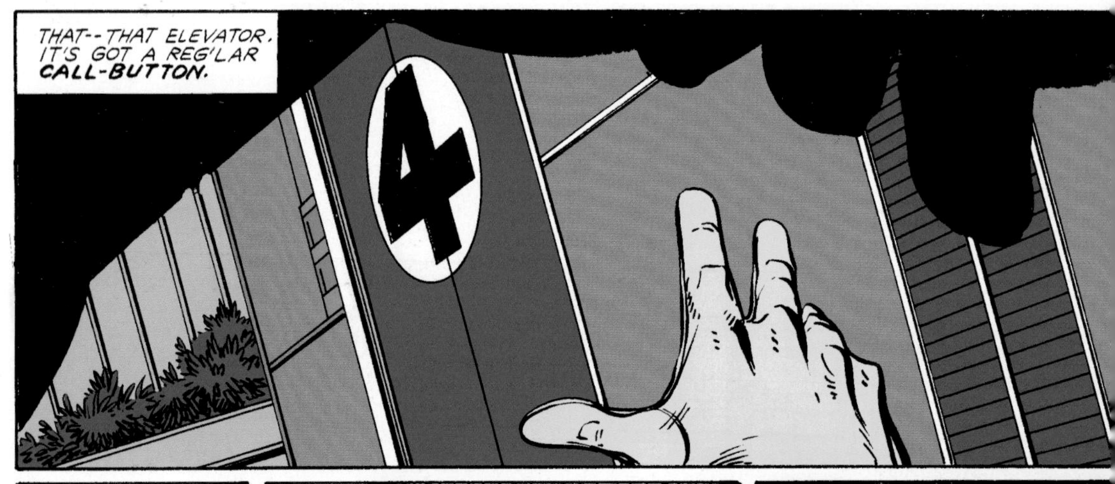
THAT--THAT ELEVATOR. IT'S GOT A REG'LAR **CALL-BUTTON.**
4

OF COURSE! THIS IS THE VISITOR RECEPTION LEVEL.

THE ELEVATOR WOULD BE DE-SIGNED TO LET ANYONE IN AND OUT ONCE THEY'D BEEN PASSED THIS FAR BY SECURITY.

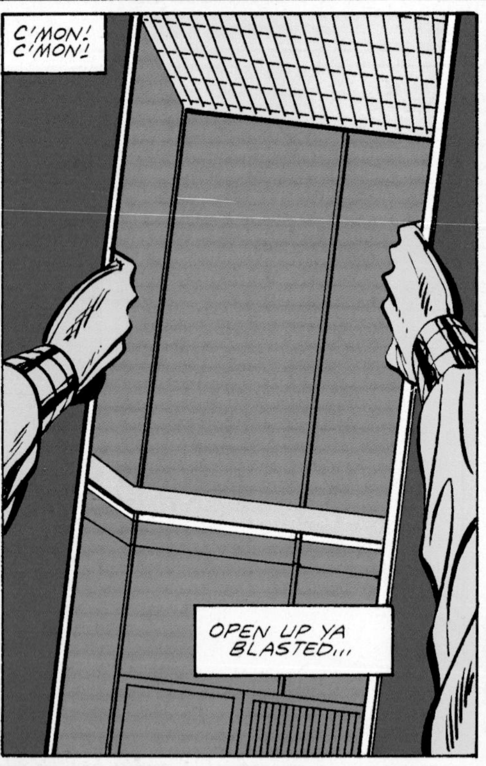
C'MON! C'MON!
OPEN UP YA BLASTED...

SUBJECT LEAVING MAX-SECUR-AREA
TOWER SYSTEMS STEP DOWN TO YELLOW ALERT

OH... HOW DID **YOU** GET INTO THE TOWER?
A RECEPTIONIST!

I CAN USE HER AS A **HOSTAGE** IN CASE THERE ARE ANY MORE TRICKS AHEAD.
OKAY, BABE. NO TROUBLE. YOU'RE COMIN' WITH ME.
OH, NO, SIR. I'M AFRAID THAT WOULD BE QUITE...

IMPOSSIBLE.

UNGH!!

POLICE?
SERGEANT QUINLAN, PLEASE.
N-NO... NO... IT AIN'T POSSIBLE.
I'M TH' **TRAPSTER!**

I CAN'T GET BEAT BY AN EMPTY BUILDING...
AN' A... A...
G... IRL...

HELLO, SERGEANT, THIS IS ROBERTA AT THE BAXTER BUILDING.
I'M SORRY TO DISTURB YOU DURING LUNCH, BUT WE HAVE A PICK-UP FOR YOU. YES, THE TRAPSTER. OH, NO, HE IS QUITE SUBDUED.
WE WERE ABLE TO DEAL WITH HIM EASILY!
11.

HOME ARE THE HEROES
MRS. RICHARDS! PLEASE!!
AVENGERS MANSION, EAST OF CENTRAL PARK, NEW YORK. A LONG AND EMOTIONALLY DRAINING WEEK IS DRAWING TO A CLOSE...
12.

OH-- HELLO, JARVIS, SORRY TO INVADE YOUR SANCTUM SANCTORUM, BUT I CAUGHT A WHIFF OF THESE YUMMY COOKING AROMAS...
... AND, WELL, I'M AFRAID MY CURIOSITY JUST GOT THE BETTER OF ME.
I APPRECIATE THE COMPLIMENT IMPLIED, MRS. RICHARDS...

... BUT THIS PARTICULAR DISH IS TERRIBLY FINICKY, AND TEMPERATURES MUST BE PRECISELY MAINTAINED.
THERE! I THINK THAT SHOULD COMPENSATE FOR THE HEAT LOSS.

I'LL... ER... JUST LEAVE IT TO YOU, THEN, SHALL I, JARVIS?
SORRY AGAIN.
OH, THAT'S ALL RIGHT, MA'AM.
I EXPECT WE'VE ALL BEEN... A LITTLE TENSE THE LAST FEW DAYS.
PLEASE DON'T GIVE IT ANOTHER THOUGHT.

"A LITTLE TENSE". JARVIS HAS A WONDERFULLY BRITISH TURN FOR UNDER-STATEMENT.
WHO WOULDN'T BE TENSE AFTER WHAT'S HAP-PENED?

"I'VE FELT SO HELP-LESS SINCE I WATCHED REED, BEN AND JOHNNY FLY OFF TOWARDS CENTRAL PARK.
"REED'S EQUIP-MENT HAD MONITORED A STRANGE FLUCTUATION OF ENERGY...

"THEY'D BARELY HAD TIME TO REACH THE SOURCE OF THAT DISTURBANCE WHEN...
THAT LIGHT!!!
13

S-SUSAN... THAT LIGHT... WHAT...?
ALICIA... YOU SAW IT, TOO? BUT YOU'RE... BLIND!!

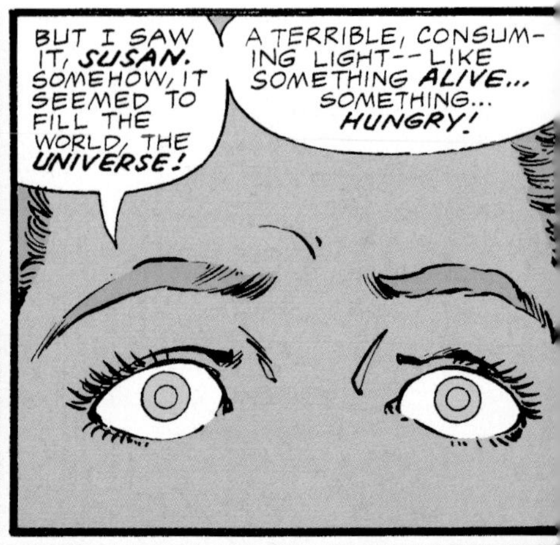
BUT I SAW IT, SUSAN. SOMEHOW, IT SEEMED TO FILL THE WORLD, THE UNIVERSE!
A TERRIBLE, CONSUMING LIGHT--LIKE SOMETHING ALIVE... SOMETHING... HUNGRY!

INCREDIBLE. IF SHE WAS SOMEHOW ABLE TO "SEE" THAT LIGHT IT MUST HAVE BEEN RADIATING ON UNIMAGINABLE WAVELENGTHS.
ALICIA, FRANKLIN IS ASLEEP IN JOHNNY'S OLD ROOM. WOULD YOU...?
SUSAN, NO! DON'T LEAVE US HERE ALONE...
...NOT AGAIN!

BLAST! I SHOULD HAVE REALIZED SHE'D BE TERRIFIED OF STAYING HERE BY HERSELF. THE LAST TIME SHE WAS NEARLY KILLED BY ANNIHILUS.*
ALL RIGHT, ALICIA. GIVE ME YOUR HAND.
*SEE ISSUE #'S 251-256.--Bob.

WHAT A STRANGE TRIO WE MUST HAVE MADE, ZOOMING AWAY FROM THE BAXTER BUILDING IN ANOTHER OF OUR FANTASTICARS.
AN EXPECTANT MOTHER, A BLIND WOMAN AND A RUDELY AWAKENED FIVE-YEAR-OLD BOY.
4

THERE'S THE SHEEP MEADOW AHEAD... AND THERE'S SOME RESIDUAL RADIANCE.
THAT MUST BE WHERE THE LIGHT CAME FROM.
14

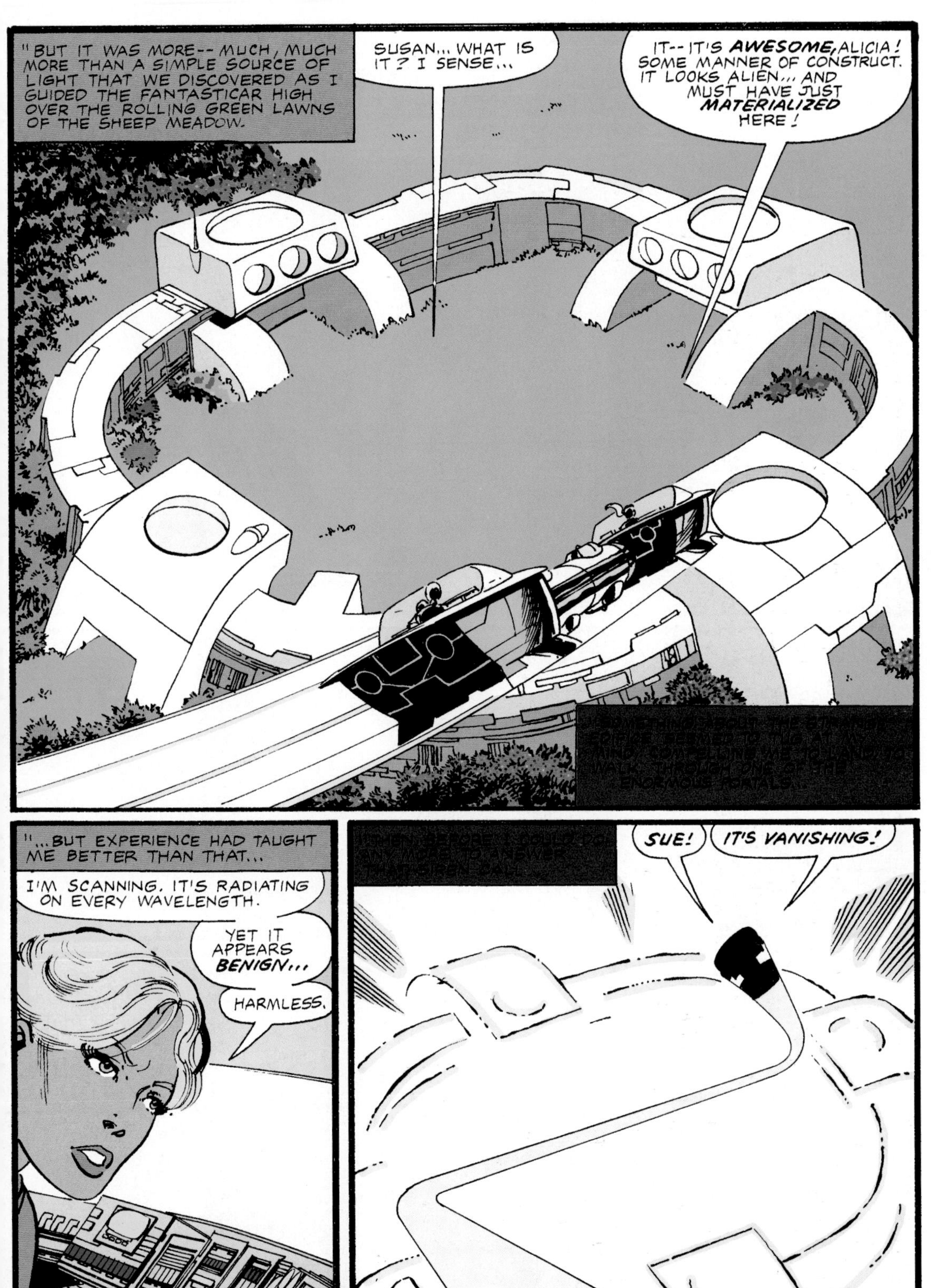
"BUT IT WAS MORE-- MUCH, MUCH MORE THAN A SIMPLE SOURCE OF LIGHT THAT WE DISCOVERED AS I GUIDED THE FANTASTICAR HIGH OVER THE ROLLING GREEN LAWNS OF THE SHEEP MEADOW.
SUSAN... WHAT IS IT? I SENSE...
IT-- IT'S AWESOME, ALICIA! SOME MANNER OF CONSTRUCT. IT LOOKS ALIEN... AND MUST HAVE JUST MATERIALIZED HERE!
SOMETHING ABOUT THE STRANGE EDIFICE SEEMED TO TUG AT MY MIND, COMPELLING ME TO LAND, TO WALK THROUGH ONE OF THE ENORMOUS PORTALS...
"...BUT EXPERIENCE HAD TAUGHT ME BETTER THAN THAT...
I'M SCANNING. IT'S RADIATING ON EVERY WAVELENGTH.
YET IT APPEARS BENIGN...
HARMLESS.
THEN BEFORE I COULD DO ANY MORE TO ANSWER THAT SIREN CALL...
SUE!
IT'S VANISHING!
15.

"I QUICKLY BROUGHT THE FANTASTICAR DOWN A FEW YARDS FROM WHERE THE OUTER PERIMETER OF THE OBJECT HAD BEEN, AND JUST AS QUICKLY DISCOVERED I WAS NOT THE ONLY ONE WHO HAD COME TO INVESTIGATE...
MOCKINGBIRD, PLEASE! TRY TO KEEP CALM. THE VISION WILL TELL US WHAT HAPPENED TO THE OTHERS AS SOON AS HE'S DONE SCANNING.
KEEP CALM? THAT'S ALL RIGHT FOR YOU TO SAY, WANDA. YOUR HUSBAND DIDN'T JUST VANISH INTO THIN AIR.

WANDA... VISION... STARFOX! ARE THE AVENGERS INVOLVED IN THIS, TOO?
SUE? BUT WHERE ARE THE REST OF THE FANTASTIC FOUR?
OH-- I PRAY THEY HAVE NOT ALSO BEEN... TAKEN?
THE INVISIBLE GIRL!
TAKEN...? WANDA... WHAT ON EARTH DO YOU MEAN?

I SUSPECT NOTHING "ON EARTH", SUSAN. I CAN AT THIS POINT ONLY HAZARD A GUESS, BUT I BELIEVE THAT ARTIFACT WAS SOME KIND OF TRANSPORTING DEVICE.
BUT WHERE IT MIGHT HAVE TRANSPORTED THE REST OF THE AVENGERS I CANNOT SAY.
T-TRANSPORTED. YOU MEAN... REED, BEN, JOHNNY... THEY'VE BEEN...

AS MY WIFE PUT IT... TAKEN. IF MISTER FANTASTIC, THE THING, AND THE HUMAN TORCH INDEED ENTERED THAT OBJECT... THEY ARE NO LONGER ON EARTH.
16

AND THAT'S WHERE IT'S BEEN FOR A WEEK OR SO NOW. WE'VE ALL BEEN ON HOLD, WAITING FOR SOMETHING, ANYTHING TO HAPPEN.
AND WE'VE ALL BEEN DEALING WITH OUR NERVOUS TENSION AS BEST WE CAN. MOCKINGBIRD HAS BEEN TAKING LONGER AND LONGER WALKS. ALICIA, FRANKLIN AND I HAVE STAYED AT THE MANSION TO BE CLOSER TO THE SHEEP MEADOW...
...AND JARVIS HAS BEEN PREPARING MORE ELABORATE MEALS.
SUSAN? ARE YOU READY TO TAKE OUR STROLL?
YEAH, C'MON, MOMMY. YOU PROMISED TO TAKE ME TO RUMPY-MYERS TODAY.
AND A PROMISE MADE IS A DEBT UNPAID, RIGHT, KIDDO? LET'S GO PIG OUT!
FRANKLIN IS SUCH A COMFORT, OF COURSE. I HAVEN'T TOLD HIM HIS FATHER IS MISSING, BUT HIS YOUTHFUL ENTHUSIASM IS LIKE A BREATH OF FRESH AIR.
ALICIA, YOU SEEM... WITHDRAWN TODAY. ARE YOU ALL RIGHT, DEAR?
I'M FINE, THANK YOU, SUSAN. I JUST HAVE A FUNNY SENSATION IN THE BACK OF MY MIND...
AS IF SOMETHING ABSOLUTELY MOMENTOUS IS GOING TO HAPPEN TODAY.
THAT SOUNDS OMINOUS. I WONDER... OH, MOCKINGBIRD. HOW ARE THINGS GOING WITH YOU?
AS WELL AS CAN BE EXPECTED, SUE. I'VE ONLY BEEN A BRIDE FOR FIVE MINUTES. SEEMS A BIT TOO SOON TO BE CONTEMPLATING WIDOWHOOD.
THE VISION KEEPS TELLING ME NOT TO WORRY, THAT MY HUSBAND, HAWKEYE, AND THE REST OF THE AVENGERS HAVE SURVIVED MANY BIZARRE THINGS IN THEIR YEARS TOGETHER.
BUT THAT DOESN'T GET ME PAST THE FACT THAT THIS TIME COULD BE THE LAST. THAT THEY COULD ALL BE...
17.

BEST NOT TO THINK SUCH THINGS, MOCKINGBIRD. IN THE YEARS OF MY RELATIONSHIP WITH THE THING I HAVE LEARNED THE LIFE OF A SUPER HERO IS THAT OF A SOLDIER IN AN UNENDING WAR, AND WE MUST STEEL OURSELVES, AS THOSE LEFT ON THE HOMEFRONT.
BUT I'M A "SUPER HERO" MYSELF, ALICIA. I CAN'T JUST...
OH... TO HECK WITH IT. HAS THE VISION MADE HIS SPEECH TO THE PRESS YET?

JUST STARTING, I THINK. BUT, IF YOU'LL EXCUSE US NOW, MOCKINGBIRD, WE HAVE A SMALL BOY IN NEED OF AN ICE CREAM FIX. AM I RIGHT, SPORT?
YEAH!

THUS, ONE HOUR AND SEVERAL THOUSAND CALORIES LATER, AS NIGHT FALLS...
THE LEAVES ARE TURNING IN CENTRAL PARK, DRAWING THEIR BRIGHT ORANGE CURTAIN OVER THE LAST ACT OF A SPECTACULARLY BEAUTIFUL FALL.

SUDDENLY...
THE LIGHT AGAIN!
BUT... IS IT THE SAME? ALICIA DOESN'T SEEM TO NOTICE IT THIS TIME.

ARE THEY... DO I DARE HOPE... ARE THEY BACK?
ALICIA, WATCH FRANKLIN, PLEASE. I HAVE TO CHECK ON SOMETHING.
SUE?

SHE RACES HEADLONG INTO THE MOTTLED WORLD BENEATH THE TREES, SUDDENLY HEEDLESS OF HER ADVANCED MATERNITY.
AND AS SHE RUNS HER CELLS WARP THE LIGHT AROUND THEM UNTIL...
I HAVEN'T USED MY POWER OF INVISIBILITY IN OVER A MONTH, BUT SOMETHING TELLS ME I'LL NEED IT NOW.

THEN, AS SUSAN REACHES THE EDGE OF THE SHEEP MEADOW...
IRON MAN!
THE FAMILIAR METALLIC FIGURE FLASHES ACROSS THE SKY ALMOST TOO QUICKLY TO BE SEEN.
THEN... THEN THE REST OF THE AVENGERS MUST HAVE RETURNED AS WELL...

YES!
THERE THEY ARE ON THE OTHER SIDE OF THE MEADOW. AND ISN'T THAT SPIDER-MAN NEARBY? AND THE HULK?
AND IF I'M NOT MISTAKEN, SURELY THAT'S THE X-MEN OVER THERE?

BUT... BUT WHERE ARE REED, AND BEN AND JOHNNY? IF THEY WERE TAKEN AT THE SAME TIME...
SURELY THEY MUST RETURN AT THE SAME TIME...?

AGONIZING MOMENTS CLICK BY. IT MIGHT ONLY BE SECONDS, BUT TO SUSAN RICHARDS IT SEEMS CENTURIES.
THEN...
WAIT... ANOTHER NIMBUS OF LIGHT. NEAR THE CENTER OF THE MEADOW?
CAN IT BE?

"IT IS! IT IS!"
"I'D KNOW REED FROM HIS POSTURE ALONE, AND THAT HAS TO BE JOHNNY TO THE LEFT..."
"...BUT WHO IS THAT WITH THEM?"
19.

WA-HOO! WE MADE IT! WE'RE BACK ON EARTH!*
I NEVER THOUGHT I'D EVER BE SO GLAD TO BREATHE NEW YORK AIR AGAIN!
OH MY GOODNESS! IT CAN'T BE! BUT IT IS! SHE-HULK! AND SHE'S WEARING A MODIFIED FF UNIFORM.
WHAT IN THE WORLD...?!?
*IF YOU WANT TO SEE WHERE THEY'VE BEEN, CHECK OUT MARVEL SUPER HEROES: THE SECRET WARS TWELVE-ISSUE MAXI-SERIES, #1 ON SALE NEXT MONTH! --Bob

REALLY NOW, PEOPLE.
I TOLD YOU I'D GET US ALL BACK. SURELY YOU DIDN'T DOUBT ME?
REED!

SUE, DARLING! YOU'RE ALL RIGHT! AND YOU HAVEN'T HAD THE BABY YET. WE MUST NOT HAVE BEEN GONE AS LONG AS IT SEEMED.
OH, REED! JUST THIS ONCE SAVE THE INSTANT ANALYSIS...

AND JUST KISS ME!

JUST THEN...
DADDY! UNCA JOHNNY! MOMMY DIDN'T TELL ME YOU WERE GOING TO BE HERE!
FRANKLIN!

GREAT TA SEE YA, JUNIOR. FOR A WHILE THERE IT LOOKED LIKE WE WOULDN'T GET BACK BEFORE YOUR COLLEGE GRADUATION!
WHO'S THE BIG GREEN LADY, UNCA JOHNNY? SHE'S SO PRETTY!
J-JOHNNY? IS BEN HERE? I DON'T...

OH--ALICIA-- I-I'D GIVE ANYTHING NOT TO HAVE TO TELL YOU THIS, BUT BEN... WELL, HE... HE ISN'T...
BUT BEFORE A STAMMERING JOHNNY STORM CAN FIND THE RIGHT WORDS...
21.

SUE!
ARRGH!

TH-THAT WAS HARD RADIATION! A SUDDEN, ALMOST EXPLOSIVE BURST.
SUE, DARLING, CAN YOU SPEAK? ARE YOU... ARE YOU...?
R-REED...

REED... IT WAS THE BABY!
I FELT IT! I FELT IT MOVE... FELT IT LASH OUT!
H-HELP... ME...

GOT TO GET HER TO A HOSPITAL IMMEDIATELY... EVEN THOUGH I RISK ANOTHER RADIATION BURST...
DON'T BE A FOOL, REED. MY TOLERANCE TO RADIOACTIVITY IS FAR GREATER THAN YOURS...

...AND NO ONE'S GOING TO WASTE MY TIME ASKING FOR FORMS TO BE FILLED OUT. I'LL GET SUE TO A HOSPITAL...
JOHNNY, FLY AHEAD TO MERCY GENERAL. LET 'EM KNOW WE'RE COMING.

ON MY WAY, SHE-HULK!
BUT THAT FLASH OF RADIATION... I'VE NEVER SEEN ANYTHING LIKE IT.
THIS IS NOTHING LIKE THE PROBLEM SUE HAD DELIVERING FRANKLIN!
THIS MAY BE SOMETHING EVEN REED CAN'T DEAL WITH!
DO WE HAVE TO SAY IT? TO BE CONTINUED!!

fantastic four # 266

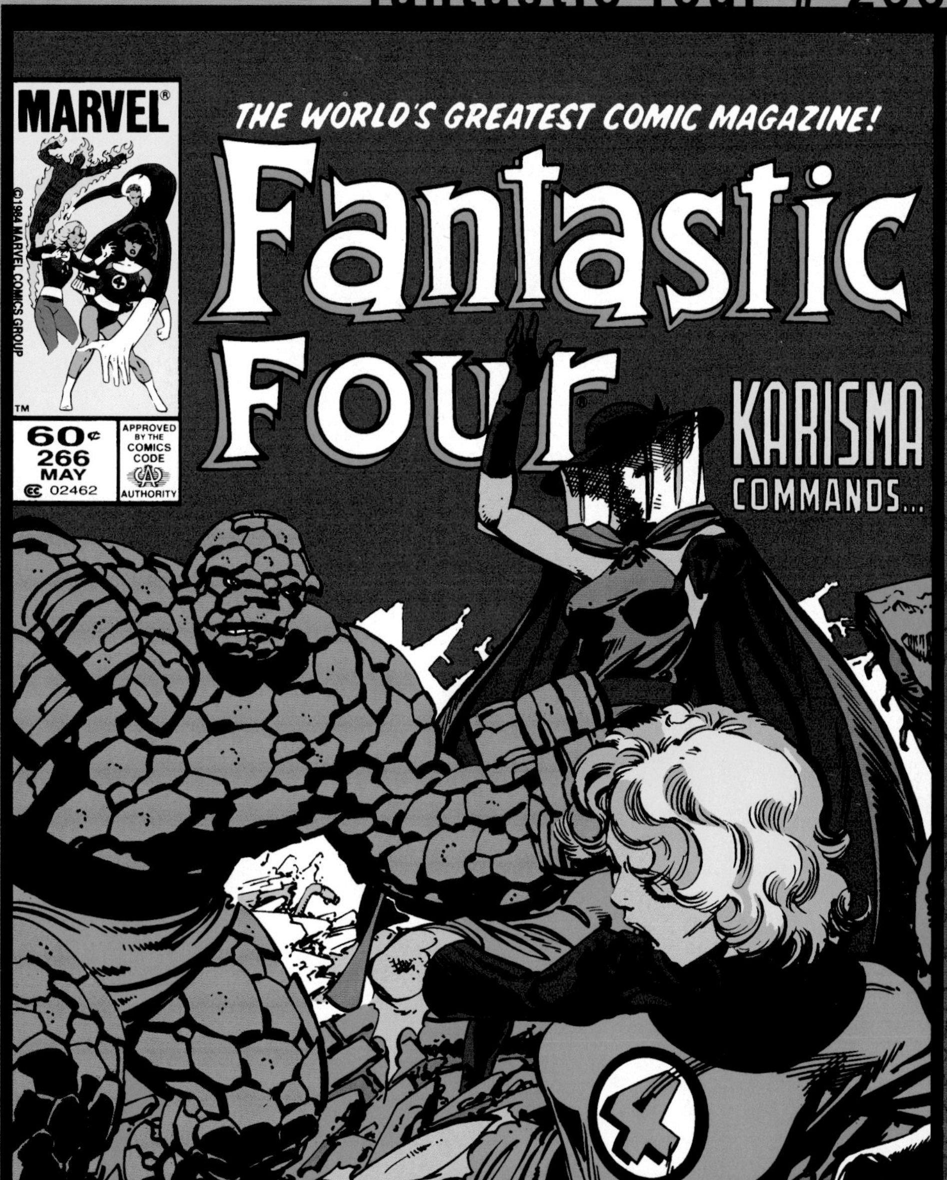

THE WORLD'S GREATEST COMIC MAGAZINE!

Fantastic Four®

60¢
266
MAY
02462

APPROVED BY THE COMICS CODE AUTHORITY

KARISMA COMMANDS...

...DEATH TO THE INVISIBLE GIRL!

MAY 1984

SOMEHOW THIS ISN'T QUITE WHAT I'D EXPECTED FROM MY FIRST DAY AS AN OFFICIAL MEMBER OF THE FANTASTIC FOUR...
HER REAL NAME IS JENNIFER WALTERS, THOUGH THE WORLD AT LARGE HAS LATELY COME TO KNOW HER BY ANOTHER NAME...
SHE HULK?

OH... MISS MASTERS, HOW ARE YOU?
I AM WELL, THANK YOU. AND PLEASE, CALL ME ALICIA. HOW IS SUSAN DOING?

SHE'S RESTING RIGHT NOW. OR, SLEEPING AT LEAST. I FEEL SO... SO HELPLESS. ALL MY ENORMOUS STRENGTH IS JUST... USELESS.
DON'T DISTRESS YOURSELF. SHE IS IN GOOD HANDS.

HER HUSBAND, REED RICHARDS, IS ONE OF THE MOST BRILLIANT MINDS ON EARTH, AND HE HAS CALLED IN THE TOP EXPERTS IN THE FIELD OF RADIATION...
WALTER LANGKOWSKI, THE CANADIAN GAMMA RESEARCHER...
BRUCE BANNER, OUR OWN LEADING EXPERT ON THE EFFECTS OF RADIATION...
EVEN MICHAEL MORBIUS, PERHAPS THE WORLD'S GREATEST EXPERT ON BLOOD RADIOLOGY.

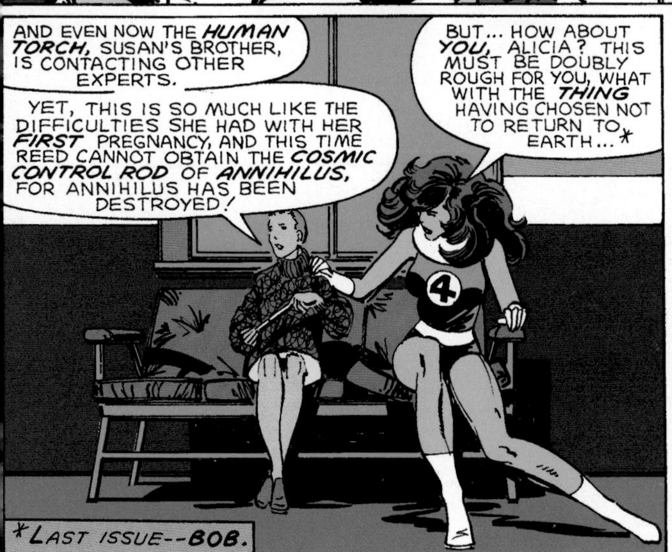
AND EVEN NOW THE HUMAN TORCH, SUSAN'S BROTHER, IS CONTACTING OTHER EXPERTS.
YET, THIS IS SO MUCH LIKE THE DIFFICULTIES SHE HAD WITH HER FIRST PREGNANCY, AND THIS TIME REED CANNOT OBTAIN THE COSMIC CONTROL ROD OF ANNIHILUS, FOR ANNIHILUS HAS BEEN DESTROYED!
BUT... HOW ABOUT YOU, ALICIA? THIS MUST BE DOUBLY ROUGH FOR YOU, WHAT WITH THE THING HAVING CHOSEN NOT TO RETURN TO EARTH... *
*LAST ISSUE--BOB.

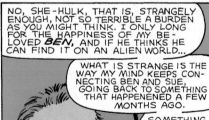

NO, SHE-HULK, THAT IS, STRANGELY ENOUGH, NOT SO TERRIBLE A BURDEN AS YOU MIGHT THINK. I ONLY LONG FOR THE HAPPINESS OF MY BELOVED BEN, AND IF HE THINKS HE CAN FIND IT ON AN ALIEN WORLD...
WHAT IS STRANGE IS THE WAY MY MIND KEEPS CONNECTING BEN AND SUE, GOING BACK TO SOMETHING THAT HAPPENED A FEW MONTHS AGO.
SOMETHING SO SILLY AND INSIGNIFICANT COMPARED TO THE MANY GREAT DANGERS THEY HAVE FACED TOGETHER...
2

Stan Lee PRESENTS:
CALL HER... KARISMA!
ALICIA'S SMALL, SOFT VOICE TRAILS ALMOST TO A WHISPER, AND SHE-HULK FANCIES SHE SEES A SUBTLE CHANGE IN THOSE SIGHTLESS BLUE EYES.
SHE IS REMEMBERING... REMEMBERING A DAY, NOT SO VERY LONG AGO, AND YET, PERHAPS AN ETERNITY PAST...
A SUMMER DAY. A DAY FOR LOVE, AND LIFE, AND WALKS IN PLACES GREEN AND GROWING.
ICE CREAM 50¢
YA KNOW, BABY, IT AMAZES ME EVERY TIME I THINK ABOUT IT. I MEAN, HERE YOU ARE, BLIND SINCE YOU WUZ JUST A LITTLE KID, AN' YET YA SEEM TA GET MORE OUTTA THIS PARK THAN ALL THE PEOPLE WITH EYES THAT WORK.
JOHN BYRNE STORY AND INKS
KERRY GAMMIL GUEST PENCILER (PGS. 3 THRU 21)
DIANA ALBERS LETTERER
GLYNIS WEIN COLORIST
BOB BUDIANSKY EDITOR
JIM SHOOTER EDITOR IN CHIEF
3

IT'S SIMPLY THAT I'VE LEARNED TO APPRECIATE THE WORLD FOR THINGS OTHER THAN COLOR AND LIGHT, BEN DARLING. THE SOUND OF BIRDS SINGING. THE TOUCH OF A BREEZE ON MY CHEEK. THE SCENT OF FLOWERS BLOOMING.
EVEN THE ROUGH HAND OF A GENTLE SOUL-- THE HAND OF SOMEONE I LOVE.

LOOK AWAY A MOMENT NOW. THE WORDS THAT FOLLOW ARE FOR THE EARS OF THE LOVERS ALONE.
AND HERE, NOT TOO FAR AWAY, ON CENTRAL PARK WEST, NEAR EIGHTY-FIFTH STREET...
MAN, I HATE THIS JOB. HAULIN' AROUND ALL THE MONEY IN THE WORLD, AN' GETTIN' PAID FIVE CENTS FER MY TROUBLES.

AH, GIMME A BREAK, LANCE. IF YOU REALLY HATED THIS JOB AS MUCH AS YOU SAY, YOU'D HAVE QUIT...
HEY...LOOK OUT!!

BREAKS SQUEAL, AND EVEN THE BLASÉ NEW YORKERS GLANCE IN THE DIRECTION OF THE SOUND.
BUT THE STRANGE WOMAN IN BLACK DOES NOT EVEN FLINCH.

IN FACT, IT IS THE PASSENGERS OF THE ARMORED CAR WHO FLINCH, AND SUDDENLY TURN GLASSY-EYED AS THE WOMAN RAISES, THEN QUICKLY LOWERS HER VEIL.
OKAY, BOYS. DO YOUR STUFF.
4

AND, NOT FAR AWAY, THIS LITTLE TABLEAU HAS SOME UNEXPECTED WITNESSES.
HEY, WHAT'S GOIN' ON?
BEN?
LOOKS LIKE A ROBBERY GOIN' DOWN, HONEY.

"BUT SOME FUNNY KINDA ROBBERY. THEM GUARDS AIN'T DOIN' NOTHIN'."
"THEY'RE JUST SITTIN' THERE WITH DOPEY GRINS ON THEIR FACES!"

WELL, YERS TRULY CAN DO A LITTLE MORE THAN THAT!
BE CAREFUL, DARLING. I SENSE...
SOMETHING STRANGE...

AND A FEW YARDS AWAY...
HOT DOG! THIS IS THE EASIEST PICKIN'S WE EVER HAD!
THINGS AIN'T NEVER LOOKED BETTER.

WELL, THANKS FER THE COMPLIMENT, PAL, OR WAS THAT JUST A POOR CHOICE OF WORDS?
GULP
HEY... REAL SHARP CAN I QUOTE YA ON THAT
5

NO, BUT YOU CAN PUT MY MEN DOWN NOW, MR. GRIMM.
WHO IN THE...

MY REAL NAME IS NO LONGER IMPORTANT. YOU MAY CALL ME...
KARISMA.

HAMANAH-HAMANAH...

UM... ER... WHAT WAS IT YOU SAID? PUT YOUR MEN DOWN?
SURE! SURE! ANYTHING YOU SAY!
THERE IS SUDDENLY A STRANGE AND ALIEN QUALITY IN THE VOICE OF THE THING-- A CLOYING, ALMOST WHIMPERING SOUND--
--THE SOUND OF SOMEONE DESPERATE TO PLEASE.

THAT'S A GOOD BOY. NOW, PICK UP THOSE SACKS OF MONEY FOR ME, WOULD YOU? THERE'S A DEAR.
6

HOLY COW! HE'S DOIN' IT! HE'S DOIN' WHAT SHE TOLD HIM!
WHAT? BEN? DARLING! WHAT'S HAPPENED TO YOU?
BOOST

BUT THE THING SEEMS NOT TO HEAR, NOT TO CARE, AS THE BEAUTIFUL BLIND GIRL RACES ALMOST UNERRINGLY TO HIS SIDE.
BEN... I HEARD THAT WOMAN... WHAT DID SHE DO TO YOU?

BEN!!
IS THERE, FOR JUST THE BRIEFEST INSTANT, A FLICKER SOMEWHERE IN HIS DEEP, BLUE EYES? A MOMENT OF RECOGNITION, OF REACHING OUT...
ALMOST, PERHAPS, A CRY FOR HELP?

WE SHALL NEVER KNOW...
GRIMM! STOP THAT LOLLY-GAGGING, YOU WICKED BOY! COME ALONG NOW!
YES'M. DON'T BE ANGRY. PLEASE DON'T?

LOOK... I GOT THE MONEY FOR YA...
BEN!
OH, MY POOR BEN! WHAT HAS SHE DONE TO YOU?
WHAT HAS SHE DONE?!
7

AND NOT TERRIBLY FAR AWAY, IN A FASHIONABLE BOUTIQUE JUST OFF BROADWAY...
MY DEAR, IT IS JUST ABSOLUTELY YOU!
HMM... WELL, I'VE WORN THIS STYLE BEFORE, BUT I'M NOT SURE THE WORLD-- OR MY HUSBAND--IS QUITE READY FOR ME AS A REDHEAD.

KEEP 'EM GUESSING, THAT'S WHAT I ALWAYS SAY. WHY JUST THE OTHER DAY I...
WHAT'S THAT? SIRENS?
OH MY WORD!

SIRENS INDEED, FOR IT SEEMS AS IF HALF THE SQUAD CARS IN MANHATTAN ARE SUDDENLY CONVERGING ON A SPOT NEARBY...

WHAT CAN BE GOING ON? I HOPE IT ISN'T SOMETHING TERRIBLE!
WELL, IT'S NOT LIKELY TO BE TOO TRIVIAL WITH THAT MANY CARS.
LOOKS TO ME LIKE SOMETHING I SHOULD CHECK OUT... BUT NOT AS SUSAN RICHARDS...

...AS THE INVISIBLE GIRL!!
UNSEEN ENERGIES FLOW ABOUT HER, AND A COLUMN OF PURE FORCE THICKENS THE AIR BENEATH HER FEET...
8

AND WITHIN SECONDS THIS UNIQUE MODE OF TRANSPORTATION HAS CARRIED HER NEAR THE HEART OF THE FRAY...
OKAY, GROUP SIX, BRING UP BEHIND. WATCH OUT NOW. HE'S MEAN!

THEY'RE BATTLING SOMEONE... FROM THE AMOUNT OF DAMAGE HERE ALREADY, SOME-ONE ENORMOUSLY POWERFUL. WHO--?
OH NO! IT CAN'T BE!

"IT CAN'T!"
ONE WAY
KEEP AWAY FROM ME, YA CREEPS! YOU HURT HER AN' I'LL BUST YA ALL INTA TH' NEXT CENTURY!

HER? WHO IS HE TALKING ABOUT? I DON'T SEE ALICIA ANYWHERE NEAR.
I'VE GOT TO FIND OUT WHAT'S GOING ON HERE.
OFFICER! OFFICER CAN YOU TELL ME...
HOLY CATS! ANOTHER ONE!

K-KEEP AWAY FROM ME! KEEP AWAY, YA HEAR? DON'T HURT ME!
HURT YOU?
HE'S ALMOST HYSTERI-CAL!

GOT TO DO SOMETHING TO CALM HIM, SHOW I MEAN HIM NO HARM.
DON'T BE SILLY, OFFICER. IF I WERE GOING TO HURT YOU I WOULDN'T APPROACH IN THE OPEN. I'D DO THIS.
WH-WHERE...?
9

I'M RIGHT HERE, OFFICER. NOW, WILL YOU STOP PANICKING AND TELL ME WHAT HAS HAPPENED HERE? WHAT'S WRONG WITH THE *THING?*
Y-YOU TELL ME, LADY. I ALWAYS THOUGHT YOU GUYS WERE ON *OUR* SIDE...
BUT SEEMS LIKE THE THING'S DE-CIDED TO CHANGE LOYALTIES... AT LEAST SINCE HE GOT MIXED UP IN THAT BANK HEIST...

BANK HEIST?
THIS MAKES NO SENSE AT ALL. CALL THE REST OF YOUR PEOPLE, OFFICER. TELL THEM TO HOLD THEIR FIRE. I'LL TRY TO REASON WITH BEN.

BEN! BEN, STOP IT! STOP IT THIS INSTANT!
KEEP AWAY FROM ME, SUZIE. I DON'T WANNA HAFTA HURT YA.
THEY'RE AFTER *HER*, DON'TCHA SEE? AN' I CAN'T LET THEM GET *HER*. I JUST CAN'T.

BEN, NOW CALM DOWN AND BE REASONABLE! WHO IS THIS *"HER"* YOU KEEP TALKING ABOUT?
HUH? ONE A' YER INVISIBLE FORCE FIELDS!
YOU... YOU'RE ON THEIR SIDE! YA WANNA GET *HER!* WANNA HURT *HER!!*
10

BUT I WON'T LET YA! I WON'T!
HIS JACKHAMMER FISTS PUMMEL THE INSIDE OF THE UNSEEN BUBBLE, SENDING REVERBERATIONS BACK THROUGH THE FIELD, POUNDING AGAINST THE VERY FIBER OF SUSAN RICHARD'S BEING.
BUT THE FIELD HOLDS.

BLAST IT! I CAN'T WASTE TIME WEARIN' YA DOWN. EVERY SECOND I'M AWAY FROM HER IS AGONY!
GRUNCH!

SO I'LL JUST TAKE ME A SHORT CUT THROUGH THE SEWERS OUTTA HERE.
BEN!

THIS IS MADNESS! I'D SWEAR SOMETHING WAS IN CONTROL OF HIM, MAKING HIM ACT AGAINST HIS WILL...
...YET HE'S SPEAKING COHERENTLY, NOT AT ALL AS IF HE WERE POSSESSED.

SURELY HE CAN'T TRULY HAVE TURNED AGAINST...
WHAT?!?
GOTCHA!
11

THE... PAIN! HE'S ALMOST CRUSHING MY ANKLE.
I CAN'T DEAL WITH THIS ON MY OWN. I'VE GOT TO CALL FOR HELP--CALL FOR REED AND JOHNNY.
MY FLARE GUN WILL...

NO YA DON'T, SWEETIE. I AIN'T SOME HALF-GASSED SUPER-BADDIE WHO DON'T KNOW TH' FF'S TRICKS.
YOU AIN'T FIRING OFF THAT FLARE TA SIGNAL TH' BIG BRAIN AN' THE KID.
CRUNCH!
NOW, I'M SORRY, SUZIE, BUT IT'S ALL OVER FER YOU!

BUT THE INVISIBLE GIRL IS NOT DONE YET...
MY POWERS ARE ALMOST USELESS AGAINST THAT INVULNERABLE HIDE OF HIS...
UNLESS...
YEOWTCH!

IT WORKED! MY FORCE BEAM STRUCK HIM ACROSS THE EYES, HIS ONLY WEAK SPOT!
I HAVEN'T DONE ANY PERMANENT DAMAGE, BUT THE EFFECT WAS LIKE WHACKING A PUPPY ACROSS THE NOSE WITH A ROLLED-UP NEWSPAPER.

NOW I HAVE TO THINK OF SOME WAY TO STOP HIM WITHOUT KILLING HIM... OR ME!!
HEY! COME BACK HERE YA BLASTID...!!!
12

THEN, ALMOST AS IF OBEYING THE THING'S BELLOW...
THIS IS RIDICULOUS. I'M GOING TO TIRE LONG BEFORE BEN. BUT AT LEAST I'VE LURED HIM AWAY FROM THE CROWDS.

I'VE GOT TO STOP HIM NOW-- BUT NOT ON HIS OWN TERMS. HIS STRENGTH IS A MATCH FOR MY FORCE-FIELDS.
BUT I CAN PUT THOSE FIELDS TO MORE THAN ONE USE...

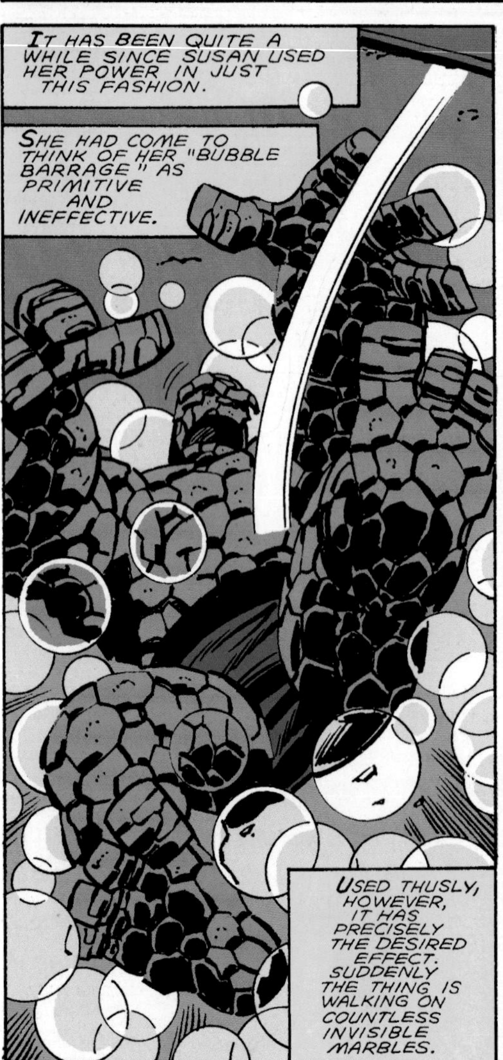
IT HAS BEEN QUITE A WHILE SINCE SUSAN USED HER POWER IN JUST THIS FASHION.
SHE HAD COME TO THINK OF HER "BUBBLE BARRAGE" AS PRIMITIVE AND INEFFECTIVE.
USED THUSLY, HOWEVER, IT HAS PRECISELY THE DESIRED EFFECT. SUDDENLY THE THING IS WALKING ON COUNTLESS INVISIBLE MARBLES.

BUT HE HAS BEEN A FIGHTER TOO LONG TO BE SO EASILY UNDONE.
AND WHILE HIS BRUTE STRENGTH IS OF NO USE AGAINST THE FORCE-SPHERES THEMSELVES...

...IT CAN HAVE DEVASTATING INDIRECT EFFECT.
OH NO!
13

IT TAKES ONLY A FEW HEARTBEATS...
...AND THE INVISIBLE GIRL IS BURIED.

BURIED, BUT NOT OVERCOME.
MY FORCE-FIELD BUBBLE PROTECTED ME FROM THE DEBRIS. MAYBE MY BEST BET NOW WOULD BE TO PLAY POSSUM...

BUT...
AH HA! I THOUGHT THIS PILE A' JUNK WAS TOO BIG FER YOU TA BE SQUASHED UNDER IT.
OH, BLAST!

TIME FOR PLAN B!

NOT BAD, SUZIE. YA KNOCKED TH' WIND RIGHT OUTTA ME.
BUT...NOT... FER...LONG...

HE'S FORCING HIS WAY BACK. PUSHING THE FIELD IN ON ITSELF!
14

I CAN REDUCE THE FIELD'S VOLUME-- THAT SHOULD INCREASE ITS STRENGTH.
BUT I'VE NEVER HAD TO GO UP AGAINST BEN'S FULL POWER BEFORE.

IN THE PAST, SOMETHING HAS ALWAYS HELD HIM BACK. AN INNER RESISTANCE TO WHATEVER WAS CONTROLLING HIM.
BUT THAT ISN'T THERE THIS TIME.

THIS TIME HE REALLY SEEMS INTENT ON *KILLING* ME!

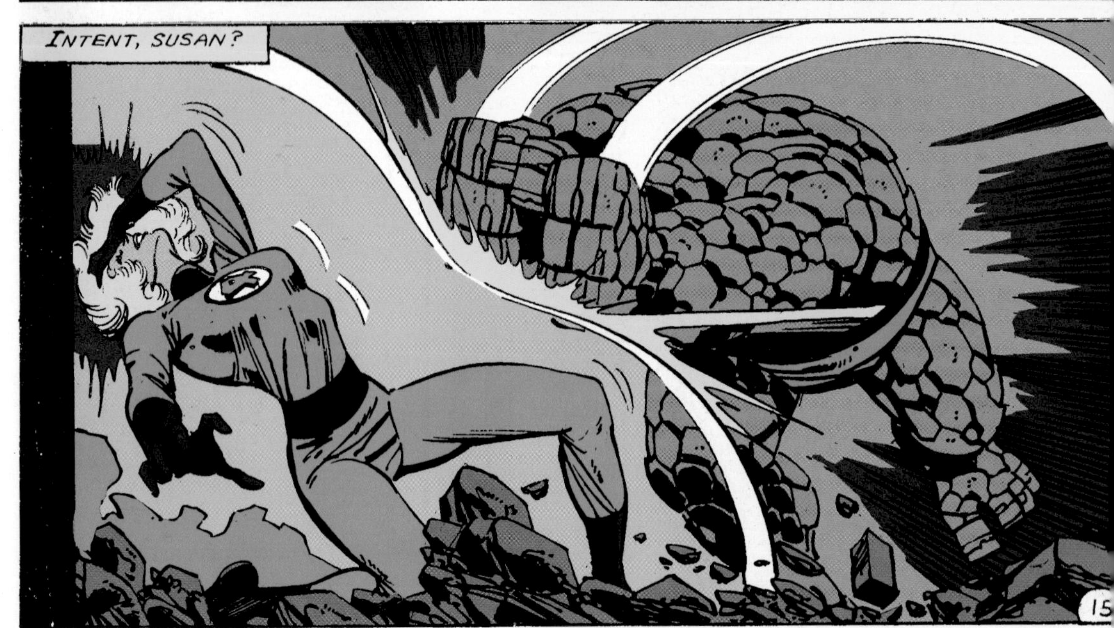
INTENT, SUSAN?
15

AS THE LAST VESTIGE OF THE PROTECTIVE FIELD DWINDLES AWAY IT APPEARS HE WILL SUCCEED!

BUT...
...S-SUZIE...

HE'S...HESITATING. AS IF WHATEVER IS CONTROLLING HIM IS WEARING OFF.
LIGHT RAYS WARP AS THEY PASS HER IRRADIATED CELLS, AND...

BLAST IT, SHE'S TURNED INVISIBLE! NOW WHICH WAY COULD SHE HAVE GONE?

TH-THAT WAS TOO CLOSE. I HAD BARELY ENOUGH STRENGTH TO TURN INVISIBLE FOR A FEW SECONDS.
GOT TO STAY OUT OF SIGHT NOW--RECOVER...

GRIMM! NAUGHTY BOY! DIDN'T I TELL YOU TO DESTROY ANYONE WHO GOT IN OUR WAY? NOW, AFTER HER!!
JUST ONE SECOND, LADY, I...
16

NO "SECONDS", YOU BAD, BAD BOY.
DO AS YOU ARE TOLD. KARISMA COMMANDS!
EEP!

AND, AS THE MONSTROUS THING LUMBERS OFF TO SEEK OUT HIS DISTAFF PARTNER...
THE WOMAN CALLED KARISMA LAUGHS, AND LAUGHTER GIVES WING TO MEMORY.

ONLY A FEW WEEKS AGO SHE WAS NOT THE GLAMOROUS FEMME FATALE SHE IS NOW.
SHE WAS ONLY MARY BROWN, A PLAIN AND SIMPLE NAME FOR ONE WHO SAW HERSELF AS A PLAIN AND SIMPLE WOMAN
SHE WORKED THEN AS A RESEARCHER FOR THE GAYLORD COSMETIC CORPORATION.

AND IT WAS THERE SHE MADE HER DISCOVERY.
THIS MAKE-UP WILL REVOLUTIONIZE THE INDUSTRY, MR. LE GUYE.
I HAVE INCORPORATED INTO IT CERTAIN LONG-CHAIN ISOTOPES THAT EMIT RADIATION ON SPECIFIC WAVELENGTHS.
THE RESULT-- THE WEARER BECOMES LITERALLY IRRESISTIBLE.
OH, COME NOW MISS... AH... BROWN...
Gaylord

THEY SCOFFED. OF COURSE THEY SCOFFED. BUT SHE SHOWED THEM.
SHE NEEDED ONLY A QUICK SMEAR OF HER LIPSTICK TO ENSNARE YOUNG MARTIN LE GUYE...
...AND TO REDUCE HIS FATHER TO A WHIMPERING IDIOT.

AND THAT WAS WHEN MARY BROWN REALIZED SHE HAD CREATED MUCH, MUCH MORE THAN A NEW COSMETIC LINE.
SHE HAD CREATED KARISMA!
17

AND THAT INFORMATION WOULD BE OF GREAT USE TO THE INVISIBLE GIRL...
...IF ONLY SHE HAD IT.
IT'S SUDDENLY GONE SO QUIET. WHERE...?

OH NO!
SKRAWG

I'M STILL TOO WEAK FOR A GOOD OFFENSE. GOT TO RISK A FORCE COLUMN...
...GOT TO GAIN TIME...

RUN AWAY AS MUCH AS YA LIKE, SUZIE. I CAN TELL JUST BY TOUCHIN' HOW WEAK YER FIELD IS.

TOO WEAK TA CUSHION YA FROM THIS!!
SLAM

THE FORCE OF THE IMPACT VIBRATES ALONG THE INVISIBLE LENGTH OF THE FIELD...
AND SUSAN STORM RICHARDS FINDS HERSELF PERCHED ATOP A QUIVERING TOWER OF JELLO.
18

FALLING... BUT AT LEAST MY WEAKEST FIELD IS GOOD FOR ONE THING...

YOU SHOULD HAVE LET YOURSELF HIT THE CONCRETE, MRS. RICHARDS.
IT WOULD HAVE SPARED YOU THE UNPLEASANT EXPERIENCE OF *DYING* AT THE HANDS OF A *FRIEND.*
SHE'S SNARED BEN AGAIN. BUT *HOW!?*

IT MUST BE SOMETHING TO DO WITH THAT VEIL. IT CAN'T BE TO HIDE HER TRUE IDENTITY. NOT THE WAY SHE KEEPS... *RAISING... IT...?*
ALL RIGHT, KARISMA. YOU MAY HAVE TURNED THE THING AGAINST ME. YOU MAY HAVE *WON.* BUT I'VE GOT ONE ACE LEFT TO PLAY...
HER POWER IS STILL WEAK, BUT IT IS ENOUGH TO RENDER THE FINE MESH OF THE VEIL TRANSPARENT, AND REVEAL...
...SOMETHING OF A SURPRISE.

WHAT IN THE NAME OF...?
YOU HAVE UNCOVERED MY SECRET, SUSAN RICHARDS. BUT DOING SO WILL PROVE ULTIMATELY FATAL!

ALL THE MALE ONLOOKERS ARE MINE--MINE TO COMMAND. AND KARISMA COMMANDS...
DEATH TO THE INVISIBLE GIRL!!

A MOMENT AGO THEY WERE HUSBANDS AND FATHERS, SONS AND BROTHERS.
NOW THEY ARE A SINGLE ORGANISM, THE MOST DEADLY OF ALL EARTHLY CREATURES.
THE MOB!

THE MAKE-UP MUST HAVE SOME HYPNOTIC EFFECT ON HUMAN MALES. YET SHE HAD TO KEEP RAISING HER VEIL TO RENEW THE EFFECT. SO IT'S NOT SOMETHING THAT OPERATES ON CONVENTIONAL RADIATION LEVELS, BECAUSE THE VEIL IS STILL THERE, JUST INVISIBLE.
IT MUST OPERATE ON VISIBLE WAVELENGTHS... AND IF THAT'S RIGHT IT SHOULD HELP IF I DO...
THIS!

KARISMA'S FACE--HER WHOLE HEAD BLINKS OUT OF SIGHT.
AND FOR THE ONRUSHING MALES IT IS LIKE A SUDDEN DELUGE OF COLD WATER.
HANH?
20

WHAT IN BLAZES IS GOIN' ON? SUZIE... WHAT ARE YOU DOIN' HERE? YOU LOOK LIKE YOU BIN RUNNIN' A GAUNLET...
DID THIS *MATA HARI* LOOKALIKE DO SOMETHIN' TO YA?
IN A MATTER OF SPEAKING, BEN. HOLD HER. DON'T LET HER GET AWAY.
GEORGE! WHAT DO YOU THINK YOU'VE BEEN DOIN??
UH... UH...
BEN!

ALICIA! BABY, AM I EVER GLAD TO SEE *YOU!*
LOOKS LIKE HE'S *OKAY* NOW, MS. MASTERS.
THANK YOU, OFFICER. THANK YOU FOR HELPING ME FIND HIM.

HOLD TIGHT, BEN. THIS STRIP TORN OFF HER CAPE SHOULD MUFFLE THE EFFECTS OF HER MAKE-UP.

AND, A FEW MINUTES LATER...
WELL! THAT TAKES CARE A' THAT!
YES, PROVIDED IT'S A FEMALE OFFICER WHO UNWRAPS KARISMA AND CLEANS OFF THAT *GUNK,* WE SHOULDN'T BE HEARING FROM HER AGAIN.
AMAZING! SO MUCH ANGUISH, SO MUCH *DAMAGE.* AND CAUSED BY SUCH A SILLY POWER.

OH, I DON'T KNOW THAT I'D CALL IT ALL THAT SILLY, ALICIA. AFTER ALL, YOU COULD SAY THAT KARISMA WAS... AHEM...
...*COSMETICALLY AWARE.*
21

HA HA. THAT'S PRETTY GOOD. I NEVER THOUGHT OF THE INVISIBLE GIRL AS HAVING QUITE THAT KIND OF SENSE OF HUMOR.

BUT HOW DO YOU KNOW ALL THIS, ALICIA? YOU WERE LEFT OUT OF THE ACTION PRETTY EARLY ON.

NATURALLY BEN AND SUSAN TOLD ME ALL ABOUT WHAT HAD HAPPENED LATER, SHE-HULK.

WAIT, DO I HEAR REED'S VOICE?

YES, IT'S ME, ALICIA. KIND OF YOU TO STOP BY. I'M AFRAID I HAVE NO GOOD NEWS.

HOW IS SUSAN FARING NOW, REED?

AS WELL AS CAN BE EXPECTED... WHICH IS NOT WELL AT ALL. I FEEL SO ***HELPLESS***. MY WIFE IS AT DEATH'S DOOR, AND EVEN THE WORLD'S LEADING EXPERTS IN RADIATION CAN'T HELP.

PERHAPS THERE IS SOMEONE WE'VE FORGOTTEN?

NO, BRUCE. JOHNNY IS CONTACTING THE LAST EXPERTS NOW. THERE'S NO ONE ELSE.

YES, THERE IS!!

I FEEL LIKE SUCH AN ***IDIOT*** FOR NOT HAVING THOUGHT OF HIM BEFORE.

HE WAS MY INSTRUCTOR FOR ONE SEMESTER IN COLLEGE. AN ABSOLUTE ***GENIUS*** IN THE FIELD OF RADIATION TECHNOLOGY.

BUT A SAD TWISTED GENIUS NOW. A MAN WHO HAS SHUNNED SOCIETY, AND ITS MORAL STANDARDS.

THE ONLY MAN WHO CAN HELP US NOW IS ***OTTO OCTAVIUS***. THE MAN CALLED...

DOCTOR OCTOPUS!

fantastic four # 267

JUNE 1984

A SMALL LOSS

A STAN LEE PRESENTATION BY JOHN BYRNE WRITER-ARTIST / GLYNIS WEIN COLORIST / MICHAEL HIGGINS LETTERER / BOB BUDIANSKY EDITOR / JIM SHOOTER EDITOR IN CHIEF

DOCTOR OCTOPUS?!? LANGKOWSKI, HAVE YOU LOST YOUR MIND?
NO, I HAVEN'T, REED, AND IF YOU'LL PUT ASIDE YOUR IMMEDIATE EMOTIONAL RESPONSE YOU'LL REALIZE I'M RIGHT!
OTTO OCTAVIUS IS THE ONLY MAN WHO CAN HELP US.
I STILL CAN'T BELIEVE I'M A PART OF ALL THIS. I'VE BEEN HANGING AROUND WITH THE AVENGERS FOR MONTHS NOW, BUT THAT DID NOTHING TO PREPARE ME FOR BEING ONE OF THE FANTASTIC FOUR!

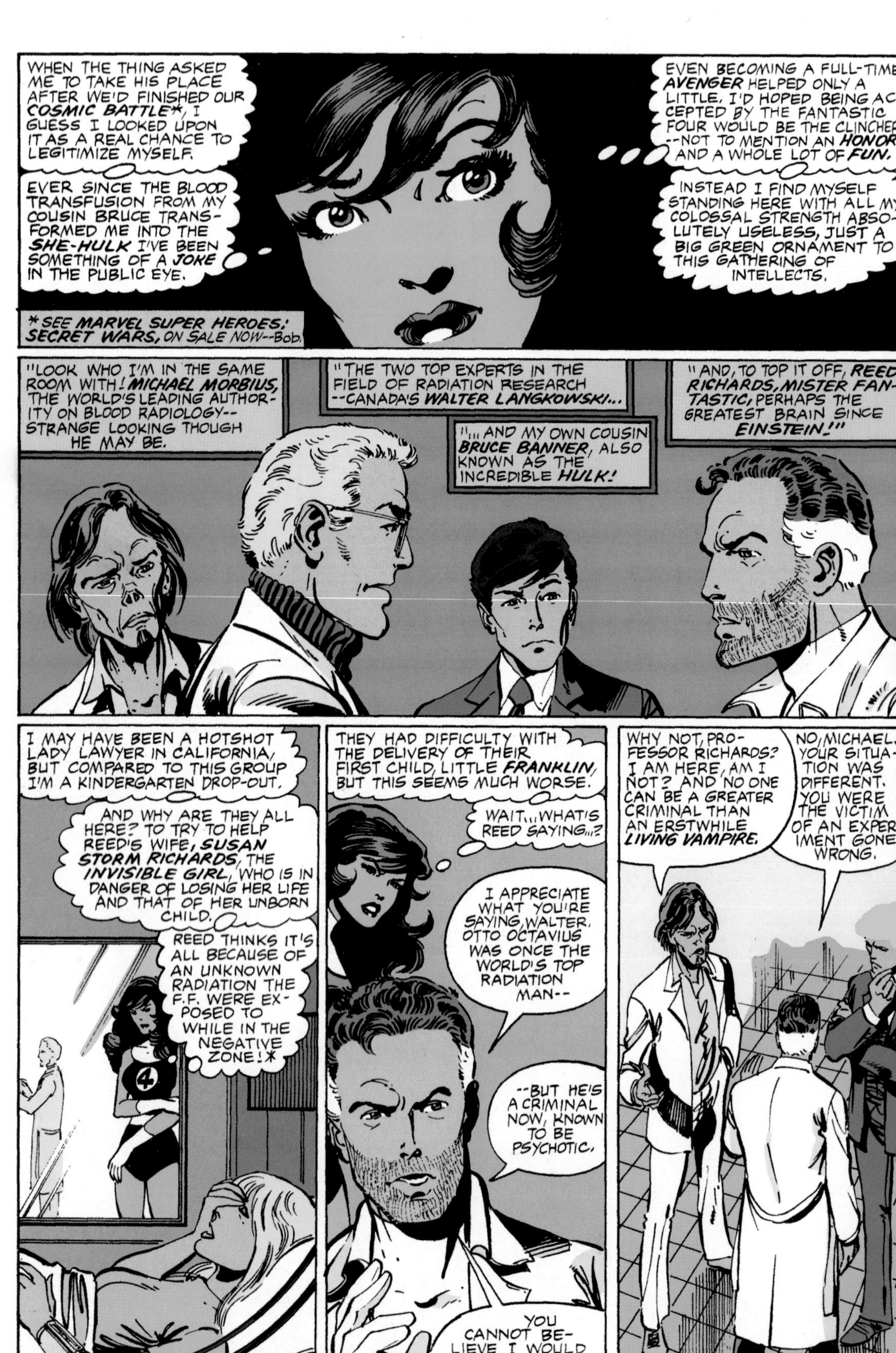
WHEN THE THING ASKED ME TO TAKE HIS PLACE AFTER WE'D FINISHED OUR COSMIC BATTLE*, I GUESS I LOOKED UPON IT AS A REAL CHANCE TO LEGITIMIZE MYSELF.
EVER SINCE THE BLOOD TRANSFUSION FROM MY COUSIN BRUCE TRANSFORMED ME INTO THE SHE-HULK I'VE BEEN SOMETHING OF A JOKE IN THE PUBLIC EYE.
EVEN BECOMING A FULL-TIME AVENGER HELPED ONLY A LITTLE. I'D HOPED BEING ACCEPTED BY THE FANTASTIC FOUR WOULD BE THE CLINCHER --NOT TO MENTION AN HONOR AND A WHOLE LOT OF FUN.
INSTEAD I FIND MYSELF STANDING HERE WITH ALL MY COLOSSAL STRENGTH ABSOLUTELY USELESS, JUST A BIG GREEN ORNAMENT TO THIS GATHERING OF INTELLECTS.
*SEE MARVEL SUPER HEROES: SECRET WARS, ON SALE NOW--Bob.
"LOOK WHO I'M IN THE SAME ROOM WITH! MICHAEL MORBIUS, THE WORLD'S LEADING AUTHORITY ON BLOOD RADIOLOGY-- STRANGE LOOKING THOUGH HE MAY BE.
"THE TWO TOP EXPERTS IN THE FIELD OF RADIATION RESEARCH --CANADA'S WALTER LANGKOWSKI...
"...AND MY OWN COUSIN BRUCE BANNER, ALSO KNOWN AS THE INCREDIBLE HULK!
"AND, TO TOP IT OFF, REED RICHARDS, MISTER FANTASTIC, PERHAPS THE GREATEST BRAIN SINCE EINSTEIN!"
I MAY HAVE BEEN A HOTSHOT LADY LAWYER IN CALIFORNIA, BUT COMPARED TO THIS GROUP I'M A KINDERGARTEN DROP-OUT.
AND WHY ARE THEY ALL HERE? TO TRY TO HELP REED'S WIFE, SUSAN STORM RICHARDS, THE INVISIBLE GIRL, WHO IS IN DANGER OF LOSING HER LIFE AND THAT OF HER UNBORN CHILD.
REED THINKS IT'S ALL BECAUSE OF AN UNKNOWN RADIATION THE F.F. WERE EXPOSED TO WHILE IN THE NEGATIVE ZONE!*
4
*F.F.'S #251-256--BOB.
THEY HAD DIFFICULTY WITH THE DELIVERY OF THEIR FIRST CHILD, LITTLE FRANKLIN, BUT THIS SEEMS MUCH WORSE.
WAIT...WHAT'S REED SAYING...?
I APPRECIATE WHAT YOU'RE SAYING, WALTER. OTTO OCTAVIUS WAS ONCE THE WORLD'S TOP RADIATION MAN--
--BUT HE'S A CRIMINAL NOW, KNOWN TO BE PSYCHOTIC.
YOU CANNOT BELIEVE I WOULD RISK SUSAN'S LIFE BY DEPENDING ON THE AID OF A FELON.
WHY NOT, PROFESSOR RICHARDS? I AM HERE, AM I NOT? AND NO ONE CAN BE A GREATER CRIMINAL THAN AN ERSTWHILE LIVING VAMPIRE.
NO, MICHAEL. YOUR SITUATION WAS DIFFERENT. YOU WERE THE VICTIM OF AN EXPERIMENT GONE WRONG.

NO, MORBIUS IS RIGHT, REED. WE CAN'T DISMISS OCTAVIUS BECAUSE HE'S ON THE SHADOW SIDE OF THE LAW. WE'VE ALL SEEN THAT SIDE OF THE STREET.
CONSIDER MY OWN SITUATION BEFORE I LEARNED TO CONTROL MY HULKING ALTER-EGO.

"ONCE OTTO OCTAVIUS WAS A SCIENTIST, A MAN MUCH LIKE YOU OR ME, SEEKING TO UNLOCK THE SECRETS OF NATURE.
"HIS CHOSEN FIELD WAS **RADIOACTIVITY**, AND HE WAS THE VERY BEST.

"HE'D CREATED A SET OF ROBOT ARMS, TO DO THE DANGEROUS WORK AT LONG DISTANCE.
"IT WAS THOSE ARMS WHICH HAD HIS CO-WORKERS CALLING HIM **DOCTOR OCTOPUS.**

"THEN, ONE DAY TRAGEDY STRUCK.
"A SMALL SCALE CHAIN-REACTION BLASTED HIM AND HIS ARMS WITH UNKNOWN RADIATION WAVELENGTHS.

"HE SURVIVED THE BLAST, BUT HE'D SUFFERED TERRIBLE BRAIN DAMAGE.
"HE BECAME **PARANOID**, INSANE -- DANGEROUS."
THEY'RE **JEALOUS** OF ME! THEY WANT TO KEEP ME FROM MY **WORK**... BUT I'LL SHOW THEM.
I'M STRONGER THAN ANY OF THEM!

"SOMEHOW HIS ARMS HAD BEEN PSIONICALLY LINKED TO HIS BRAIN.
"THEY NOW OBEYED HIS EVERY THOUGHT.'

"SO **DOCTOR OCTOPUS** QUICKLY BECAME A NAME TO BE FEARED, AS HE SOON PUT A DENT IN THE CAREER OF A YOUNG AND INEXPERIENCED **SPIDER-MAN**.
"THE WALL-CRAWLER FINALLY DEFEATED OCTOPUS, BUT SINCE THEN **DOC OCK** HAS RETURNED TIME AND TIME AGAIN...
"AND EACH TIME HE HAS BEEN DEFEATED, AND DRIVEN DEEPER INTO MADNESS."

BUT HOW DIFFERENT IS HIS STORY FROM THAT OF YOURS OR MINE, REED? WE MIGHT ALSO HAVE LOST EVERYTHING TO OUR OWN EXPERIENCES WITH RADIATION, MINE WITH THE **GAMMA BOMB**, YOURS WITH **COSMIC RAYS**.
PERHAPS ALL OCTAVIUS NEEDS IS, JUST ONCE, FOR SOMEONE TO APPEAL TO THE MAN HE USED TO BE.
AND, REED, I THINK **YOU'RE** JUST THE ONE TO DO IT!
3.

PERHAPS... PERHAPS YOU'RE RIGHT, BRUCE. OCTOPUS WAS RECENTLY CAPTURED AGAIN. THE LAST I HEARD HE WAS BEING HELD AT THE SOUTH BROOKLYN PSYCHIATRIC FACILITY, FOR OBSERVATION. I SUPPOSE I COULD...
OH, DOCTOR LANSING, HOW IS MY WIFE?
STABLE, FOR THE MOMENT. WE'RE STILL GETTING SOME DISTURBING RADIATION LEVELS FROM THE CHILD, BUT FOR THE MOMENT THOSE SEEM TO HAVE PEAKED.

THEN, IT WOULD BE ALL RIGHT FOR ME TO GO IN AND SEE HER, ONE MORE TIME?
YES, BUT JUST YOU ALONE THIS TIME, PLEASE. THESE OTHER GENTLEMEN CAN WAIT OUT HERE.

"I DON'T WANT HER EXPOSED TO ANY MORE STRESS THAN SHE ALREADY IS."
SOON...
SHOULDN'T BE GONE FOR TOO LONG, THIS ONE LAST EXPERT IS...NEARBY.
THERE'S MORE TO IT THAN THAT, ISN'T THERE? I KNOW YOU TOO WELL, DARLING. YOU'RE TRYING TO KEEP SOMETHING FROM ME.

NO, SUSAN... IT'S JUST THAT I...
DON'T, REED, PLEASE. SOMEHOW... THERE'S SOMETHING GOING ON THAT YOU DON'T LIKE... POSSIBLY SOMETHING DANGEROUS. I KNOW ...I KNOW THERE'S NOTHING I CAN SAY THAT WILL STOP YOU DOING WHAT YOU FEEL YOU MUST...
...BUT BE CAREFUL. BE VERY, VERY, CARE-FUL, REED.

I WILL, MY DARLING. NOTHING CAN STOP ME COMING BACK TO YOU AND OUR CHILD.
MY LOVE...

"...MY...LOVE..."
SHE SOUNDED SO WEAK, SO TERRIBLY FRAIL.
I'VE NEVER SEEN HER SLIP SO LOW.

PERHAPS OCTOPUS IS OUR ONLY HOPE, BUT IF I AM TO SECURE HIS ASSISTANCE I'D BEST STOP OFF AT OUR BAXTER BUILDING HEADQUARTERS.
SINCE THIS WILL BE AN OFFICIAL VISIT, I NEED TO CLEAN UP AND GO GET...

...THE FANTASTICAR.
IF I AM ABLE TO PERSUADE THE DOCTORS TO RELEASE OCTAVIUS INTO MY CARE I'LL NEED THIS VEHICLE TO GET HIM BACK TO THE HOSPITAL.
NOW, IT SHOULDN'T TAKE MORE THAN A FEW SECONDS TO REACH...

...THE SOUTH BROOKLYN PSYCHIATRIC FACILITY."
I'LL LAND ON THEIR ROOF, SO AS NOT TO STARTLE THE PATIENTS IN THE YARD.
NOW, IF I REMEMBER CORRECTLY, THE PRESENT HEAD IS...

...DOCTOR JEFFERSON, IT WOULD SEEM OTTO OCTAVIUS IS MY LAST HOPE.
THAT'S AN AWFUL SITUATION YOU'RE IN, PROFESSOR RICHARDS, AND I WISH I COULD HELP.
BUT... OCTAVIUS IS... IS...
WELL, PERHAPS I SHOULD JUST SHOW YOU...

WILSON, OPEN UP NUMBER SEVEN, WOULD YOU?
YES, SIR.
5.

THEY TOOK AWAY HIS ROBOT ARMS, OF COURSE, TO BE PUT UNDER LOCK AND KEY.
NEVERTHELESS, **THIS** IS OTTO OCTAVIUS, THE MAN CALLED **DOCTOR OCTOPUS!**
GREAT SCOTT!

DOCTOR JEFFERSON? IS IT TIME FOR MY SHOT?

NO, OTTO, YOU HAVE A VISITOR... A VERY SPECIAL VISITOR, A VERY FAMOUS MAN WHO WANTS TO SEE **YOU!**
OTTO, YOU'VE HEARD OF REED RICHARDS, HAVEN'T YOU?
MISTER FANTASTIC?

THAT'S RIGHT... **DOCTOR OCTAVIUS.** I'M REED RICHARDS, THE LEADER OF THE FANTASTIC FOUR, AND I NEED YOUR HELP.
MY... HELP...?

THAT'S RIGHT, **DOCTOR OCTAVIUS.** MY WIFE IS VERY SICK. SHE HAS A KIND OF **RADIATION POISONING.** SOMETHING ONLY **YOU** CAN UNDERSTAND.
RADIATION?

YES, DOCTOR OCTAVIUS, YOU ARE ACKNOWLEDGED AS THE LEADING EXPERT IN THE FIELD. YOU ARE THE ONLY ONE WHO CAN HELP ME SAVE MY WIFE, THE ONLY ONE!
REMARKABLE! I WAS NOT AWARE OF RICHARDS HAVING HAD ANY PSYCHIATRIC TRAINING, YET HE IS TAKING PRECISELY THE CORRECT APPROACH, REINFORCING THROUGH REPETITION OCTAVIUS'S TRUE IDENTITY.
IT'S AN ABSOLUTELY BRILLIANT STRATEGY, AND, UNLESS I'M VERY MUCH MISTAKEN...

"...I BELIEVE...

"...IT'S GOING...

"...TO WORK!"
L-LET ME HELP...

OH, PLEASE, PLEASE LET ME HELP. LET ME GET BACK TO MY WORK... BACK TO HELPING PEOPLE. IT'S BEEN SO LONG. SO VERY, VERY LONG...
YES, DOCTOR OCTAVIUS. YOU CAN HELP. YOU MUST HELP.

CONGRATULATIONS, PROFESSOR RICHARDS. YOU'VE DONE WEEKS-- PERHAPS MONTHS--OF WORK IN MINUTES!
I HOPE SO, DOCTOR JEFFERSON. NOW, IF WE CAN GET THE RELEASE PAPERS TAKEN CARE OF...
7.

OF COURSE. COME ALONG NOW, OTTO. WE'RE GOING TO LET YOU TAKE A SHORT TRIP WITH PROFESSOR RICHARDS.
HI, FRANK. WHAT'S HAPPENING?

HMM? OH, HIYA, MYRT. JUST A LITTLE MEDICAL MIRACLE, I GUESS.
YOU MEAN, SOMEBODY FINALLY GOT THROUGH TO DOC OCK? WHO WAS IT?

NONE OTHER THAN MISTER FANTASTIC HIMSELF.
SWEETEST BIT OF PSYCHE-TALK I EVER DID SEE-- AN' I'VE BEEN FITTIN' STRAIGHT-JACKETS FOR A LOT OF...
...YEARS...?

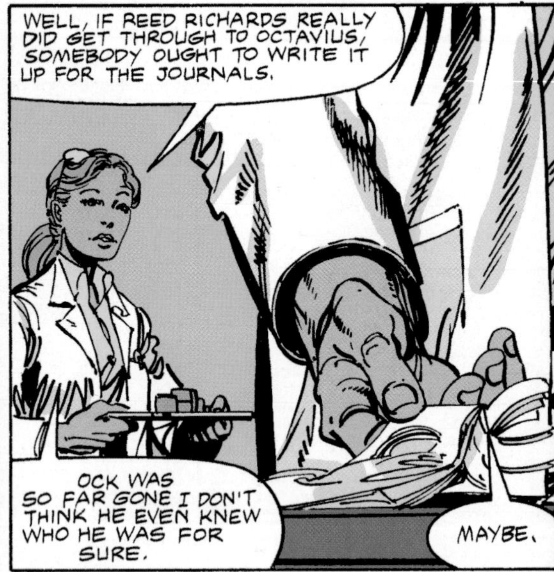
WELL, IF REED RICHARDS REALLY DID GET THROUGH TO OCTAVIUS, SOMEBODY OUGHT TO WRITE IT UP FOR THE JOURNALS.
OCK WAS SO FAR GONE I DON'T THINK HE EVEN KNEW WHO HE WAS FOR SURE.
MAYBE.

I WONDER...
8

I JUST WONDER..."
CAN YOU DESCRIBE THE SYMPTOMS MORE FULLY BEFORE WE GET THERE, RICHARDS?
OF COURSE, DOCTOR OCTAVIUS.
BRUCE WAS ABSOLUTELY RIGHT. OCTAVIUS IS COMPLETELY HIS OLD SELF ONCE AGAIN.

I ONLY HOPE AND PRAY HE WILL BE ABLE TO STAY THAT WAY!

THE PRIMARY MANIFESTATION SEEMS TO BE PURELY RATIONAL-- A STEADILY INCREASING LEVEL OF UNKNOWN WAVELENGTHS FROM THE FETUS.

YES...

G-GO ON...

...I...
...I...
...FEEL... MOST... UNWELL...
9.

"... MOST... UNWELL...

STAND BACK! STAY CLEAR! WE'RE TRANSPORTING DOCTOR OCTOPUS'S ARMS TO THE SUPER-MAX SECURITY HOLDING CELLS.

SUPER-MAX? ARE YOU KIDDING? WE'RE SEVENTY FEET UNDER-GROUND, SURROUNDED BY TWELVE-FOOT THICK REINFORCED CONCRETE AND GUARDS.

WHAT'S MORE SECURE THAN RIGHT HERE?

EMERGENCY!
EMERGENCY!
ALL PERSONNEL TO SECURITY CORRIDOR 17B! EMERGENCY!

WHAT IN THE NAME OF...?

UNGH!!
LOOK OUT!

ORDER... THE MEN TO FALL BACK. WE... CAN'T STOP... THOSE ARMS THIS WAY!
SECURITY CENTRAL! SECURITY CENTRAL! THIS IS NUMBER TWO, BAKER SQUAD. ORDER OUR MEN OUT! CLOSE CONTAIN-MENT DOORS!
NYPD
NYPD
EXECUTE PROGRAM C-57-D...
REPEAT... C-57-D!
11.

C'MON! MOVE IT! MOVE IT! DID EVERYBODY GET CLEAR?
NOT EVERY-BODY.

"HANSON'S STILL IN THERE!!"

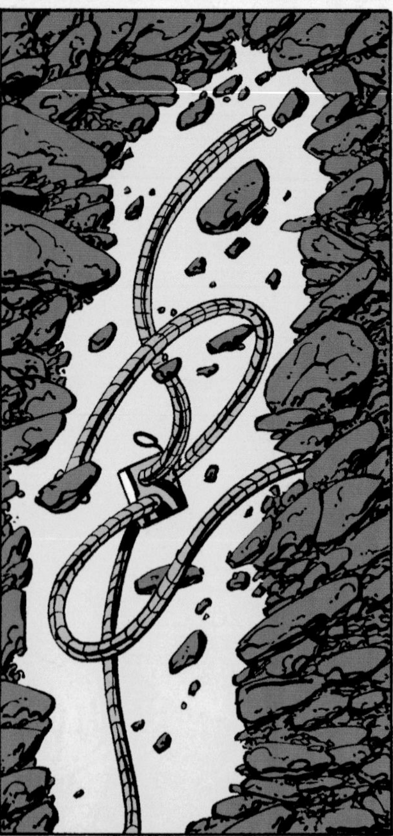

OFF TAXI DUTY

"ATTENTION ALL UNITS! ATTEN-TION ALL UNITS!
"DOCTOR OCTOPUS'S ARMS ARE ACTIVE AND AT LARGE. REPEAT, ACTIVE AND AT LARGE!"

...MOST UNWELL...
OCTAVIUS... WHAT IS IT? WHAT'S...?

...WRONGGHH!!
HIS ARMS! GREAT SCOTT! IT'S OCTOPUS'S ROBOT ARMS!!

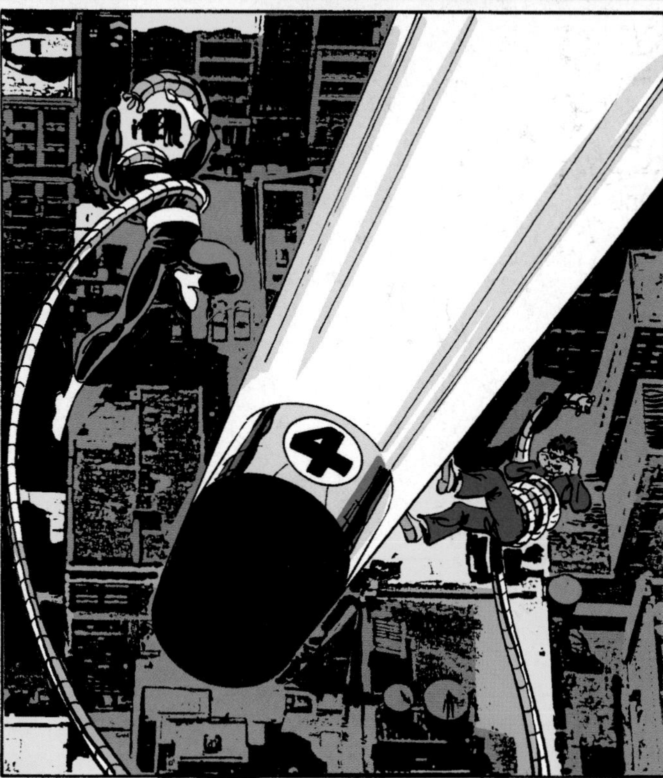

13.

BLAST IT! SOMETHING MUST HAVE TRIGGERED HIS PSYCHOSIS!
BUT WHAT? WHAT? SURELY ONLY SPIDER-MAN COULD...

OF COURSE!
IT MUST HAVE BEEN ONE OF THOSE WRETCHED DAILY BUGLE POSTERS!
J. JONAH JAMESON HAS "SPIDER-MAN-- THREAT OR MENACE?" PLASTERED ALL OVER THE CITY!

UNGH!!
THESE ARMS ARE TAXING THE LIMITS OF MY DUCTILITY.
GOT TO TETHER MY SELF SO I CAN FIGHT!

MY ELASTIC BODY HAS BEEN A TREMENDOUS BONUS IN MY SCIENTIFIC WORK, AND IN OUR BATTLES AGAINST EVIL.
BUT, I'VE NEVER HAD TO DEAL WITH AN UNLIVING ANALOGUE TO MY POWERS.
14.

BUT WHERE IS OCTAVIUS HIMSELF?
I SAW HIM LIFTED FROM THE FANTASTI-CAR, THEN...
THERE!

"HE'S ON THAT ROOFTOP, BUT... HE'S NOT *DOING* ANYTHING. HE SEEMS... CONFUSED, DISORIENTED.
"COULD IT BE THAT SOME *OTHER MIND* IS CONTROLLING HIS ARMS? THAT THIS ATTACK HAS NOTHING TO DO WITH HIS PSYCHOSIS?
"OR... OR COULD IT BE THAT HE HAS SO TOTALLY SUBMERGED HIS DOCTOR OCTOPUS PERSONA THAT IT IS HIS *UNCONSCIOUS MIND* THAT IS CONTROLLING THE ARMS?"

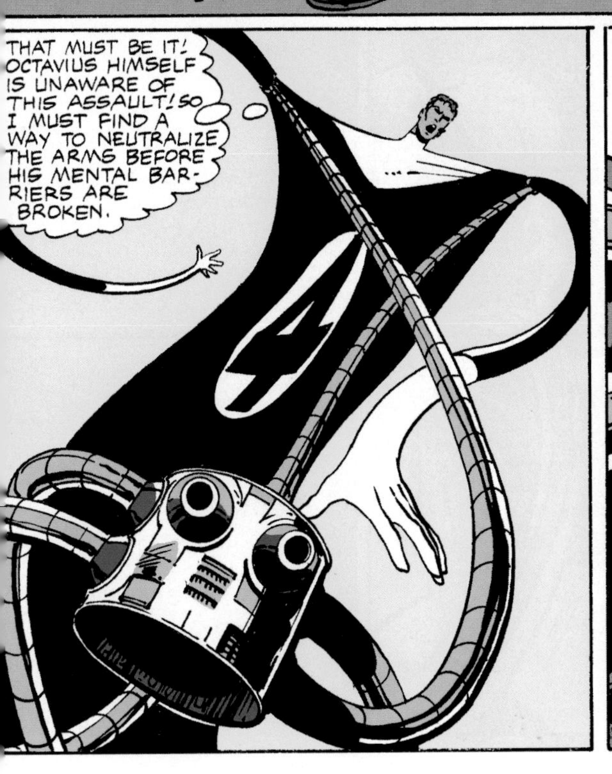

THAT MUST BE IT! OCTAVIUS HIMSELF IS UNAWARE OF THIS ASSAULT! SO I MUST FIND A WAY TO NEUTRALIZE THE ARMS BEFORE HIS MENTAL BARRIERS ARE BROKEN.

UNNHH!!
BUT, FIRST I HAVE TO *SURVIVE* LONG ENOUGH TO COUNTER-ATTACK.
EVEN IN MY ELASTIC STATE MY BODY STILL HAS THE USUAL NERVE ENDINGS AND GANGLIA--AND THE ARMS ARE HITTING *PRESSURE POINTS*.
15.

SKRASH
THE ARMS SEEM TO HAVE "DECIDED" TO CARRY THE BATTLE IN-DOORS.

LUCKILY IT'S AFTER THE WORK-DAY. I DON'T HAVE THE ADDITIONAL CONSIDERATION OF PROTECTING CIVILIANS.
BUT... THERE'S SOMETHING HAPPENING...

YES.
IT'S... UNGH... SUBTLE, BUT THE ARMS ARE ALTERING THEIR ATTACK...

"...AS IF THEY ARE NOW BEING MORE DIRECTLY GUIDED.
"BUT THAT CAN ONLY MEAN..."
PERFECT! WHILE THE OTHER TENTACLES PIN REED RICHARDS THIS FOURTH ARM WILL CARRY ME UP TO THE BATTLE.

I FEEL AS IF SOME GREAT, NUMBING CLOUD HAS BEEN LIFTED FROM MY MIND. I SEE THINGS ONCE AGAIN WITH THE ICY CLARITY OF REVELATION.
DO YOU HEAR THAT, REED RICHARDS?
YOUR STUPID SCHEME WILL NOT WORK. I AM TOO BRILLIANT TO ALLOW YOU TO TRY TO SHOW YOUR SUPERIORITY OVER ME LIKE THIS.
OCTAVIUS, PLEASE! THIS IS NO TRICK, I PROMISE YOU!

WORDS! WORDS! BUT YOUR WORDS ARE YOUR UN-DOING.

YOU APPEAL TO OTTO OCTAVIUS, AND HE *MIGHT* HEED YOUR WORDS.
BUT HE IS A WEAKLING, AND A FOOL.

AND HE IS *NO MORE!*
DOCTOR OCTOPUS LIVES!!
17.

AND DOCTOR OCTOPUS KILLS!

THIS IS POINTLESS! HE'S EASILY AS ADEPT WITH HIS TENTACLES AS I AM WITH MY OWN PLIABLE LIMBS.
YET THERE MUST BE SOME WAY TO DEFEAT HIM.

"SOMETHING I'M OVERLOOKING...
"OF COURSE! THE MANUAL CONTROLS ON THE CHEST PLATE!

"OCTAVIUS NO LONGER USES THEM, BUT THEY STILL RESPOND TO EVERY MOVEMENT OF HIS ARMS."

IF I CAN JUST REACH THEM...

"I DID IT!"
WHAT...
...THE...
18

UNHAND ME! HOW DARE YOU! HOW DARE YOU LAY HANDS ON DOCTOR OCTOPUS!
UNH... IT'S QUITE A STRAIN HOLDING THOSE CONTROL DIALS STATIONARY, ESPECIALLY WITH MY ARMS AT EXTENSION.
I'LL UNHAND YOU, OCTOPUS, BUT FIRST YOU'RE GOING TO LISTEN!

I CAME TO YOU IN GOOD FAITH, OCTOPUS. THERE WAS NO PRIDE INVOLVED. NO NEED ON MY PART TO PROVE ANY SUPERIORITY TO YOU, INTELLECTUAL OR OTHERWISE. IN THIS FIELD YOU ARE CLEARLY MY BETTER. IT COSTS ME NOTHING TO ADMIT THAT.

WHAT, THEN, DOES IT COST YOU, OCTOPUS? WHAT DOES IT COST YOU TO PUT ASIDE YOUR EGO FOR A MOMENT, PUT ASIDE YOUR LUST FOR POWER?
AN INNOCENT WOMAN AND HER UNBORN CHILD ARE AT YOUR MERCY, OCTOPUS. WOULD YOU LOSE VERY MUCH IF YOU HELPED THEM?

WELL, OCTOPUS? HOW GREAT A LOSS WOULD THIS BE FOR YOU, FOR YOUR EGO?
A SMALL LOSS PERHAPS.
BUT HOW CAN I KNOW THAT YOU ARE TO BE TRUSTED?
YOU'LL KNOW. YOU'LL KNOW BECAUSE OF THIS DEMONSTRATION OF GOOD WILL.
I RELEASE YOU NOW, OCTOPUS. YOUR ARMS ARE YOURS AGAIN TO CONTROL.
NOW, MAKE YOUR DECISION, OCTOPUS.
19.

"MAKE YOUR DECISION!"
I CAN'T BELIEVE IT!

IT CAN'T HAVE ENDED LIKE THIS! IT CAN'T!
JOHNNY?

A-ALICIA. I'M OVER HERE.
MAY I STAY WITH YOU, JOHNNY? SHE-HULK HAS BEEN TRYING TO BE COMFORTING, BUT...

YEAH--I KNOW. SHE MEANS WELL, BUT SHE'S JUST NOT FAMILY.
AND THIS IS A TIME FOR FAMILY. OH, HOW I WISH BEN WERE HERE.

HOW CAN THIS HAVE HAPPENED, ALICIA? AFTER ALL THE FF HAVE BEEN THROUGH, ALL THE LIFE AND DEATH BATTLES, ALL THE COSMIC ADVENTURES.
WE'VE CROSSED THE UNIVERSE TIME AND TIME AGAIN, AND COME BACK WITHOUT SO MUCH AS A SCRATCH. NOW... NOW THIS! SOMETHING THAT'S SO... SO NORMAL, SO EVERYDAY! TO COST US SO MUCH!
TRY TO BE STRONG, JOHNNY. REED WILL NEED YOUR STRENGTH, NOW THAT BEN IS NO LONGER WITH US.
AND SUSAN--I CANNOT BELIEVE SHE WOULD WANT YOU TO LET THIS DESTROY YOU. WE MUST GATHER OUR STRENGTHS TOGETHER. WE ARE A FAMILY, AS YOU SAID, AND WE MUST SURVIVE AS A FAMILY.

ALICIA, WAIT! HERE COMES REED!
WITH DOCTOR OCTOPUS!

JOHNNY! GOOD TO SEE YOU BACK, LAD! DID YOU CONTACT THOSE OTHER EXPERTS?
R-REED--SIS--SUE... THE BABY... THEY...

JOHNNY...?
S-SUE...?

SUE! NO! NO!!

BRUCE! WHERE IS SUSAN? WHAT...?
REED! THANK HEAVENS YOU'RE BACK. WE DID EVERYTHING WE COULD, BUT... BUT...

BUT WHAT? WHAT'S GOING ON? WHY CAN'T ANYONE GIVE ME A WHOLE ANSWER?
ERGENCY
DOCTOR LANSING MY WIFE HOW...?

...HOW IS SHE...?
SUSAN IS AS WELL AS CAN BE EXPECTED, REED, UNDER THE CIRCUMSTANCES...
21.

BUT I'M AFRAID SHE LOST THE BABY A LITTLE OVER THIRTY MINUTES AGO...